P9-BJQ-707

Death
in the
Long
Grass

By the same author:

Death in the Silent Places
Death in the Dark Continent
Safari: The Last Adventure

The Peter Capstick Library

Chosen by, and with introductions by,
Peter Hathaway Capstick:

The Man-Eaters of Tsavo, J. H. Patterson
Hunting the Elephant in Africa, C. H. Stigand
African Hunter, Baron Bror von Blixen-Finecke

Death in the Long Grass

Peter Hathaway Capstick

Photographs by M. Philip Kahl

ST. MARTIN'S PRESS
NEW YORK

Copyright © 1977 by Peter Hathaway Capstick
All rights reserved.
For information, write:
  St. Martin's Press
  175 Fifth Avenue
  New York, N.Y. 10010
Manufactured in the United States of America
Library of Congress Catalog Card Number: 77-9224

45 44 43 42

Library of Congress Cataloging in Publication Data

Capstick, Peter Hathaway.
  Death in the long grass.

  1. Big game hunting—Africa.   I. Title.
SK251.C27   799.2'6   77-9224
ISBN 0-312-18613-4

Acknowledgements

The author wishes to express his thanks and appreciation and admiration to the following persons who, in an astonishingly wide variety of ways, contributed to the production of this manuscript:

Col. Charles Askins, unquestionably one of the world's greatest living hunters and firearms experts for his encouragement and companionship.

John W. Cox for kind permission to quote his reminiscences of a hairy night in Central Africa.

Tom Siatos, Howard French and Ken Elliott of Petersen Publishing Company for their aid, encouragement and generosity in permitting me to include material from GUNS & AMMO and Petersen's HUNTING Magazines.

Malcolm C. A. Lyell and Carey Keates of Holland & Holland Limited for their help in the matter of record elephant tusks.

Robert P. Mills, my agent, for his efforts and guidance.

Les Pockell, my editor, who proved that 10 pounds of potatoes can fit in a 5-pound bag without mashing them first.

Alan Root, the intrepid wildlife photographer of Kenya, for kind permission to quote his episode with a killer hippo.

M. Philip Kahl, Ph.D., one of the finest wildlife photographers in the world, for making available some of his best work for this book.

Silent, Invisible, Debalo and Amos, my African family, who did yeoman duty keeping my tail from those snapping jaws.

Lastly, yet foremostly, my wife, Mary Catharine, to whom I can never repay the months of loneliness when I was in the bush or the hours of creeping uncertainty spent locked away from terrorists with only a pair of automatic shotguns for company.

To the memory of my good friend Dean Witter, Jr.,
who had to leave early.

Contents

"I speak of Africa and golden joys; the joy of wandering through lonely lands; the joy of hunting the mighty and terrible lords of the wilderness, the cunning, the wary and the grim."

Theodore Roosevelt
Khartoum, March 15, 1910

Death in the Long Grass

Foreword

I have often been asked how a Wall Street stockbroker and investment banker goes about swapping his chalk-stripe for camouflage, a change in life styles no less than polar. I suspect that the answer to that one is rooted in my early years, although it did not blossom into a decision until I was nearly thirty years old. Me and Gauguin.

Born in that part of New Jersey that strangers, used only to the ferro-concrete squalor of the New Jersey Turnpike, find hard to believe exists, my childhood I spent in the deep mountainous woods and waters around Lake Valhalla, Montville, in Morris County, where my father was an owner/developer of a club community. My infancy was centered in nearby Boonton, where my grandmother played Elizabeth Regina in a huge gargoyle of a Victorian house that today would give Vincent Price the crawlies.

From the start, the family suspected there was something a bit spooky about young Peter. From about age six, my whole world was centered on stalking and actually catching live songbirds with my bare hands on the lawn.

They were healthy, adult robins, grackles, and the like, and I suspect the neighbors took to crossing themselves and wearing garlic as they watched me ease up with the stealth of a cat and grab them, then run off to show poor mother my latest prey, which I then released. I believe my high score was five in one afternoon.

When we moved to the lake in 1944, I found I had several thousand acres all to myself and, with only three playmates—one younger and one a girl—I lived the life of a young Abominable Snowman, hunting, fishing, frogging, and generally sweeping the countryside like a Zulu *impi* on a rampage. Nights were spent with pet opossums and raccoons devouring David Corey, Selous, Roosevelt, Baldwin, Harris, Baker, Stanley and the works of anybody else I could borrow or ransom that had anything to do with my new fascination: Africa. By the time I was twelve, I had a vocabulary of a couple of hundred KiSwahili words (a hell of a lot of good that did me).

Through prep school at Morristown and college at the University of Virginia, I spent every spare moment either hunting and fishing or dreaming about it. Vacations were spent bass fishing with my brother Tom or prowling the grouse and woodcock covers. After college, a monument of mediocrity, and a short stint in the army, I bit the bullet and went into the securities brokerage business, learning the ropes as an order clerk and finally passing my examinations for customers' man. To the intense surprise of anybody who knew me, I did pretty well financially, well enough to decide after five years of my life sentence that there just *had* to be something else in life besides commuter trains, slush, strikes, and muggings. Perhaps I had been overexposed to Thoreau's "quiet desperation," I couldn't say. I simply decided that I wanted to be a professional white hunter and, as I wasn't getting much younger very fast, determined to give it a go.

Perhaps a word of semantical direction is in order. The term "white hunter" is, with all due apologies to the Tanzanian government, not a racist title. It merely designates a non-African who conducts safaris for sport in Africa. The job is also called "professional hunter," PWH, or PH, and has nothing to do with the use of the word "guide" as applied in North America. In Africa a guide is one licensed to drive tourists on photographic safaris only and has no bearing on hunting. More and more I hear myself referred to as a "Great White Hunter." I have no idea where the term comes from, though I suspect it is probably an Americanism. So, to set the matter straight, there are Great White Whales, Great White Hopes, even Great White Ways. There are no Great White Hunters. Mediocre, at best.

To simplify the story I found myself in Central and South America as an apprentice jaguar hunter learning one side of the safari trade. A year later I started a travel agency for sportsmen, booking hunting and fishing trips worldwide. As president I was able to travel considerably, which widened my knowledge and experience quite a bit. I finally sold this firm and became hunting and fishing director of Winchester Adventures, Inc., a subsidiary of the famous arms manufacturers. After two years of traveling for them as a "professional" client, checking out the facilities of safari firms all over Africa and most of the world, I decided to go for broke. I resigned and joined the old Luangwa Safaris, Ltd., out of Chipata, Zambia, and soon gained my full professional hunter's license. From Zambia I also became licensed in Botswana and Rhodesia as well as spending some time in Ethiopia, usually hunting six months per year and returning to the United States to write for magazines the other six. My wife, Mary Catharine, whom I met in 1970, was with me in Africa until 1975, when we finally left Rhodesia after political difficulties made booking clients too difficult.

That's the how; the why may not be so simple. In these days of mouth-foaming Disneyism, with ten or more hours a week of thinly veiled, antihunting, network wildlife shows drumming into every twelve-year-old mind that man is slaughtering everything in sight in the name of horrid bloodsport, it is fashionable to look upon hunters, especially professionals, as depraved, moronic, insensitive buffoons. That the sport hunter is more responsible for wildlife conservation, through habitat preservation and species management (financed through donations, whopping fees, licenses, and stiff excise taxes on his equipment), than any preservationist group is not widely understood. If you doubt this, remember that the government brought out a special stamp a few years ago for $5, the proceeds of the sale going directly into wildlife and environmental conservation. The general public, who hoot and sneer at the hunter, didn't buy enough to fill three S & H stamp books, a tiny fraction of the monies generated by the sportsmen who pay the bird watchers' way. Of course, you can't blame the networks; they're selling dog and cat food and have learned to give the people who believe in such shows what they want.

My father once advised me, wisely, I think, not to waste time trying to change folks' opinion about religion, politics, baseball, or redheaded women. That's good advice for this book. If you are an ardent hunter hater, you're likely to stay that way. If, however, you are simply a nonhunter and don't have too much of an opinion one way or another, let me try to explain the sportsman's thinking in the face of the negativism so popular these days.

Let's try a domestic example. How about quail hunting? The nonhunter, if asked the purpose of quail hunting, would usually reply that it was to kill quail. Actually, it's not. If the object was dead quail for the table, logically the cheapest, easiest, most practical method of achieving this end would be to buy a box of commercially raised, professionally cleaned, pan-ready birds for about $1.75 apiece. This saves one the bother of such matters as keeping and training bird dogs, securing licenses, risking snakebite, laying out for guns and shells, breaking teeth from biting into pellets, and paying for the hundred fringe items that probably cost the quail hunter an amortized average of at least $15 per bird per season, and possibly as much as $25. Yet, he chooses to spend the money, walk the miles, train and care for his dogs, all for possibly taking his limit while refusing to murder a bird on the ground, which, from a meat standpoint, would be many times more rewarding than wing shooting if the objective was merely dead quail.

So it is with elephants. Or lions. Or brown trout on the dry fly. Just as a man may indeed slaughter an elephant from a safe distance, he may also *hunt* a particular one under a code of rules that is part of the same ethic that forbids passing signals to a partner at bridge, shooting sitting ducks, or using night crawlers in fly-only trout streams. With elephants, however, the difference in playing the game honestly may have other consequences than the embarrassment of a card infringement, the missing of a whistling teal with both barrels, or the drive home troutless. It can get you very dead, which is what makes elephant hunting among the most moral of all sports when practiced honestly, with relatively equal risk to life of man and elephant.

What, after the fat is boiled away, is the essence of hunting dangerous game? In a word, it is challenge in its most elemental form, the same challenge that provided the drive that brought the hairless, puny-toothed, weak, dawn-creature that became man down out of the trees to hunt meat with his rocks, clubs, and pointed sticks. This daring still lives, in various degrees of mufti, under the flannel breast of the meekest shoe clerk although, like every other primeval drive that elevated early man, it has been watered down in direct disproportion to our rising self-estimation. We have ritualized every facet of our behavior that linked us to our bestial past. Our eating, procreation, and elimination habits have been vastly modified and closeted so we don't have to face the fact that we once did things much the way the rest of the mammal world still does. Our greatest and most developed ability—our skill at hunting—has, in most Western cultures, been under attack. Well over 99 percent of the time man has been on earth, he has been a hunter by profession. Today, man does not hunt for food in modern societies as he did in his recent past. Today, he hunts for the vestigial, ancestral memory of the thrill of the hunt itself. Even though his basic weapon is the *ability* to make weapons through brain capacity, haven't you ever wondered why human eyes face forward as do those of every other land predator or bird of prey? Think of the herbivores, the prey, the nonmeateaters such as deer or cattle or bluebirds. They have side-facing, defensive eyes. This alone is enough to qualify man, despite the denials of the Bambi-ites, as predators.

You may not like it, but it is your heritage. We hunt for the same reason an English Pointer puppy points before it can wobble: generations upon generations of evolutionary selectivity urge that course of action. Does this mean that you—yes, you—are an instinctive killer? In my opinion, hell yes, although you have covered it up so you can live with your own image of yourself, as that image was taught to you. We are all killers to the extent that we recognize it, in as much as the death of the prey in a humane manner is the logical conclusion to the modern hunt. We hunters have modified our behavior, too, in that most of us who play by the human ethic are classified under the heading of "sportsmen." It is the hunt itself that matters rather than the kill.

Let's try another tack. Take the example of the rock climber. Is his objective to reach the pinnacle of the rock? Only indirectly. What matters is *how* he achieves his aim. If the only point was to reach the summit, then why wouldn't he save a lot of risk and energy and take a helicopter? What matters is that he places a risk on his life, the degree of which he alone determines, to achieve his aim the hard way—pitting his strength, skill, and endurance against the element of gravity. Getting the golf ball into the hole is the conclusion of the challenge; how one gets it there and how many strokes it takes is the challenge itself. The putt is to golf what the shot is to hunting.

The object of the sport of hunting big, dangerous game under adverse conditions is not to get killed any more than the object of the rock climber is to fall to his death. It is rather the deliberate exposure of one's life to the real possibility of death purely for the sake of the experience itself. Sneer if you will, but you only will have half-lived your life is you never feel the icy clutch of danger for its own sake.

In hunting big game, facing danger is the height of the hunting ethic. Any bloody fool can, without encountering the smallest modicum of risk, murder a bull elephant at 200 yards with a lung shot. This is not elephant hunting, but elephant killing. Yet, to walk for a week, thirsty and foot-sore over hot, dry, thorn-spiked terrain, disappointed a dozen times by small or broken tusks, frightened witless by the female of the species or seemingly unshootable bulls, and then finally to track down a big tusker in heavy cover for a confrontation at less than fifteen yards—well, that is elephant hunting. That is man against himself, the last and purest of the challenges that made us men, not animals.

Peter Hathaway Capstick
Naples, Florida
April, 1977

1

Lion

It is nearly three o'clock in the sweltering morning of September 2, 1974. In four hot, still hours dawn will hemorrhage like a fresh wound in the sky over the eastern Muchingas, the great, towering walls that confine the upper reaches of the Luangwa River in Zambia's Eastern Province. In the anemic wash of a dying Central African moon, three canvas tents gleam bluely in a sparse grove of sausage trees near the water's edge. One of them, older and more weather worn, is pitched fifty yards from the others. Behind its bleached cloth and netting walls, a slender white man sleeps fitfully, tossing in the humid spring silence as greasy sweat darkens the sheets of his camp bed. On the dirt floor beside the tent's walls, a watery moonbeam glows on the scratched white stencil of a footlocker: *Peter Hankin, Box 72, Chipata*. Inside the travel-dented locker lie three flat five-packs of Kynoch 300-grain soft-point cartridges for the battered, silver-worn, old rifle, a Cogswell and Harrison, .375 Holland and Holland Magnum in caliber. But the rifle, as bush-scarred as the face of its owner, is not leaning in its usual place beside the bed. Operating in a photographic safari area, professional hunter Peter Hankin has had to leave it at his hunting camp, Chitangulu, forty miles downstream. His friends will later decide that even if he had the rifle now he would still have less than one minute to live.

Fifty yards from Hankin's tent, in the shadowy skeleton of a fallen *muSassa* tree, there is a tiny, silent movement. Dilated wide to gather the pale light, two hard, amber eyes flicker across the broken ground and lock on the indistinct form of the man sleeping behind the netting. Seconds pass, then the lioness rises and begins to ooze forward, gliding like a tawny wraith between deep clumps of shadow. There is no sound as she slips along on thick pads, the white sickles of her claws sheathed, the aching throb of hunger hollow in her chest and loins.

At twenty yards she freezes, the thick, acrid man-scent dank in her nostrils. She stifles an involuntary growl, her black upper lip curled back to show thick, long fangs. For a moment she hesitates, but her ancestral fear of the smell is washed over by the desperation of her hunger. At five yards she gathers her hind legs beneath her flattened, lean body, the hind claws gripping the earth for purchase. The man-thing is still asleep, unaware of crouching death so near, his breathing deep and regular in the cat's lain-back ears. In a flash of dark motion she is in the air, claws extended like naked linoleum knives, the light mosquito netting shredding before her charge. Her impact hurls the man from his bed and onto the ground. Before he is even awake, there is the soggy snap of crushing vertiebrae, then silence. For Peter Hankin, one of central Africa's most experienced professional white hunters, the last safari is over.

It is light before Hankin's clients, unarmed and cowering in their tents while listening to the wet feeding sounds, can escape and seek help. In a few hours Joe Joubert, a professional hunter employed by Hankin's safari firm, a Zambian game guard, and Joubert's safari client, Samuel Lenher of Wilmington, Delaware, are driving hard along the bush road from Joubert's camp at Zokwe to the scene of the tragedy. When they arrive, the lioness is still feeding on Hankin's corpse, which has been dragged a few yards out of the tent. Before Joubert can come up with his express rifle, the Zambian foolishly wounds the man-eater with a blast of SG buckshot from his single-barrel-issue Greener shotgun-/carbine. The big cat runs off into the bush where Joubert takes up the blood spoor.

Over the next hour the lioness inscribes a large circle through the heavy riverine cover and incredibly, despite her wounds and the men following her, returns to the man she has killed and resumes feeding. Joubert, half-retching with horror and disgust, executes her with a shot from his .458 Brno, the 510-grain Winchester soft-point dropping the man-eater lifeless across the body of her victim. Inspection establishes that the lioness is in the prime of life and previously uninjured or disabled although very lean and, with macabre obviousness, hungry. A post-mortem on the body of Peter Hankin determines that, mercifully, he died instantly of a broken neck from the lioness' first bite.

America in the last quarter of the twentieth century is something of an odd place from which to contemplate the fact that, contrary to popular belief, man-eating lions (not to mention leopards, crocodiles, and hyenas who will receive their due later in this book) are still very much in evidence in large areas of Africa. Due, most likely, to the Sea-to-Shining-Sea garbage we are force-fed by the Network Nature Fakers, including such prime-time pap as the happily now-defunct *Born Free* television series, it's understandable that most Americans don't regard the average lion as much tougher or more dangerous than Rima the Bird Girl.

And speaking of the Adamson lions, you might be interested to know that one of those cuddly creatures sprang upon an open car driven by one of Kenya's top game officers, who was riding with his wife and young son in a game reserve a year or so ago. It grabbed the boy by the skull from between the unarmed mother and father and dragged him out of the Land Rover, severely mauling him until, somehow, the father was able to reclaim his son. At the time I was given this report by the father, who stayed several days with us in Rhodesia this past season, the complete extent of the boy's injuries was yet unknown, although some brain damage was suspected. That lion still roams free. I was also given an unconfirmed report during this same conversation that one of George Adamson's lions killed and ate one of his African domestics, a cook as the tale goes. Knowing the reputation of the man who told me this, I do not personally doubt the information offered, but cannot prove it.

There are several very good reasons why, despite the surprising number of maneating incidents that occur today in Africa, most are hushed up like an epidemic of social disease at a bible school. It's the same reason that Florida

5

Chambers of Commerce don't go out of their way to spread the word of shark attacks along their beaches. One doesn't tend to pack the tourists in when word gets around that there is an outside chance of seeing the inside of a lion on a trip through the Tsavo National Park. How many Detroit schoolteachers do you think the tour mongers in Kenya's national parks would have signed up last year if word had gotten out about the photographer who was pulled out of his tent by the head and eaten down to his toenails by a solitary *Simba* with a taste for white meat? If most of the emerging, game-rich countries ever published figures on how many people are killed and eaten by a variety of carnivores within their borders, there would be a tourist recession that would make Black Tuesday look like St. Swithin's Eve.

Of course, nobody knows for certain exactly how many people are eaten, the very nature of man-eating having a decided tendency to make evidence somewhat scarce. Man-eating lions, if undisturbed, commonly eat almost every vestige of their victims, even the blood-soaked clothes and shoes as well as the bones. Whatever may be left falls to the African Sanitary Department and, after even a few days, it's difficult to examine a piece of skullcap the size of a demitasse saucer and state unequivocally that the cause of death was a lion. Yet, in only one six-month season as a professional hunter in Zambia, I learned of six definite cases of man-eating by lions in just one concession area of twenty by sixty miles. I wonder how many more there were who were simply reported as "missing" or, considering the primitive conditions of the more remote tribes, never reported at all.

Certainly, there are any number of cases of men being killed but not eaten by lions. Unlucky bwanas and unfortunate natives get pounded with monotonous frequency by running inadvertently into females with small cubs, mating lions, feeding lions, and the like. Wounded lions' scores for homicide are probably about as high as genuine man-eaters, but obviously the moral considerations are quite different. However, unless you've promised your carcass to

Harvard, the difference between being nabbed by a certifiable man-eater or having your face bitten off by an irate lady lion are, at best, academic. After all, if the lion doesn't eat you personally, you won't have to wait long until the vultures, ants, hyenas, and jackals do. Africa is astoundingly efficient in the disposal of protein.

The non-African attitude toward man-eating lions is typical of the whistling-in-the-graveyard humor of cartoons showing missionaries in the cannibal pot. Large, well-fed lions are drawn burping over a rifle and pith-helmet with the caption: "I never met a man I didn't like. . . ." To nearly all of us, the concept of being eaten, *actually eaten*, is so remote as to be unthinkable. However, if you spend the best part of eleven years, as I did, living with big, live, genuine lions all around, you might discover that your balding head never hits your pillow without that little niggling of doubt. Just maybe tonight . . .

Man-eating lions have had an almost unbelievable influence on the continent of Africa since the first European explorers and developers began to open up the bush in earnest. A classic example took place at the close of the last century when no less a power than the empire of Queen Victoria was thwarted in its imperial designs by eight man-eaters who halted construction of the so called Lunatic Express, the Uganda Railroad, as it passed through southeast Kenya. The Man-eaters of Tsavo treated the project as one extended buffet table, their accomplishment having been to have eaten more imported Indian coolies than it took to film *Bhowani Junction*. These incredibly brazen killers finally had their hash settled by a pith-helmeted paladin working for the railway, a Lieutenant Colonel J. H. Patterson, DSO, but only after a period of several months of frustrating hunting, during which time the colonel very nearly got the chop himself on several occasions. His book on the episode is a classic of hunting literature and, due to its immense popularity, is still often available in used bookstores. *The Man-Eaters of Tsavo* has been so widely quoted in works about lions and man-eaters as to make a further retelling merely lily gilding, save to mention that, a bit after Patterson killed the Tsavo pride, a single man-eater of considerable talent took residence further up the line displaying, to quote Colonel Patterson, "an extraordinary taste for the members of the railway staff," culminating in the catching, killing, and eating of the superintendent of police, a Mr. Ryall. Very bad form, indeed. The lion, as if he had a shopping list, entered a railway car and killed the man in the company of two other whites, one of whom the lion had to stand upon to reach the sleeping Ryall in an upper berth. He was later trapped and, after being displayed, shot.

Although there is virtually no area in Africa that has not recorded a degree of man-eating activity, some localities are historically much more dangerous than others. One of the worst is Central Africa, especially near the Great Rift Fault that crosses the continent perpendicularly. There have been literally hundreds of man-eaters reported in the area since 1900 and, as the case of Peter Hankin so horribly demonstrates, there is still not much of a shortage.

One pride, for example, the Ubena man-eaters, had been in operation for a full ten years before George Rushby, a game officer of Tanganyika (now Tanzania), and one of the greatest man-eating lion hunters of all time, began to put the screws on them in their thirty by fifty mile range in 1942. In the two years of hard hunting he needed to wipe out the pride, the lions added an additional 249 human kills to their record. Imagine the number of people they had eaten in the ten years they operated unmolested! Four years later, in the Njombe District of Tanganyika's Southern Province, Rushby was again enlisted to hunt the Njombe man-eaters, a collectivity of feline mayhem that, between the fifteen members of the grisly pride racked up a confirmed score of over 1,500 natives and colonists. And, remember, those are just the ones we know of.

The scores of other man-eaters in central and southeast Africa, such as the Mpika lions, the Revugwi man-eaters, the Chabunkwa lion that I killed, and literally dozens of others, less famous because of remoteness, have killed without question many tens of thousands of people in this century alone. All indications are that the end is far from near.

One of the most consistant danger points of this area is the Luangwa Valley of Zambia (formerly Northern Rhodesia), a northern tributary of the Zambezi and one of the better hunting grounds of Africa. The death of Peter Hankin in the Luangwa Valley came to me as more than a news item; I had worked for him as a professional hunter in the area quite near where he was killed. I knew him as one of the most experienced and talented professional hunters in all Africa, an immensely respected gentleman and a good friend. But, he knew the odds and they caught up with him. One night they nearly caught up with me, too.

I was on a twenty-one-day safari with two Italian clients, hunting from a base camp called Nyampala, an Awiza tribal area located at the juncture of the Munyamadzi and Luangwa rivers. It was near midnight on a cool winter's night in July, and I was asleep in one of the grass and pole huts we preferred to canvas tents because of better ventilation when the weather warmed up later in the season. I was awakened by one hell of a commotion—roaring, snarling, and growling some hundred yards away where my native staff was quartered in similar huts. Grabbing my big, five-cell torch, I stuck a pair of soft-points into my .475 No. 2 Jeffery's express double-barreled rifle, flipped up the ivory night-bead sight, and burst out of the door in my sandals and *kikoy*, a wraparound loincloth. As I neared the huts, I caught the flash of a big, male lion in the probing beam, moving off into the bush and high grass. Silent, my gunbearer, heard my call and stepped out of the hut with his brother, Invisible. In Fanagalo, our common language, I asked them what had been going on.

Silent had been asleep near the door on his rush mat,

his brother at the rear of the hut. He wasn't certain what had awakened him but realized that he could hear the breathing of a heavy animal just through the grass of the walls. The next instant a lion crashed into the door, closed and jammed with a stick through the frame. One paw ripped through the grass like shredded newspaper, the lion tearing chunks from the hard *mopane* wood frame with his teeth. Snarling fit to freeze the man's blood, he tore away a section of the grass wall and squeezed his head through, right next to Silent's waist.

The little gunbearer scrambled around the floor trying to find his spear without success. Then he touched something smooth and hard, snatching up a bottle of beloved Coca-Cola, a still unopened gift from the Italians. With all his strength he belted the lion across the muzzle with it, then again. It grunted at the blows and pulled its head back partially, then with a furious roar stuck it back into the hut. Silent hammered the lion one in the nose twice again until, probably confused by my torch and shouting, it ran off into the darkness. Silent finished the story sucking at the gashes on the heel of his hand that the cap of the bottle had cut. It had to be the only recorded instance of a man driving off a marauding lion with a Coke bottle!

Not much fancying the probable results of following a hungry man-eater into the dark, I gave Silent my Beretta over/under 12-bore shotgun and a handful of buckshot shells, sending him and Invisible over to the large hut where the rest of my staff slept. I stopped by the Italians' hut to advise them of the state of affairs and was able to talk them out of their .460 Weatherby magnum elephant guns, figuring that a pair of tyros opening up blindly at some night noise with those cannons could well have tragic consequences. I told them, and myself, that the odds of the lion returning were pretty slim, but when I left, that hut was better defended than the Alamo. Pinching a bottle of cold beer from the condensation bag, I went back to my hut and lashed the door shut with a long piece of buffalo hide thong.

Anybody who is not at least slightly terrified by the

prospect of a man-eating lion dropping by for a late snack is, in my opinion, suffering from soft spots in the head. I have no soft spots. I checked the Jeffery, shook the panatella-sized cartridges to hear the satisfying rattle of cordite against the cool, brass cases, closed the rifle's action and, sitting on the bed with a cigarette and the bottle of beer, waited to see what would happen.

Perhaps an hour went by, a hell of a long time when you are sitting in the dark wondering if something big and hairy is going to burst through the frail grass walls and grab you. You will likely recall the sensation from your first childhood camping trip. There were the usual bushveldt sounds of insects, the wet swirls of catfish and crocs on the river, the honking of hippos and the sleepy chatter of insomniac baboons in the grove of fever trees over the ridge. Then, somehow, with prehistoric certainty I *knew* he was there, very close. I could absolutely sense him. The hackles were crawling around on my neck like a nest of maggots, and my palms were slippery cold on the Circassian walnut stock of the rifle. My heart slammed in my ears like Gene Krupa on speed as adrenalin pumped through my system. With my heightened senses, I could now hear the animal padding through the soft dirt outside the hut, looking for a weak point. There was a long pause and I knew he was coming. A low, incredibly sinister rumble welled up through the dark, and the hut shook under a heavy shock. Pieces of dry grass and dust shook down cloudlike from the roof into my hair and eyes. Frantically, I tried to locate the lion, but his roars drowned everything out, a solid vortex of impossible sound saturating the hut. Then, against the eighteen-inch open strip that ran under the flat roof for ventilation, a dark lump was silhouetted against the slightly lighter sky. It was the lion's head, looking in, and I realized in a flash that he was crouched or lying on the roof, a flimsy network of slender poles and bunched grass. Two big feathers of flame erupted from the muzzles as I raised the double rifle, sighted on the spot where the cat seemed to be, and pressed the triggers. As the thousand grains of lead tore through the roof (happily without setting fire to it with muzzle blast), there was a tremendous roar that blended with the twin crash of the shots. There followed a scratching, thrashing sound and a thump like a meal sack dropped down an empty elevator shaft. I automatically broke the action and dunked in two fresh rounds from between the fingers of my left hand, the greasy cordite fumes stinging my eyes.

The thrashing continued outside the hut for a few seconds less than it took me to untie the rawhide lock with quivering fingers. The bare, beaten earth outside the hut was empty. My back flat to the wall, I swung the torch in a slow, wide arc, the dark, grape-jelly gleam of blood spoor reflecting in the lightbeam. I stopped and fingered it. Arterial. One pussycat that wasn't going far. Forty yards away, collapsed in a heap of tan putty, lay the dead lion. One big slug had taken him from below at a slight angle, punching a cantaloupe-sized hole through his chest that broke his off-shoulder into atoms, the other just creasing his side in a long, red welt that cut the short hair of his flank like a barber's razor. I released a very large breath that I had been holding for the past hour and wandered over to the dining hut for a similarly proportioned Scotch before the shakes arrived.

The whole camp poured out and came over to view the punctured pussy. The killing of a lion seems to excite Africans more than any other species, and this was no exception. I eventually declined the presidency of the republic and got to thinking about the consequences of having bashed this chap. Aware, from related incidents, of the Zambian Game Department's policy on the killing of unlicensed game, I knew that the department would conclude that since the lion had not actually eaten me, there was no proof that it was a man-eater, and I was therefore guilty of lion poaching. If I had let it eat maybe a leg or two before shooting it, all would have been well. Catch-22, Afro style. One of the Italians kindly took it on his license for me, solving a very real legal problem.

Interestingly, a rash of killings that had been taking

place over the past few months in an area some fifty miles upriver abruptly stopped after the incident. There was no proof, but circumstantial evidence pointed to the fact that the big, healthy, glossy-coated cat (who is now a full-mount in Milano) had decided that things were getting a bit hot where he was operating and moved south, just happening to pick the wrong hut for his first foray in a new zone. If he wasn't a man-eater, what do you suppose he had in mind trying to get into Silent's house and then returning to give me a try? Perhaps he just wanted to borrow a cup of zebra.

Over the years since the first Europeans began writing about African game, there has been a consistent controversy over just why lions and other *Felidae* become man-eaters. In researching this book among many hundreds of previous works that date as far back as the first decade of the eighteenth century, I have noticed one conclusion as to the cause of man-eating that seems to recur. Almost without exception, until the publication of Patterson's book on the Tsavo lions in 1907, man-eaters were traditionally reported to be poor, broken-down, tooth-worn, crippled "brutes" who ate people for a living only because they had been injured by nasty hunters, porcupine quills, and the like. The fact is, it's not necessarily true.

It is my experience and belief that there are many classes of man-eating lions. Although injured carnivores who cannot fend for themselves in a normal hunting manner may, indeed, turn to sneaking a native or two between meals, most people-preying lions are generally healthy, sleek, and often oversized specimens more than fit to pursue their normal food. Actually, all of the man-eaters I have shot or inspected after someone else killed them have been in the blush of health with the exception of one old lioness in Ethiopia who had a horribly deformed lower jaw, from the bone of which I extracted a two-and-a-half-inch chunk of iron curtain rod shot there by a hydrocephalic moron with a muzzle loader. I can only hope he was her first victim. Most of her frontal lower teeth were missing, but she still managed to gum fourteen Galla tribesmen with quite definitive results.

Possibly, the practice of the early explorers to consider all man-eaters as "mangy brutes" is better rooted in psychology than fact. Human nature being what it is, Homo sapiens are somehow loathe to entertain the thought that any mere animal would possibly want to eat them for food. For proof to the contrary, it is interesting to consult the excellent table compiled by Peter Turnbull-Kemp, the well-known South African game ranger and author, on the age and condition of eighty-nine known lion man-eaters at death: 91 percent of the killers were either in "good" or "fair" condition when disposed of; only 13.3 percent were "aged" and uninjured, and a mere 4.4 percent aged and injured by any cause, including man.

Aside from those lions forced through injury to a life of homicide, there are many ways that normal lions may take up man-eating. They may be the offspring of man-eating parents, weaned on human flesh and taught to hunt man as a normal activity. In heavy bush country men sometimes stumble onto lions that have no sense of humor. Lions may or may not eat people killed under these circumstances, but if they do, they don't seem to forget how easily the meal was obtained and *voilà*, you have a budding, new man-eater. Look at it this way: why fool around with Cape buffalo and zebra when man is such a pushover?

There are many natural catastrophes, such as plagues and epidemics that litter the bush with corpses, that may lead to lions' learning to eat man. The Tsavo man-eaters may have picked up their culinary preferences by dining upon the bodies of Indian coolies discarded along the railway line. Many African tribes still cling to the custom of discarding their aged and dying members without burial in the bush, which, when you think about it, is tantamount to teaching lions to feed on man. Lions are not at all above scavenging and take to moderately decomposed carrion quite nicely, thanks very much.

* * *

Authorities have likened man-eating lions to homocidal maniacs among men; indeed, there are apparently some lions that kill just for the hell of it, but the most common cause of man-eating in Africa is the most obvious: hunger. If a lion is hungry enough, he will eat you. Period. Consider the recent case in Wankie National Park, Rhodesia, of the lions that in 1972 gave two white families a night of indescribable horror. Here is the story as I obtained it from direct interview at the time.

Len Harvey, a Rhodesian game warden, had recently been married and was honeymoon camping with his wife, Jean, at an old elephant control station near the Shapi *pan*, as natural ponds and flowages are called. At Shapi was another semivacationing ranger and his family, an experienced man named Willy De Beer, his wife, daughter, and her husband, a student from Salisbury called Colin Matthews. In a two-day period, three lions had become increasingly bold, even to the point of entering the camp and eating chickens belonging to the native staff. However, since they had attacked no one and were within the borders of the national park, nothing could be done despite their threatening behavior.

The second night, firearms locked away in accordance with regulations designed to prevent their theft for guerrilla purposes, Len and Jean were asleep in a pole-and-dagga (mud) hut. Slightly after 11 P.M. a large lioness leaped through the window of the hut, hurling Jean from her bed to the floor. Instantly the lioness bit her through the small of the back and shook her like a terrier with a lamb chop. Shrieking with pain and terror, the woman struggled to escape. Shocked awake, Len Harvey realized what was happening and, with the incredible bravery of the desperate, threw himself on the lioness barehanded, punching and scratching to make the big cat drop his wife. It did. In one lightning movement it flattened the man, driving long fangs deep into his shoulder. Still conscious, Len screamed for his wife to get out of the hut and run. She rolled under the bed and, hysterical with agony and fear, emerged from the far side of the hut near the door. Covered with gore from her wounds, she fled the black hut but, halfway to the De Beer house, she stopped, giving a desperate thought to helping her husband. As she neared the hut again with steel nerve, there was a scuffle of movement, and although she was a young woman who had never listened to anyone die, the sound that came through the darkness left no doubt that Len Harvey was beyond help.

Banging on the De Beers' door, she poured out her story and collapsed. Willy awoke his son-in-law and sent him to start the small Honda generator while he went to the storeroom for the guns. In the light of the small plant he grabbed a Model 70 Winchester in .375 H&H caliber, and a Parker-Hale .243, both bolt-action rifles, along with a handful of cartridges for each. Fumbling, he loaded them both, jacking a round into each chamber. Locking the safety catches, he handed the .243 to Colin Matthews as he came up. Both men, still in their underwear, ran for the Harvey hut. The door was shut.

De Beer looked the hut over carefully. Seeing and hearing nothing, he called Harvey's name softly. A deep, warning snarl cut the thin light of the naked bulb outside the hut and De Beer cursed. Still inside. He edged up to the window, a small, black orifice in the mud wall. The safety snicked off the .375 as the Rhodesian paused. What if Len wasn't dead but only unconscious? A blind shot might kill him. He would have to be able to see the lioness to risk a safe shot. Gritting his teeth, he eased his head into the window, catching a glimpse of Harvey's bloody legs in a thin bar of light. But he did not see the paw stroke that tore through the skin of his forehead and grated on his skull bone. A sheet of blood burst into his eyes as he threw himself backward, gasping in pain.

Most men who had just had their foreheads ripped open by a man-eating lioness would not be anxious for an encore performance. Willy De Beer was not most men. Directing Colin Matthews to rip his T-shirt into strips, he had the young man bind the wound to keep the blood out of

16

his eyes. Shortening up on the rifle, he approached the window once more. Waves of agony made him gag and wobble, but he pushed the rifle barrel through the window again. This time the lioness was ready and waiting for him. She lashed out of the blackness and caught De Beer behind the head at the base of the skull, the two-inch talons driving to bone and holding him like great fishhooks. The cat tried to drag him into the hut with her, but De Beer screamed, let the rifle fall through the window into the hut, and, gripping the edges of the opening with both hands, tried to push away. The lioness' breath gagged him as she tried to get his face into her mouth, but, because the paw she was holding him with was in the way, she failed. The man-eater gave a terrific tug and the claws ripped forward, tearing De Beer's scalp loose from his skull until it hung over his face like a dripping, hairy, red beret. The man fell backward onto the ground, and the lioness immediately launched herself through the window after him, landing on his prostrate body.

Although barely conscious, Willy De Beer had the presence of mind to try to cover his mutilated head with his hands, a feat he accomplished just as the man-eater grabbed his head in her jaws and started to drag him away. Perhaps covering his head was a conscious gesture, perhaps reflex. Whichever, it probably saved his life. As the lioness lay chewing on his head, she may have thought that the crushing sounds she heard beneath her teeth were the breaking of the skull bone instead of those of the man's hands and fingers. De Beer, completely blind and helpless, could only scream as the lioness ate him alive.

Ten feet away, petrified with terror, Colin Matthews stood watching the cat ravage his father-in-law. In his white-knuckled fists was the .243 rifle, loaded with four 100-grain soft-point slugs and a fifth in the chamber. Colin could have easily shot the man-eater, but he did not. Never having fired a rifle before, he did not know where the safety catch was or even that there was one. As he fought with the little Parker-Hale to make it fire, the incredible, unbeliev-

17

able, unthinkable happened: Colin Matthews put his foot into a galvanized bucket hidden in the shadows, lost his balance, and fell, dropping the precious rifle.

The lioness looked up, her bloody mouth twisted into a snarl. She had been too busy with Willy De Beer to realize Matthews' presence but suddenly dropped the ranger and, with a hair-raising roar, charged the prostrate boy. Matthews was still struggling to remove the bucket from his foot when the lioness slammed into him. As if in a dream, he shoved his right arm as far as it would go into the enraged animal's mouth, the wood-rasp tongue tight in his fist. White flares of agony rocketed up his arm as the powerful teeth met against his bones, crushing them like pretzel sticks.

Slowly the blind, semiconscious De Beer realized that the great weight was gone, that the lioness wasn't biting him anymore. As from a long distance, he could hear Colin shrieking over his pain. He rolled over, face-up on the dirt, listening to the lion chewing on the young man. Automatically his crushed hands began to feel around for a weapon, anything. His broken fingers touched something hard: in a flash he realized that it was a rifle barrel, the fallen .243. Ignoring the agony of broken bones, he tried to grasp it. It seemed stuck. It dawned on him that the lioness must be standing on the stock. Somehow he tugged it free, the sudden release making him fall backward. Awkwardly, he reversed the rifle, found the safety, and, still unseeing, listened to determine where to fire. By the sounds, the lioness was standing over Colin's body. He triggered the first shot, then, as fast as his smashed hands could work the bolt action, fired twice more. Silence blanketed the camp.

"Colin! Are you all right? Colin!"

"Yes, Dad, I'm all right," answered a pain-tight voice. "But you've shot my hand off."

Before De Beer could answer, Matthews gave another scream, which mixed with a grunt from the dying lioness. In her death throes, she had moved down the young man's body and, in a final reflex, bitten the kneecap completely off Colin's leg. On De Beer's legs and Matthew's eyes, they staggered back to the house where Mrs. De Beer drove the thirty miles to Main Camp, Wankie, for the Rhodesian army helicopter that evacuated the victims at five the next morning.

Rescuers found Len Harvey's body where it lay in the hut, partially eaten by the lioness. He was buried the next day. A post-mortem on the lioness revealed no reason for her attack beyond hunger. Her stomach contained a small snake, a wad of chicken feathers, and most of Len Harvey's face. The first shot fired by De Beer had caught her in the lungs, the second in the shoulder, and the third, traveling at a muzzle velocity of 3,000 feet per second, pierced the cat's right cheek, completely smashed Colin's hand and knuckles, which were inside the lioness' mouth, and then passed harmlessly through the left cheek. An inch or so higher or lower would have broken either her upper or lower jaw and prevented her from snapping off Colin's kneecap a few seconds later. The luck of the draw.

Willy De Beer, surprisingly, survived his wounds. He had 222 stitches in his head alone and immense skin and bone grafting work on both head and hands. Two months after the attack his head was still swollen twice the normal size, and he continued to suffer from dizziness and ringing in the ears. Colin Matthews has had many operations on his hand, but it is not expected to be of much use to him again. His knee may someday support his weight once more, but that won't be determined until years of grafting operations have been completed. Widow Jean Harvey recovered from her bites, if not her nightmares, and was released from the hospital within two months of the tragic night.

I have often wondered what became of the two other starving lions that were reported as accompanying the lioness that killed Len Harvey. They have not been heard from. Yet.

Hunger can, of course, have many causes. As previously mentioned there are some lions injured or aged past the point where they can take their natural prey and therefore turn to man. Hunting conditions, such as the scarcity of game in an area or very high and dense grass after a wet season making hunting difficult, may also be responsible. Although it is almost a cardinal rule that a man-eating lion, once established in his profession, will kill and feed on man to the exclusion of other prey, there is one area of Africa where man-eating is decidedly seasonal. In the grasslands of Tanzania and parts of Portuguese East Africa (now Mozambique) as well as in Malawi (formerly Nyasaland), man-eating activity rises to a crescendo when high grass inhibits normal hunting for lions. Yet, taking Africa as a whole, this behavior is definitely exceptional.

The brazen dedication of the experienced man-eating lion to his art can be spine chilling. Just as a normal lion learns techniques of killing and hunting animal prey in specific manners, so does the man-eater develop a *modus operandi* for catching humans. The fact that a man-eating feline is the most difficult animal in the world to hunt can be explained by the cat's ability to learn well and quickly. As most men who have written about the hunting of man-eaters have confirmed, the majority of really high-scoring lions have been hunted badly by an amateur or clumsy professional before. Most often it's an amateur because you don't live very long as a pro if you get careless. The first time a lion returns to a human kill to finish his meal and receives a whiplash of bullet from a bad shot, you can bet the beer money he won't make the same mistake twice. If you can catch him the first time and make an effective shot, you will end his career right there. But if you blow it, it may cost many dozens of lives before you have another chance.

Just as he does when hunting zebra or wildebeest, a lion, having chosen a victim, will usually stick with his choice, no matter how many other animals pass within easier reach. The singlemindedness of a man-eater was amply demonstrated by C. A. W. Guggisberg in his definitive work on lions, *Simba*. In the vicinity of Fort Mangoche there was an isolated hut some hundred yards from the main village. At dusk one evening a woman was mixing a meal of *posho* while her husband sat nearby chanting, playing a small drum. A large male lion had been stalking him from cover and charged, grabbing him, presumably in the chest, with its teeth. He managed to shout that a lion had him, and his wife bravely snatched up a flaming stick from the campfire and beat the lion in the face with it. Surprised at her audacity, the cat dropped the man, and the woman was able to pull him into the hut, closing and jamming the door shut. Unfortunately, her heroism was for naught since the man died shortly from his wounds. Seconds later, as the woman sat mourning her husband, she was terrified to hear the lion scratching at the hut. Many times the animal tried to break in, and finally the woman's nerve broke. Snatching up a new flaming brand, she opened the door and ran for the village, right past the lion, who let her go. The lion simply walked into the hut, dragged out the body of the man, and carried it off to eat.

When a man-eating lion takes a human from a hut or from a ring of sleepers around a campfire, it is usually by the method of a bite in the skull, which causes instant death. Curiously, there have been many cases of lions actually stepping over one man to pick another, like a bored matron at the canapé platter of a cocktail party. Sometimes, however, the victim is grasped by the body and dragged off to be eaten alive. A "big" bite in the thoracic region by a lion is almost sure death, but victims caught by a shoulder or leg can live a long time in the most unspeakable horror and agony. Hans Besser, a German hunter early in this century, told of a missionary of the White Fathers in Tanganyika being carried off and taking fifteen minutes to die while the lion ate him. Nobody had the nerve to go to his aid. In East Africa there are several cases recorded of a lion eating his victim within the sight of paralyzed onlookers.

I still get the old flutter-guts when I recall the night in Ngamiland, Botswana, in 1970 when I was sharing a tent with Daryll Dandridge, a fellow professional hunter at the time with Ker, Downey, and Selby Safaris, Ltd. Our camp was pitched hard on the edges of the Okavango Swamp, and, the night being warm, we had not zipped the ends of the tent closed. There had been lion noises throughout the night, but since we were used to them, neither of us had any trouble sleeping. I was shaving at first light when I heard a muffled curse from Daryll, who was sitting up in his camp bed, staring at the powdery dirt of the floor. Two feet from the end of my bed, where my head lay, was a very fresh set of immense lion pug marks. He had almost without doubt stood there to sniff my head as I slept blithely on. To add insult, he then had walked smack between our beds and out the other side of the tent.

Lions in camp are a fairly normal state of affairs in Africa today. I personally suspect that the increase of tourism and the expanded game reserves have taken the edge off the traditional fear lions have had of man since he first developed the sharp stick. If they have less apprehension about the scent of man through familiarity, I feel they are more likely to attack. In 1969 on the Luangwa I was sharing a hut with Brian Smith, a young professional hunter, in Mwangwalala camp, which was located about 150 yards from the main camp used by the clients. I had just poured a sun-downer and, armed with nothing more formidable than a fly switch, walked through the half-light down the path along the river separating the camps. I should have known better since Martin, my head waiter, had reported seeing a lioness with three cubs that very afternoon close to camp. A very attention-getting grunt sounded from the grass about twenty feet away, and a most determined-looking lioness stepped onto the path and flattened herself. I froze. The banks of the river in this area are perhaps forty to fifty feet high, and below them is one of the niftiest collections of large crocodiles and hippos you would ever want to see. My mind raced like a flywheel: What'll it be, boy, lion or crocs? Interesting choice. I finally decided, after locking eyes with her for at least six months, that I would prefer the devil I didn't know to the one lying there watching me like a butcher reading a cuts chart. I marked a spot on the trail that would allow me to go over the edge out of her reach. Slowly, and I do not misuse the word, I eased a step back. She came forward one. Impasse. There was no way I could possibly make it the seventy-five yards back to the rifle. Still measuring our relative distances carefully, I decided to take a step toward her. It worked, since she backed up, but not without some violent muttering. Another yard and she seemed uncertain. Well, I reckoned, double or nothing. I dropped the drink, clapped my hands as loud as I could, and screamed a very unprintable phrase, tensed for that long fall to the water if she took it unkindly. My heart hit the top of my skull as she growled and dashed almost past me to disappear into the grass. I did not make that walk ever again without a rifle.

Another night in Sidamo Province, just across the Ethiopian border from the Northern Frontier District of Kenya, I was camped with the late, great Christian Pollet, a famous professional hunter from the Congo. By visual count we had eleven lions wandering around the trucks and tents at once, possibly a couple more in the murk we could not see. They stuck around for almost an hour, probably attracted by the odor of our hung meat, a fringe-eared oryx I had shot that afternoon. Our safari crew was scared white, but none of the big cats showed any aggressiveness and eventually melted off into the night. One, an absolutely immense black-maned male, was the biggest lion I have ever seen, certainly over ten feet in length. I have never seen his like since.

I am indebted to John W. Cox, my good friend and a noted sportsman, once the owner of such larger-than-a-breadbox items as Yankee Stadium, for permission to print an account of his adventures one dark night in the 1950s in Chad. It's one of the more interesting lion-in-camp tales I have heard.

It was the first shooting day of Cox's safari with the French hunter M. Cornon, and the party had driven all day from Fort Archambeau, on the Bahr Aouk, to their hunting area on the Chari River. Reaching their campsite, Cornon had some mechanical difficulty with the truck that hauled provisions, tentage, and such. Deciding that repair was imperative, Cornon elected to drive back through the night for spare parts. As Johnnie Cox tells it:

"We would miss him, but, after all, we were well ensconced at our water hole. Actually, before Cornon left, a group of nomads came to camp adjacent to us, so we had quite a gathering."

"As night closed in, we retired to our cots and mosquito netting. I had heard lions roaring in the distance but thought nothing of it at the time. Although I was tired, sleep came fitfully; possibly the ever-nearing roar of those lions helped keep my mind occupied. A murmur of voices arising from somewhere in our camp indicated that I was not alone in my apprehension. Before long, these mutterings rose to a crescendo of gabble in a strange language which left me totally uninformed as to what was going on."

"It didn't take long to find out about the disturbance. The whole camp and our nomad neighbors broke into an uproar, people screaming and running all over the place. I looked out and saw the world's biggest lion walking past my cot, growling in that low, gutteral tone they apparently use to scare things. It worked in my case. Those lions can't do that for pleasure, because it has to scare them, too. There was nothing between me and that lion but a fairly fragile mosquito net, so I felt it incumbent on me to take a dive out the opposite side of the cot."

"Where were my guns? Good God, we hadn't unpacked them! I ran into Marie (a friend of Cornon's) on her way to the top of a truck and implored her to find out where the guns were. She came through, and soon I was assembling my .308 rifle and shotgun. Where was the ammunition?

Meantime, the whole camp and the nomads were frantically seeking higher ground. People were climbing on top of trucks, scaling trees and shouting in terror. Lions were everywhere. I was too scared to either climb or shout, but got some false courage by possession of my rifle and my over/under with pockets full of ammunition for both."

"As I could see lions within what looked like biting distance, I started blasting away with the .308. They were dimly-lit in the semi-darkness of the camp. I didn't hit one as far as I know, but the shots scared them out of camp. They did not go away, though; they just stayed out in the high grass adjacent the camp and growled. I wished they would quit doing that."

"No one had been bitten. Marie, Marcel (Marcel Brochard, owner of the Studio de Bologne, a major Paris movie studio and Cox's nonhunting companion), one of our trackers and I were the only ones left on terra firma. Everybody else was ensconced aloft somewhere except my partners, Steiner and Sherwin, Americans from Chicago."

"What to do now? I tried to arouse those tired, intrepid hunters, Steiner and Sherwin, but I'll be damned if they had not slept through the whole thing and told me I was nuts to wake them out of a sound sleep with such a wild tale."

"I then entered into the stupidest misadventure of a mis-spent life. It seemed obvious that these lions were regrouping for another raid on the camp. I had learned in Asia that the best weapon against a thin-skinned animal at close range was a 12-gauge shotgun with magnum loads of buckshot. I beckoned to the remaining grounded tracker to go with me out into that black, high grass where all those lions were loitering. We started out to where a lion was grunting about 20 yards from the camp perimeter. Courage is a fleeting fault. We got within what seemed like inches of that lion, when he let out a fine roar, almost as if he didn't like us there. That did it. That tracker turned and ran like a scared-ass ape toward camp, leaving me all alone except for one vocal lion. I passed that tracker before he got out of the grass."

"In the security of camp fires and lanterns which had been lit, I just happened to check the shotgun in case those lions did return. *Both barrels were empty*! I had bearded that lion in deep grass at night with an empty gun! My dear, dumb friend, who had never fired a gun in his life, Marcel, had unloaded it without my knowledge. He thought it unsafe to have a loaded gun around the camp."

"What remained of the night, I spent firing at lion noises in the grass with the .308. At least those shots might keep the lions in the grass and out of camp. Sometime before dawn, the lion sounds stopped. Apparently, the pride had left, so I went back to my cot and fell asleep, lions or no lions."

"There was a large tree in our camp area. In the dawn light, that tree proved to be the residence of all the nomads as well as most of our crew. Nobody had any interest whatever in coming down until we found out what 'gave' with those lions. With a loaded rifle and shotgun, I ventured into the now-lighted grass which had so nearly proved my undoing. We found two dead lions, which were triumphantly dragged back to camp by the now-intrepid occupants of the tree. One of the lions had a shot which had broken its tail—a testimony to my marksmanship. Shooting a lion in the tail in high grass with a rifle in the dark of night is difficult."

The fact that those lions were not driven off or particularly intimated by repeated rifle fire is fair evidence, I believe, that they were reasonably desperate. Presumably, since the natives were nomads, there were some livestock, camels, or horses in camp. Yet, the lions paid them no appreciable interest. Were they a man-eating pride? We'll never know, but the odds surely tilt in that direction. At very least, it was quite a first night on safari for Johnnie Cox.

In a life of professional hunting one is never short of potential close calls. With most big game, especially the dangerous varieties, one slip can be enough to spend the rest of your life on crutches, if you're lucky, or place you or sundry recovered parts thereof in a nice, aromatic pine box. Of course, many individual animals stand out in one's mind or nightmares as having been particularly challenging or having come extra-close to redecorating you. One of the hairiest experiences I have had was with the Chabunkwa lion, a man-eater with nine kills when my gunbearer Silent and I began to hunt him in the Luangwa Valley. We came within waltzing distance of becoming still two more victims.

The spoor told the whole story. A rounded edge of half-moon was just beginning to creep over the black horizon as the lion covered the last few feet to the edge of the sleeping village. He could surely smell the human odor mixed with the smoky scent of dying campfires, urine, and stale *tshwala* beer. His preying eyes slipped carefully across the village, but all was still—none of the hairless animals in sight.

In a low, hunch-shouldered crouch, he slinked toward the rear of a darkened hut, his huge paws soundless against the packed red clay. He stopped. The heat of the African night pressed heavily against him, and, as he paused, the hush of quiet breathing came to his pricked-up ears. Flattened to the ground, he crept across the open space between two huts and froze into tawny stone as he saw the three huddled forms in the shadows against the side of a hut, near the dying embers of a small fire. He lay perfectly still for several moments deciding which man would die, then began to flow through the shadows toward the three deeply sleeping men.

He passed the first two, sniffing softly at their heads, and stood over the closest to the mud wall. His jaws opened and the long, white canines drove into the unsuspecting victim's temples, piercing the thin bone past the eye sockets, and sank into the brain like driven spikes. The man gave a single, convulsive tremor and lay still. Without releasing his grip, the lion tugged, gently pulling the body from between the hut and the sleepers a few inches away. When it was clear, the man-eater straddled the corpse and, holding it by a limp shoulder, dragged it across the open and into the blackness of bush.

The lion easily carried his kill for three miles, pausing only twice to shift his grip. A dark green stretch of towering *conbretum* loomed ahead in the moonlight, and the killer made for it, dragging the man deep into one of the tunnels of the tangled boughs. A single hyena had crossed the blood spoor and followed the lion, but a threatening rumble from the man-eater kept the other animal shuffling twenty feet away.

The big cat rolled the body over and, holding it down with his forepaws, began to feed. The scissor-shaped incisors sheared away huge chunks of meat from buttocks and thighs, the lion chewing with the side of his muzzle until his face and chest were covered with dark gore. By the time dawn lightened the sky there was little left, but still plenty to interest the hyena. The Man-eater of Chabunkwa, thirsty from his ninth kill, padded from the thicket to drink at the nearby river.

The safari season was over and I was puttering around camp, taking care of the last-minute details of tagging trophies and sorting and packing equipment when I heard from the district commissioner of the area, who had sent a runner with a note wedged in a cleft stick asking me to come on my SSB radio as soon as I got it. When I had the aerial rigged after breakfast, he answered my call immediately. We went through the usual amenities, the Thin-Red-Line-of-Empiah voice hollow over the speaker. I asked him what was up.

"Sorry to bugger your holiday," he told me, "but something's come up. . . . I thought you might be able to help me out. That bloody Chabunkwa lion chopped another Senga last night. The Tribal Council is screaming for action. Suppose you might spare a day or so to pop over there and sort him out? Over."

"Stand by, please," I answered. We both knew that man-eating lions didn't usually get sorted out in a day or so. I lit a cigarette from the flat thirty-pack of Matinees. Well, I reasoned, I'm stuck. He must have already cleared it through my company or he wouldn't have known I was free. Also, one just doesn't turn down official requests from district commissioners, not if one wants to hang on to one's professional hunter's license. I reached for a pencil and pad.

"Right, Cyril," I answered. "What are the details? Over."

"Bugger hit the village just this side of the Munyamadzi—know it?—around midnight last night, so far as the report goes. Grabbed a young man sleeping off a beer bust with two others, but neither of his pals awoke. Smells like that same chap who ate the other bunch over at Chabunkwa, about five miles from this village. We don't have any Game Department people in the area and it'll be a few days before we can get somebody up from Valley Command or Nsefu. Can you give it a try before the trail cools? Over."

"Roger, Cyril. Roger. I'll leave in an hour. Shall I give you a radio sched at eight tonight to see if anything's new? Over."

He reckoned that would be a fine idea. We went through the usual jolly-goods and signed off. I whistled up Silent and told him to get cracking with the normal *katundu* for a three-day trip. Less than an hour later we were boiling through the growing heat and billowing dust to the village of Kampisi.

Kampisi looked like most in Zambia's Eastern Province—shabby and dusty with a ragtag collection of snarling curs and tired-looking people, hordes of spindle-legged children who would not reach puberty. We were greeted by the headman, a born politician who always wore eyeglasses and carried a fistful of ballpoint pens despite the fact he could see perfectly well without glasses and couldn't write a letter. Status symbols are as important in the African *miombo* as they are on Park Avenue. He treated all within earshot to a tirade on the lack of government protection from the horrors of the bush. I asked him why in hell the three men had been sleeping outside when there was a known man-eater in the vicinity.

"The young men thought it was too hot to sleep inside their *kaia*, Bwana," he replied. "Also," he said, shuffling the dirt with a big toe, "they were a little bit drunk." He shrugged with typical African fatalism. Most Africans believe it can never happen to them, something like the attitude of front-line troops. The millet and sorghum beer the tribes brew and drink keeps fermenting in their stomachs until the celebrants pass into a comatose sleep wherever they happen to lie down. In this case the price of the binge wasn't a headache, but death.

The headman pointed to the north when I asked him in Fanagalo where the lion had carried his kill. Silent whistled for me, and I walked over to see the pool of dried blood on the crusted blanket where the man had received his fatal bite. He had backtracked the lion's stalk, showing where he had lain watching the village, how he had stalked the sleepers, and where he had begun to drag the body. I loaded my .470 Evans double-express rifle with soft-points and stuck another clump of the big cartridges into various pockets of my bush clothes where they wouldn't rattle against each other. Silent started off on the now-cold trail carrying the water bag, a pouch of biltong (wind- and shade-dried meat), and his long spear.

The afternoon sun seared our shoulders as we followed the spoor into the bush and finally found the spot in the *conbretum* where the lion had settled down for his meal.

The prints of the hyena were over those of the cat, and the most we could recover was a tooth-scarred chunk of lower jawbone and some splinters of unidentifiable bone. Silent wrapped the pitiful fragments in *ntambo* bark fiber and we started back to the village. Too late. There was no point in continuing to follow the cold trail since darkness was only an hour off and we both knew the most heavily armed man is no match for a lion's stealth at night.

Arriving back at Kampisi about dark, I had two hours to kill before my radio schedule with the D.C. I fished out my flask of Scotch and poured a hair-raising shot into the little, scratched plastic cup while Silent recruited men to cut thorn for a *boma*, or as it is called in East Africa, a *zariba*, a spiky barrier or fence to keep out nocturnal unpleasantries. I felt the first lukewarm slug burn the dust from between my teeth and form a small, liquid bonfire in the pit of my stomach. It was that sun-downer or three that made you forget the saber-toothed tsetse flies and the pain in the small of your back, like a hot, knotted cable from too many miles bent over tracking. Four wrist-thick sticks of the biltong washed down with a cool Castle Pilsner from the condensation bag on the Land Rover's bonnet completed my dinner. I sent one of the tribesmen to fetch the headman, who came over to my fire. In a few curt sentences I gave him the succinct impression that anything found wandering around tonight would be shot as the man-eater, so he'd better keep his boys on the straight and narrow. He looked hard at the two asparagus-sized cartridges in my hand and decided that would be a fair idea.

The commissioner came on the radio right on schedule to report everything quiet, so far, from the other villages. "Keep on it, Old Boy," he told me.

I did not think the man-eater would kill again tonight because of the size of his meal the night before. Still, I knew that there had been cases of lions killing as frequently as twice the same night and that, anyway, man-eaters have an uncanny way of showing up where least expected. To be on the safe side, I would sleep in the open car with the big rifle against my leg. Not overly comfortable, to be sure, but those two barrels contained better than 10,000 foot-pounds of wallop, which gives a man considerable peace of mind. I'm not the squeamish sort, but when you have just finished putting what is left of a man in a coffee tin for burial, it does give pause for thought. I had hunted man-eating cats twice before this experience: the Okavango man-eater, a famous killer-leopard, and a lioness who had developed a sweet-tooth for Ethiopians. I had come close enough, theoretically, to being a statistic on both occasions to never again underestimate a man-eating feline.

I rigged the mosquito netting and took my weekly malaria pill as Silent maneuvered the extra thorn bushes across the barrier. The humidity hung about like a barber's towel, and sweat poured from my body. After fifteen minutes of tossing, I took another bite at the flask and dozed off shortly after.

You don't have to live in the African bush surrounded by dangerous or potentially dangerous game very long before you develop a sixth sense that may mean the difference between life and the alternative. After enough experience, you find your brain never goes completely to sleep, but, like an army posting sentries, keeps partially awake while the main body sleeps. A parallel may be found in the case of the new mother who awakes instantly at her infant's faintest cry. This reflex seems better developed in humans than in most big game, who have few if any natural enemies. I have walked up to within a few feet of sleeping lions, elephants, and rhinos, who never noticed me. But then, what do they have to fear?

I don't know what awakened me a few hours later— perhaps a sound I didn't remember hearing, but more likely that sixth sense of apprehension. I sneaked my eyes open but saw nothing in the pale moonlight filtering through the tall acacias. I lay listening for long minutes but decided it must be only nerves. Just as my eyes closed, the night was slashed by a shriek that would curdle Bearnaise sauce. Three more unearthly screams followed. I grabbed the rifle and electric torch, pulled the thorn fence away, and dashed barefoot toward the screams. The beam showed nothing as I pounded through the village until I came to a hut at the far side with the door hanging from a single leather hinge. A gibbering man was inside, his bloodshot eyes wide as poached eggs with terror.

I flashed the light around the interior of the *kaia*. No blood. The walls seemed intact, as was the roof. The soft snapping of Silent's fingers attracted my attention back outside the hut. In the beam of the light was clear evidence of a scuffle, the smooth earth torn by striations of long claw marks. Bending down, I defined the clear pugmark of a big, male lion. I went back into the hut. The man was still staring in horror, mumbling gibberish. Silent entered with my flask, and we were able to get a gagging shot down his throat. Finally, he calmed down enough to tell us what had happened.

He had awakened when his wife stirred to a call of nature. He told her not to go outside, but she insisted. Anatomically unequiped, as was he, to perform the function through the door, she had stepped out into the night, and the lion had immediately nailed her. The man, named Teapot, heard the struggle and the first scream and bounded off his mat to the door. His wife had reached it and was gripping a crossbar that formed a frame for the lashed-on *tshani* grass. He recoiled in terror as he saw the lion pulling her by the leg until she was suspended off the ground between his mouth and the door frame. Suddenly, the upper hinge had broken, and the woman lost her hold. The lion immediately swarmed over her upper body and, with a crush of fangs, dragged her quickly off.

I looked at my wristwatch. The scratched, old Rolex said two hours until dawn, perhaps just about right to permit the lion to feed and get careless. We might be able to stalk him while he was actually eating his kill or intercept him on his way to water before he went to lie up for the hot hours.

"*Chabwino*, Bwana," commented Silent. "It is good. I

think we will find this eater of people this day." I couldn't share his enthusiasm. Rooting man-eating lions out of thick cover is not my idea of good fun. Still, we had our best shot at him yet.

We took up the trail at half-past five as the false dawn began to turn the trees into gnarled monsters. I felt that just as the day before, the lion would travel a few miles, then stop to feed, although after the meal he had taken the previous day, he couldn't have been terribly hungry. Silent ruled out the possibility of this being another lion; one glance at a set of week-old prints and my gunbearer could tell you that lion's favorite color as well as his probable political leanings. The tracks showed definitely that we were on the trail of the right lion.

The spoor led through thinning, winter-dry bush studded with thorn, scrub *mopane*, and towering ant hills for a couple of miles, then turned off to the dense riverine vegetation that bordered the shallow Munyamadzi for about 500 yards of depth along each bank. I had tried hunting lion in this cover before, harrying them through the jungles of waxy, green *conbretum*, a dense, house-high shrub that grows like a beach umbrella with the handle cut off, in hope of getting my clients a quick shot as the cats crossed the open channels between the heavier clumps. It was hard, dangerous hunting that I had quit rather than risk a client's being chewed up. Half the time was spent on hands and knees peering under the dense growth for a patch of tawny hide, hoping, when you saw it that it wasn't attached to a growing halo of teeth hurtling at you in a close-quarter charge. Everything was in the lion's favor in this growth, and I hadn't kidded myself that the man-eater had left it. After all, he had already proven ten times that he had no natural fear of man—the fear that can give the hunter an edge.

I thought about Paul Nielssen's mauling in the past year within this same strip of bush, about five miles upriver. A Spanish client, Armando Bassi of Barcelona, a fine hunter, had wounded a good-maned lion, but it had escaped into the thick *conbretum* before Paul could get in a finishing shot. As the professional, Paul was obliged to earn his $25 per day salary by following the lion and killing it. Nielssen put Bassi up a tree, as is standard practice, and went in alone after it with his double rifle, a .458 Winchester converted from a .450. The lion lay under a bush, after doubling back on his track in a short loop, and watched Paul track past. Nielssen later told me he heard a slight sound behind him, but as he spun to fire, the lion was on him and knocked him flat.

The infuriated cat grabbed Paul by the shoulder and sank his fangs through meat and bone, while shaking the puny human like a jackal with a mouse. For some reason the lion then turned on Paul's legs and began chewing, as I recall, on his left thigh. Armando Bassi, hearing the mauling, jumped out of his tree and ran blindly after Paul. Coming up, he shouted and yelled at the lion to draw its attention and blew the cat's head into pudding with his own .458. Lord, give us more clients like Armando Bassi! Paul owed the man his life and escaped crippling injury, although he suffered a broken femur and a collection of stitches that would have done a Bond Street tailor proud. An animal that can and does kill Cape buffalo with a single bite doesn't waste much time sorting out a mere human.

As we approached the thick cover, Silent and I stopped to peel off our bush jackets lest they scrape against a branch or thorn giving away our presence or position. We left them behind with the water bag after I removed the cartridges from mine. Entering the green tangle, Silent moved just ahead of me in a low crouch, his eyes on the spoor and his spear held in front of his body like a lance. It is normal between a hunter and his gunbearer/tracker that the first spoors while the other covers the possibility of an ambush charge. It's impossible to hunt and track at the same time. The safety was off the .470 and the night sight, an oversized bead of wart hog ivory, which doesn't yellow like elephant ivory, was flipped up for fast sighting in the deep shade. We drifted slowly through the bush listening for the crunch of bone or a low growl as the lion fed in the leafy stillness. The damp, soft soil muffled our stealthy walking on the outsides of our feet, the quietest way to stalk, as we slid through the mottled murk with pounding hearts, ringing ears, and stomachs full of bats.

My mind went over the lion charges I had met before: the quick jerking of the tail tuft, the paralyzing roar, and the low, incredibly fast rush, bringing the white teeth in the center of bristling mane closer in a blur of speed. If we jumped him and he charged us, it would be from such close quarters that there would be time for only one shot, if that. Charging lions have been known to cover a hundred yards in just over three seconds. That's a very long charge, longer than I have ever seen in our thick central African hunting grounds. In tangles like this, a long charge would be twenty-five to thirty yards, which gives you some idea of the time left to shoot.

Ahead of me, Silent stiffened and solidified into an ebony statue. He held his crouch with his head cocked for almost a minute, watching something off to the left of the spoor. The wild thought raced through my skull that if the lion came now, the rifle would be too slippery to hold, since my palms were sweating so heavily. What the hell was Silent looking at, anyway?

Moving a quarter of an inch at a time, he began to back away from the bush toward me. I could see the tightness of his knuckles on the knobby, thornwood shaft of the spear. After ten yards of retreat, he pantomimed that a woman's hand was lying just off the trail and that he could smell the lion. The soft breeze brought me the same unmistakable odor of a house cat on a humid day. Tensely I drew in a very deep breath and started forward, my rifle low on my hip. I was wishing I had listened to mother and become an accountant or a haberdasher as I slipped into a duck-walk and inched ahead. I was certain the lion could not miss the thump-crash of my heart as it jammed into the bottom of my throat in a choking lump, my mouth full of copper sulphate. I could almost feel his eyes on me, watching for the opportunity that would bring him flashing onto me.

I lifted my foot to slide it slowly forward and heard a tiny noise just off my right elbow. In a reflex motion, I spun around and slammed the sides of the barrels against the flank of the lion, who was in midair, close enough to shake hands with. His head was already past the muzzles, too close to shoot, looking like a hairy pickle barrel full of teeth. He seemed to hang in the air while my numbed brain screeched SHOOT! As he smashed into me, seemingly in slow motion, the right barrel fired, perhaps from a conscious trigger pull, perhaps from impact, I'll never know. The slug fortunately caught him below the ribs and bulled through his lower guts at a shallow but damaging angle, the muzzle blast scorching his shoulder.

I was flattened, rolling in the dirt, the rifle spinning away. I stiffened against the feel of long fangs that would be along presently, burying themselves in my shoulder or neck, and thought about how nice and quick it would probably be. Writing this, I find it difficult to describe the almost dreamy sense of complacency I felt, almost drugged.

A shout penetrated this haze. It was a hollow, senseless howl that I recognized as Silent. Good, old Silent, trying to draw the lion off me, armed with nothing but a spear. The cat, standing over me, growling horribly, seemed confused, then bounded back to attack Silent. He ran forward, spear leveled. I tried to yell to him but the words wouldn't come.

In a single bound, the great cat cuffed the spear aside and smashed the Awiza to the ground, pinning him with the weight of his 450-pound, steel sinewed body the way a dog holds a juicy bone. Despite my own shock, I can still close my eyes and see, as if in Super Vistavision, Silent trying to shove his hand into the lion's mouth to buy time for me to recover the rifle and kill him. He was still giving the same, meaningless shout as I shook off my numbness and scrambled to my feet, ripping away branches like a mad man searching for the gun. If only the bloody Zambians would let a hunter carry sidearms! Something gleamed on the dark earth, which I recognized as Silent's spear, the shaft broken halfway. I grabbed it and ran over to the lion from behind, the cat still chewing thoughtfully on Silent's arm. The old man, in shock, appeared to be smiling.

I measured the lion. Holding the blade low with both hands, I thrust it with every ounce of my strength into his neck, feeling the keen blade slice through meat and gristle with surprising ease. I heard and felt the metal hit bone and stop. The cat gave a horrible roar and released Silent as I wrenched the spear free, the long point bright with blood. A pulsing fountain burst from the wound in a tall throbbing geyser as I thrust it back again, working it with all the strength of my arms. As if brain-shot he instantly collapsed as the edge of the blade found and severed the spinal chord, killing him at once. Except for muscular ripples up and down his flanks, he never moved again. The Chabunkwa man-eater was dead.

Ripping off my belt, I placed a tourniquet on Silent's tattered arm. Except for the arm and some claw marks on his chest, he seemed to be unhurt. I took the little plastic bottle of sulfathiozole from my pocket and worked it deeply into his wounds, amazed that the wrist did not seem broken, although the lion's teeth had badly mangled the area. He never made a sound as I tended him, nor did I speak. I transported him in a fireman's carry to the water, where he had a long drink, and then I returned to find the rifle, wedged in a low bush . I went back and once more put the gunbearer across my shoulders and headed for the village.

Silent's injuries far from dampened the celebration of the Sengas, a party of whom went back to collect our shirts and inspect the lion. As I left in the hunting car to take Silent to the small dispensary some seventy-five miles away, I warned the headman that if anyone so much as disturbed a whisker of the lion for *juju*, I would personally shoot him. I almost meant it, too. That lion was one trophy that Silent had earned.

The doctor examined Silent's wounds, bound them, and gave him a buttful of penicillin against likely infection from the layers of putrefied meat found under the lion's claws and on his teeth, then released him in my care. We were back at the Senga village in late afternoon, the brave little hunter grinning from the painkiller I had given him from my flask.

I snapped a couple of pictures of the lion with the self-timer and began to skin him. I would later report that the hide had spoiled and was not taken, so I wouldn't have to turn in more than the ears to the Game Department, which claims all unlicensed trophies. Actually, I had it salted and presented it to Silent, who believed that sleeping on it would bring back much of the romance of his youth. When I dropped him off at his village, near my safari camp, his fat, young wives seemed to concur as they bore him off to his hut with much giggling.

The Sengas retrieved the body of the lion's last victim, which was about half-eaten. That night, back in my own camp, I took a long bath and sat smoking in the tub, with a tall glass of man's best friend at my elbow. Only now did I realize how close I had come to being the Chabunkwa lion's eleventh victim. My side was starting to turn a lovely black and blue where the lion had hit me, but whether it was from a paw stroke or just the 450 pounds of impact, I didn't know. Academic at best. In this kind of business you learn to remember close calls only for what they taught you, not for how they might have turned out. I took away one lesson for sure: the next time a district commissioner asks me for a favor, I'm going to have a severe attack of radio trouble.

A very strong case, both historically and morally, can be made that the lion is *the* classic big game animal. Because of the great personal danger inherent in sport hunting for lions under modern conditions, it might be said that hunting lion on foot in the thick covers of central Africa is the purest expression of the honest sport of hunting. I use the term "honest" because there are many ways to get a cat to skin; to safely bust a *Simba* across 200 yards of cover such as the putting green grass of the Kenya flats is a much simpler proposition than rooting one out of the scrub *miombo* of central Africa, where eyebell-to-eyeball confrontations are as common as not. Crawling into the nightmare tangles of thorn on your hands and knees after a big male lion may have very different consequences from kicking a cottontail rabbit out of a Connecticut brush pile, although in each case the sport is called hunting.

But for his skin as a personal trophy, the lion is hunted entirely as a personal challenge. He has no prized ivory or horn; you cannot eat him, although there are some tribes who do so for sympathetic magic; his pelt is not made into coats. Lions are hunted for the same reason people skydive, race cars, or, in extreme cases, play Russian roulette. They are hunted for the oldest of motives: the challenge of man against a fast, deadly animal on the animal's terms. When you pick up a rifle and take the first step on a lion hunt, you know that you are taking a fair chance of being maimed or killed. It is the clearest case of not just the ancient confrontation of man against beast, but also of man deliberately putting himself in harm's way. It is, in fact, man against himself.

Over the incalculably hoary ages, lion hunting has been considered one of the most noble sports, and the lion the most respected adversary of the hunter. From the time of the interglacial Pleistocene, the period in which, incidentally, Africa still finds itself zoologically, man has had a direct relationship with the lion. *Panthera leo* once roamed throughout Europe, North America, Asia, and, of course, the whole of Africa. Certainly early man confronted him in the Paleolithic and Mesolithic periods, and the tradition of lion hunting as one of the most respected pastimes continued well into the earliest civilizations, which have left us records of early hunts.

Many of the first advanced cultures' monarchs must have concentrated a great deal of their time on perforating lions for fun and profit. I have seen the *scarabaeus* in the British Museum, dating from approximately 1400 B.C. and bearing the cartouche of Amenhotep III, progenitor of Ikhnaton, or Amenhotep IV, which records his killing 102 "fierce-looking" lions during the first decade of his pharaohship. Of course, a pharaonic lion hunt must have made a duke's Scottish grouse drive look like a girl scout outing. Huge bands of beaters concentrated the game while the pharaoh shot them with arrows from his chariot. I think, considering the number of lions killed, that the pharaohs' personal bodyguards must have formed quite a rank, or surely, inevitably, a wounded lion would have caught up with somebody's royal hindside.

Tiglathpileser I, a Middle Eastern monarch in a later time slot, is recorded to have made Amenhotep III look like a beginner by smiting "120 brave-hearted lions in heroic battles on foot [I'll bet!] and 800 lions from my chariot." Assurnasirpal II claimed to have done in "370 lions like caged birds" with a spear.

In ancient Greece, lion sticking was all the rage. Surviving illustrations appear to demonstrate that warriors surrounded their lion in much the same manner of the Masai or Nandi of East Africa, throwing spears or javelins and then relying upon the tall shields they carried for protection when the lion charged.

Most early European sportsmen hunted lion from horseback with muzzle-loading rifles in Africa, not quite as safe a proposition as one might immediately presume. Many of them, at one time or another, were severely mauled or killed through failure of their primitive arms or foolhardy pursuit of wounded lions. I have never decided in my own mind which animal, the elephant or lion, has killed more people. Hippo is is at the top of the list for herbivores, and crocodiles lead the category of man-killers in the carnivore section, yet neither are true sporting animals in the classic sense. At any rate, lions certainly have a creditable record for killing the famous. Nairobi has an impressive cemetery of lion-killed white men, including Sir George Grey, brother of the then prime minister of Great Britain early in this century. In the 1920s it was fashionable for young British bloods to amuse themselves lion hunting on horseback in such areas as the Athi Plains. Sir George made the last mistake of his life by trying to stop a determined charge from a big lion with a little .280 Ross rifle, firing a 140-grain bullet. He bravely held his ground and made the shot nicely, only the bullet broke up in the massive chest muscles of the lion, who proceeded to chew Sir George into small, easily digested chunks before anybody could come to his aid. The nobleman joined a double carload of other defunct sportsmen who learned the hard way that you only make one mistake with a lion: your last.

Modern lion-hunting techniques are somewhat diverse, dependent upon terrain and other physical considerations. Probably, most legally shot lions today are killed by stalking, usually after they have been heard roaring near dawn. There is no form of lion hunting that is not exciting, but this is one of the methods most likely to continue fluttering your stomach twenty years after you first tried it. It is chancy hunting, since the lion is on the move at this time of day, and, in thick bush, you are unlikely to see him until he is quite close.

Another extremely interesting form of lion hunting is practiced mostly in arid countries such as the *gussu* Kalahari shield of northwestern Botswana, formerly the Bechuanaland Protectorate of South Africa. Botswana lions are generally among the largest in Africa. They are also, I can promise you, the most consistently nasty. It has been suggested that this may be due to the fact that Bushmen commonly taunt them off their kills for the meat, and their patience with man is therefore somewhat short. I couldn't say for sure, but in my experience a Botswana lion is as likely to charge on sight at close quarters as not.

Because of the loose, sandy texture of the soil, tracking is quite easy in this area. During the course of a safari, one or more lion kills of natural game are usually discovered. If they were made the night before, the standard procedure is to say your prayers, load your heavy rifle, and follow the tracks to the point where the lion has "lain up" for the hot daylight hours, usually sleeping in the thickest tangle of crud it can find until it cools off and darkness falls.

The impossibly slow and hopefully soundless creeping through the blast-furnace heat of midday, with visibility often less than ten yards, is enough to rattle the nerves of a snake charmer. The average shot will be about fifteen yards, if you are lucky, and if you can determine which part of the lion the shadow-dappled patch of hide covers. At such a short range it is impossible to overestimate the degree of danger a hunter is subjected to. A lion can cover forty-five feet quicker than you can pronounce it. Also, there is the small consideration that he probably won't be alone. One day, with a client from Philadelphia, we shot a very fine male lion at about ten yards after tracking him off the carcass of a wildebeest for three hours. At my client's shot, six other lions appeared, none showing any particular inclination to move off. We looked at them and they looked at us. Discretion being the better part of lion hunting, it was we who cleared off, returning a few hours later for the old boy's skin. I was almost positive that I was going to have to shoot our way out of there, but, fortunately, they let us back off.

Baiting for lion is widely misunderstood. As opposed to leopard baiting, where the object is to actually kill the animal over the offering, the use of baits for lion serves mainly to draw a lion to an area and hold him so he can be followed up for a shot. Baits may be deliberately laid out and hung at chest height by wire from a tree or may take the form of previously killed large game such as elephant. Over the years, my clients have probably killed 25 percent of their lions off dead elephant carcasses or nearby, where the lion has gone to sleep off his meal.

Although many harassed lions will charge unwounded, the vast majority of human maulings and deaths under hunting circumstances are, logically, from wounded lions. There are things I would less rather do than follow up a wounded lion into thick bush, but none come to mind immediately. I've done it nine times and I certainly hope it never comes to ten.

There are several factors that make a wounded lion so

incredibly dangerous. First among them is his inclination to charge from close quarters where only a brain or spine shot will anchor him. You may blow a hole in his heart big enough to accommodate a navel orange, but in his condition of hyperadrenia, there will still be enough oxygen in his brain to carry his charge for a surprising distance and enough moxie left over to turn you into something that would give a hyena the dry heaves. A lion with a bullet in his guts will do everything he can to repay the favor by lying in wait until the last moment before he charges.

The second factor contributing to a lion's dangerousness is the combination of his speed and strength and the small target he offers in a frontal charge. If I had to pick a common trait of all dangerous game, besides the fact that they can kill you, it would have to be that they are all so unbelievably fast. In times of stress their movements are virtually nothing but blurs, a very unnerving fact at a time when you yourself are probably scared witless. A typical charge by a lion from sixty feet takes a blinking of an eye. Add to this the blood-curdling vocal display that accompanies the rush, and you will see why there have been many men who never even got a shot off, let alone a winner. Many lion charges are successful because, considering the velocity, the gunner doesn't hold a low enough lead factor. Also, the anatomy of a lion is such that he has no skull above the eyebrows, usually just a mass of fatty tissue and mane. I almost blew my first lion charge by not compensating for this, but luckily the slug passed through the scalp and broke the spine above the paunch. I didn't miss the second time as he dragged himself toward me with his front paws.

Lion charges are usually, but not always, preceded by a short grunt, which is a great aid in locating the cat. Leopards, on the other hand, almost never make a sound when charging. I do not enjoy following up either one, but if I had to make a choice between digging a lion or a leopard out of grass, I would take the leopard simply on the basis that although he was much more likely to chew a couple of sirloins off me, he probably would not be as likely to kill me.

You get nailed by a lion with one good body bite and, brother, your problems are all over.

I am absolutely delighted to tell you that, as of this writing, I have no idea whatsoever of what it feels like to be bitten by a lion. Jaguar, yes. But, I've had plenty of friends who are firsthand experts on the subject. There has always been something of a controversy about the pain experienced, some maulees claiming that there is little pain, mostly a dreamlike sensation caused by shock, others that the bite of a lion is extremely painful. Undoubtedly, both may be correct, depending upon mental condition at the time, location of the bite, and other such factors. David Livingstone was severely mauled in his early days by a lion he had wounded in Bechuanaland, the cat grabbing him by the shoulder and shaking him until he felt no pain at all. Others, such as Willy De Beer and Paul Nielssen say that the pain was excruciating.

The fact that I have never been seriously injured by an animal, save a bite on a booted foot by a Brazilian jaguar, is owed both to luck of the purest form and an absolute dedication on my part to caution with any game. Some professionals show their assorted scars with pride, but I don't feel that way. If you are a professional, every stitched seam on your body shows that you're probably not very good at it. I am, however, a believer in the sooner-or-later theory, sort of an offshoot of Murphy's Law, which, paraphrased, states that if you stick your neck out with the stuff that bites back enough times, you're going to get it sooner or later. The only possible way to counter the odds of this happening is to be so incredibly careful as to forestall the inevitable as long as possible. Africa has no patience with careless hunters.

Still, many of the really fine hunters from time to time get caught through flukes and plain bad luck. John Kingsley-Heath, a very well-known pro, was badly mauled by a lion he wounded with a light rifle while in a leopard blind several years ago. He followed it up with his .470, but despite two head shots that gave erratic bullet performance, was badly chewed up by the lion. His gunbearer, Kiebe, saved him by shooting the cat off him. Brian Smith, with whom I made several safaris, has been twice mauled by lions and once by a leopard. I believe that an educated guess would be that of those professional African hunters who have plied their trade for more than ten years, perhaps 25 percent go to their graves with lion scars.

Lions are intensely interesting animals to hunt, and to say that no two lion hunts are similar is nearly axiomatic. For example, let's just take one season, May through September 1975, when I was a professional hunter in the Matetsi region of northwest Rhodesia.

Since lions, like all other game, are allocated on a careful quota system by the Game Department to concessionaires of safari areas, lion licenses are only available to those clients who stay for long safaris. My first clients who had lion licenses were Americans on a thirty-day safari. Most clients consider their safari highlighted by the taking of a lion, so this is the species upon which we normally start concentrating. Also, the killing of a good lion early in the trip takes a great deal of pressure off the professional hunter.

The clients arrived in camp late one afternoon and settled in. As we sat around the fire getting to know each other, a pair of lions started the evening serenade. By the sound of their calls they were probably at a bait I had hung some three miles from camp. Well before dawn had broken we were off, trying to get as close as possible to the last calls before first light to begin tracking as soon as we could see.

We picked up the spoor without any trouble and tracked for an hour, the lions, by the sign a pair of large males, not stopping as I thought they would after eating a good portion of the zebra bait.

After the second hour, tracking in more difficult terrain, my gunbearer, a half-Kalanga, half-Bushman named Amos, suddenly stopped and held up his hand to listen. Perhaps a mile away a lion's roar could be heard, although somewhat indistinctly. Instantly Amos diagnosed that the animal was in a deep valley at the base of a hill called "Insholoinyati," Sindebele Zulu for a buffalo-horn boss because of its shape. Carrying rifles at high port arms, our party of five ran for the end of the valley and began to stalk up it, much as one would when trying to flush guinea fowl or francolin. We had not gone 300 yards when we froze at a low hiss from Amos and Rota, his apprentice tracker. An easy forty yards away, lying down and looking at us from the edge of a thicket, was a magnificent male lion with a full, auburn mane. I pointed at it and grabbed the nearest client saying in a whisper, "Lion! Bust him!"

The man looked confused but raised his rifle and sighted. I held my breath as I waited for him to fire, praying it would be quickly since I could see that the lion had pretty well satisfied his curiosity and was about to melt back into the thicket any second. Still, the man did not fire. "Bust him! Bust him," I kept urging, but he just kept looking through the scope at the lion. Finally, the huge lion sat up, yawned, and walked slowly into the grass. I was practically beside myself at having missed the chance to take a beautiful trophy like that the first morning, right out of the box.

We chased further up the valley, hoping for another glimpse of the lion or the one with it, but it was too late. When, after a half-hour, I decided to give it up rather than risk scaring the lions out of the concession, we stopped for a smoke and I asked the man as gently as possible why he had not fired. To my amazement he answered that he thought I was out of my mind and that he was looking at a wart hog! By the time he realized that it was a lion, it was already mostly obscured by the grass and he was afraid to fire in case he only wounded it.

Oddly, that was that client's third safari, and he had never seen a live lion outside of a zoo before. Yet, he was to have another chance the third day.

The original two lions had pushed off to parts unknown, and I had hung a series of other baits in strategic locations within reach. The morning of the third day we were driving slowly toward a bait I had near a wide, grass-choked *vlei*, an area swampy in the rains but dry in winter. Since the previous year had been a record one for heavy rainfall, much of the grass was twelve to fourteen feet tall and offered the visibility of minestrone soup. I have seen more attractive places to hunt lion. Except for a very small percentage of the acreage that the buffalo herds had knocked down, it was practically impenetrable. As we drove along, I felt an urgent tap on the shoulder from Amos, riding in the back of the old Land Rover. I slowed further and he explained in Fanagalo that he had seen the flicker of an ear beneath a small thorn shrub in the grass but wasn't certain if it belonged to a lion or a hyena. Rather than risk spooking whatever it might be, I continued another half-mile down the road before stopping. Finally, we stopped and, checking the wind, swung in a wide arc to bring us as close as possible to the shrub yet offer us maximum visibility under the difficult circumstances.

Finally, we came up to the thorn bush and, the three armed men leading the trackers and gunbearers, sneaked up on it. At twenty yards there was the familiar Whuff! as two huge male lions broke into a run across our fronts. I shouted to the client to take the second one since it seemed to have a better mane. He wing-shot it, though a bit far back, and it rose into the air with a terrible roar, rearing like a hooked tarpon. In a blink it was gone into the high grass, but not before I was able to stick a .375 into it with undetermined effect. Quivering with adrenalin we listened to it growling ferociously thirty yards in the cover.

I led the men back a few yards to have a cigarette and hoped the bloody thing would die before I had to go in and drag it out. I was sure it was badly hurt, perhaps crippled because it stayed in the same position without moving away or attempting a charge. In the impossibly heavy grass, the visibility could not have been over ten feet, and I wanted to give it every conceivable opportunity to expire before I went in. Also, I knew there was more than one wounded lion in there, not forgetting the companion who had not reappeared nor shown himself after disappearing into the hardwoods that ringed the *vlei*. Finally an idea formed that would give me an edge. I sent Amos back for the Rover and my driver, Elias, who pulled up on the road shortly.

Although this particular car was open, a raised plank on a pipe framework over the pickup bed had been built for photography and better visibility in heavy cover. Installing the two clients atop this with me, I had Elias carefully drive toward the continuing growls, the bumper of the car's front flattening the grass ahead of us.

As we came closer, perhaps seven or eight yards, we saw some movement at the place from which the growling was coming and instantly fired. The lion thrashed and roared for several minutes, then seemed to die. For good measure, we both shot it again until I was sure it was dead. As if I was walking on a pile of sleeping mambas, I dismounted and approached the lion. It was still breathing. I had refilled the magazine but was afraid to shoot since I did not know where the other lion was and dared not risk a zero-range charge while working the bolt. It was an interesting few minutes. My nerves were further jangled when the second client screamed, "Watch it! Your right!" I swung around a half-turn and looked smack into the puss of the second lion, who uttered a low sound that you didn't have to speak lionese to understand. Through all the firing, he had stayed not ten feet from the wounded one and, if the American had not spotted his creeping up on me, I would likely have been given the New Look. I put a shot into the ground right between his legs and he did a back flip and disappeared, finally showing himself again as he cleared the grass 200 yards away. I aimed carefully and paid the insurance on the first one.

Although nothing to write home about in the mane department, these two were extremely large and heavy lions, probably about 500 pounds, and in their prime. Hell, I'm in my prime, and I don't have much of a mane! He taped out at a bit over nine feet, one inch, a very fine trophy.

* * *

The man I worked with in Rhodesia, a concessionaire of about 800 square miles of hunting grounds adjoining the Wankie National Park, had another typical experience on a safari the month before. Hunting with a Southwest African, he climbed a low hill the first day and, just across a small valley, saw a very good lion resting under a shady tree.

They made the stalk very well—too well in my opinion—getting to within ten yards of the lion, but they were unable to see him because of intervening brush and thorn scrub. Trying to find a passage to shoot in the cover, the hunter almost stepped upon a second, unseen lion, which, happily, was as surprised as he was. Of course, it spooked the other and the chance was lost.

The two men hunted from long before dawn until last light for the next twenty-nine days, often arriving back in camp chilled to the bone from the long, icy rides in the open car as late as 10 P.M. *Aziko Silwane. Nikis*. No lions. At all. No spoor, no roaring, no kills. Yet, they kept at it until, almost at dark the last day of the safari, they heard a lion roaring a mile away. Since the sun was already down, they ran as fast as they could toward the sound and actually caught up with a big lion within shooting distance. The client fired, but because he was so blown and shaking from lack of breath after the long run, he just creased the forepaw. The lion ducked into a thicket, raising vocal murder.

The professional, muttering unprintables, bulled in after it to save his reputation for never letting a client with a lion license go home empty-handed. It was so dark that he could hardly see, but he heard the short Chuff! that the lion coughed before beginning his charge. At ten feet he put his .458 bullet into the center of a growing, dark shape that seemed to float up at him and was fortunate to remove the top of the lion's skull.

As they built a fire to skin the cat, two men had to stand guard against the other several lions and lionesses who came practically up to the fire. Finished, they backed away to the truck and got out of there.

Lions do very odd things to otherwise stable, sober

people. I had a client in Zambia once, who shall go un-
named, who had a great chance at a lion that was very well
known in the area, a tremendous black-maned monster
called the Mwangwalala lion. As lions go, he was a real
beaut, well over nine feet and with an anthracite neckpiece
that grew down to his cuticles. We were checking a bait one
morning when I caught a movement out of the corner of an
eye and saw this lion walking sedately across a small *dambo*,
or flat, as casually as you please.

I told the gentleman to please place a large hole in it
with all dispatch, and he got into shooting position. Five
times he worked the bolt of his .338 custom Mauser, but the
lion did not fall. In fact, he hardly hurried his stately exit
after a disdainful glance at us. My client was doing everything right except for one minor item: he had forgotten to
pull the trigger. As the saying goes, I kid you not. He was
positive he was firing the rifle, in fact, became furious at me
when I told him he had merely worked the bolt of the
action. Only when I picked up his unfired cartridges and
gave them back to him did he believe me. In the excitement
he was *positive* he was actually shooting at the lion, and to
this day I suspect he wonders if I pulled some sort of
practical joke.

Another hunter friend of mine reports that, upon
seeing his first lion at close range, his client threw away his
rifle and ran like a lunatic straight after the big cat. The
lion, fortunately, wasn't having any, although what might
have happened if the client had caught him might have
made interesting reading.

I don't know about you, but I still get a funny feeling in
the pit of my stomach when I flip on the Late Show and see
the poor old MGM bloke doing his thing. Even though most
African lions are afraid of man on general principles, Africa is a mind-bogglingly big place, and it's going to be some
time before you can bet the beer money that the next lion
you bump into won't be the wrong one.

2

Elephant

Silent's low hiss slithered through the dry, noon heat like a cold, thin blade. The old gunbearer stiffened and slowly passed the .375 Magnum back over his shoulder, edging to the side to clear my field of fire. To our front, deep in the bewildering tangles of second-growth *mopane*, a low, cracking sound could be heard blending with a soft, gurgling undertone. Silent's muddy, malarial eyes probed the grove, then turned on me. "*Njovu*," his lips quietly formed in Chenyanja. "Elephant."

I retreated a few paces, motioning for Antonio, my client, to follow. When we had covered thirty yards, we stopped and I whispered in his ear, using the weird admixture of Italian, Spanish, and English we had developed over the first few days of safari to communicate. In this case the simple word "*elefánte*" was sufficient. His eyes widened, staring back into the wood as he wiped the sweat from his forehead and licked his lips. Gripping my arm, he whispered, "Pedro, for mee ees feerst wahn!"

I have always wondered what his reaction might have been had I leaned over and confided that, for me, his hairy-chested, smell-like-leather bwana, thees was feerst one, too.

Everybody has to start somewhere. I had never seen a live African elephant in the wild before this day on my first professional safari in Zambia. If this seems a bit inconsistent with the finest traditions of the hunting profession, let me explain that I had come to Africa from South America, where I had been a jaguar hunter, then, before arriving in Zambia, I had been conducting safaris in areas that were not in elephant country. Since I had a slight reputation as a "cat man," specializing mostly in lions and leopards, nobody ever dreamed of asking me if I had ever seen an elephant. I had a professional hunter's license, didn't I? Who ever heard of a white hunter who'd never seen an elephant? Had the question come up, the most I could have said truthfully was that I had read a lot on the subject. That's me, the correspondence school bwana. Since this sort of revelation doesn't tend to put the paying clients aquiver with confidence in their intrepid guide, and since nobody *had* asked me, I didn't volunteer the information. Nothing like on-the-job training to learn a trade, anyway.

I jerked my chin at Invisible, who padded over and fished out a five-pack of Kynoch nonexpanding, solid-bulleted cartridges for Antonio's magnificent .475 No. 2 Jeffery's double-barreled express rifle. It had, according to my pal, once been owned by a member of Mussolini's cabinet. Antonio had picked it up from the man's estate for a song, although these days such a rifle was worth about as much as a platinum-plated Maserati. He removed the panatella-length soft-point cartridges from the chambers and dunked in a pair of wicked looking blunt-nosed solids, swinging the action shut with the precision of a vintage Chubb safe. Since I always load with solids anyway, I just checked the magazine on the bolt-action Mauser, stuck a couple of hedges against disaster between the fingers of my left hand, and quietly hyperventilated to slow my heart down to 300 beats per minute. Well, I thought airily, let's go look at an elephant.

As the rest of my safari crew headed back out of harm's way, I could smell the familiar barnyard, zoo-stall odor of big game on the edge of the breeze. Silent motioned for me to give him a cigarette, which I lit. He studied the wafting of the thin, smoky tendril and nodded. It was straight back into our faces. With Antonio gripping the Jeffery's like the true cross, we started into the grove for a reconnaissance of the situation. I can think of things I would rather have been doing.

Since that day, it has always amazed me how anything as god-awful big as a bull elephant can be so hard to spot in cover. Possibly, it is the optical phenomenon of its very size not offering a recognizable view of the whole animal when the silhouette is broken by even fairly light bush. Elephants, under most close-range hunting conditions, appear as small patches of whatever color dirt they have been dusting or wallowing in. Even when he locates the animal, the hunter faces the problem of determining the size of the ivory, which way the animal is facing, and what portion of the anatomy the patch of hide showing represents. In any case, had something the size of a townhouse not stuck its nose into the air and snapped off an arm-thick branch to strip off its bark and leaves with a sound not unlike driving a Buick through a rotting picket fence, we might have stopped for a rest in the bull's shade. He was just fifteen yards ahead, facing three-quarters away when we picked him out, his left tusk a lovely arc of sap-stained ivory.

As we stared chunks and pieces of his outline began to fall into place like the pieces of a jigsaw puzzle. The edge of an ear appeared, and then the shadowy lines of flank and back materialized. Beyond him, a slow movement betrayed something else big and gray looming indistinctly. I raised the binoculars and tried to gauge the ivory of each. From the pictures I had seen, the nearest bull was carrying about sixty pounds per tooth, a fair trophy. The second had slightly heavier tusks, although the right one was broken off two feet shorter than its mate. I looked back at the near bull and nodded to Antonio.

Now, the books I had read never got across how big elephants really are. It may be that the only way to find out for yourself is to walk up to one with a steel and wood toothpick in your shaking hands with the ridiculous intent of doing it harm. You suddenly note all sorts of details you never saw in the zoo: the dark patch from the temple gland, the ragged tatters and holes in the ears, and the strange, pale gray circle around the eye's iris set between impossibly thick lashes. The burbling sound is still heard, which, according to all those books, is just fine. If it stops, prepare to repel boarders. As the ammonia of his urine slaps you in the face, like a public men's room in Atlanta in August, you recall that this digestive sound is not what it appears to be, but just a low, communicative device elephants use to stay in touch in heavy cover.

Swell. So what's next? You have the same feel of rising panic as realizing your fly is open while lecturing to your wife's garden club. You can't simply stand there and tell

Antonio to shoot him in the arse. Just not done. Completely un-*pukka*. Think now. If you try to shunt your shivering carcasses around to the flank for a side brain shot, he'll probably either see you or hear your teeth clacking out the accompaniment to *Malaguenã*. But, you had better think up something clever pretty quick, chum, because he's too close. Way too close. And the wind may shift or he'll take a look astern, and things may become intensely unpleasant.

Grabbing $50 worth of Antonio's tailored bush jacket in one fist, you decide to back off a touch for more shooting room. You don't like the unnerving way Silent is starting to show too much white around the eye, either. With the casual grace of a landslide, the bull shifts a few feet, opening the angle between you. You freeze. Look at the bloody *size* of him! He's gained at least four tons and five feet at the shoulder in the past fifteen seconds. You see the great pads of cartilege in his feet expand with his shifted weight until they are bigger than coffee tables. If only you weren't so damned close. Still ruining Antonio's crease, you start to drift back with infinite care, avoiding each dry leaf and branch as if they were the wire trigger prongs of *teller* mines. You actually manage to cover five big yards before it happens.

Maybe he has felt the touch of all those eyes on him; perhaps the tiniest rustle of vegetation has alerted him. Whatever. With a trumpet so loud that it reverberates in your stomach, he spins around. It is a microsecond before he picks out your forms with those myopic eyes guided by the slick, metallic slide of the safety catches. The huge, raggedy ears swish open wide and the trunk coils up against the chest, a tensed, spring-steel pile driver, a 500-pound bullwhip neat and ready to lash out with irresistible power. Then, he comes, unbelievably fast for his looming bulk, great clumps of dirt and bush debris exploding from his smashing feet as he eats up the precious yards. You throw up the puny rifle, screeching for Antonio to shoot. The twin slaps of concussion from his muzzle blasts cuff the side of your face and deafen your right ear. A fountain of dirt blows from the ground in front of the elephant's feet, a spurt of dust from a skull crease hangs bright in a shaft of sunlight. You had better do it, and do it now.

He is less than ten yards away when the ivory bead of the foresight nestles into the vee of the express leaf on your .375. The head, bigger than a Volkswagen, is tossing, the spot for the frontal brain shot shifting. Then, reflex takes over and the Mauser seems to fire by itself. You never hear the flat whiplash of the shot, never feel the slamming recoil. Somebody else is working the bolt automatically, your eyes stuck on the magical, white-edged hole that has just appeared in a puff of dirt in the middle of the forehead—a ridiculously small hole that is now red-rimmed. You never touch off the second round although it is ready, snug and deadly in its chamber as a mamba in its hole.

The tremendous, gray skull is lifting, pulled backward as the hindquarters collapse and the huge bulk crashes down in the same slow motion as an office building receiving a demolition charge. The thick, wet noise of six tons of blood, bone, and muscle striking earth sounds hollow as he rolls over onto his side, the top, rear leg stretching, stretching, then relaxing. If you are stupid enough to try it, you may take three medium steps forward and touch him with the muzzle of the rifle. But you are too clever for that. You've read too many books. Before the shakes start, you calmly walk around him, sight carefully, and drive another 300 grains of copper-jacketed lead through the nape of his neck—the same spot where the *Matadores de Toros* stick that nifty little leaf-shaped mercy knife. The elephant doesn't seem to have any objection.

You finally get the cigarette lit at the proper end and the desire to festoon your lunch over the back of a *muSassa* stump has somewhat abated. Robert Ruark always said it was proper to cry upon slaying one's first elephant. We'll see. At the moment you're still too scared. Antonio looks like one of those people you see wandering about roadsides near the sites of head-on collisions, although some of the color is creeping back under the tan. Silent slaps his back and pumps his hand. So do I. What the hell? He didn't cut and run, and if his shooting was something less than exemplary, well, it's not every day a Milan businessman gets charged from tennis-court range by a bull *elefánte*. Antonio had taken his bull the hard way, the honest way, with his life on the line against that of the elephant on the animal's own grounds. Before the safari is over, he will collect better trophies than that 120 pounds of billiard balls and piano keys, but it will always be those stained, twin pillars of ivory flanking his den fireplace that will yield the strongest memories of an afternoon in the Central African bushveldt.

If you wonder why a sane man treasures memories of near-death by a bull elephant, I am not sure I can explain the sentiment to your satisfaction. Perhaps the best way to put it would be to say that that bull elephant was Antonio's Matterhorn or Everest, his swim with a Great White Shark, his win of the Grand Prix. It was Antonio's victory over his own mortality.

The African bush elephant, *Loxodonda Africana*, is the largest extant land animal still open for business. Most people who have never hunted elephants tend to think of them as big, gray, good-natured slobs who spend their time running in terror from mice, vacuuming up peanuts, and remembering things. But, if you will spend even a short time in jumbo country, you will rapidly learn that there is as much in common between wild elephants in hunting areas and those park animals accustomed to man's presence as between crocodiles and chameleons. Nothing, but nothing, is as overwhelmingly attention getting as an elephant that has just decided he doesn't like you; and nothing in the animal world is better equipped to do something about it.

For sheer ferocity and determination to get you, he has no match. He will spread his ears in threat display like a windjammer in a line squall, screaming like a bass calliope with all stops lashed down. He will tuck his trunk up against his chest, and he'll start coming. If you are very cool and lucky, and can get a shot through cover that could stall a tiger tank, a heavy bullet, precisely placed, may turn or kill him. Then, again, it may not.

As he gets closer, it will dawn on you that there is simply no place you can go to avoid his six tons of murder. He can easily outrun the fastest sprinter with his deceptive shuffle, and if you're thinking about climbing a tree, don't bother. He'll either knock you out of it personally or toot up a couple of chums to share in the festivities. If 12,000 pounds of screaming, screeching, infuriated elephant bearing down on you has somehow rattled your nerves to the point that you miss that six-by-four-inch spot on his forehead, or your bullet fails to penetrate the two- and one-half feet of tough, spongy, honeycomb bone that protects his brain, then you may as well forget it. The most talented mortuary cosmetician in the world couldn't rewire you so your own mother would know if you were face up or down.

Angry elephants are highly inventive and develop quite individual modes of operation in their sorting out of careless bwanas and locals. After all, there's a lot to the old saw that the black stuff between an elephant's toes is really the remains of slow natives. A favorite procedure is to grip the victim firmly by an arm or leg (experienced elephants prefer the leg as being sturdier) and methodically beat him to furry guava jelly against the handiest solid object. A convenient tree trunk is favored as a mortar by many, but a few show a marked preference for a concrete-hard termite heap. Either way, it's academic as far as the victim is concerned after the first swing or so. One uncoordinated gentleman I used to know in Kenya was brought home in three plastic buckets after a prolonged session of this type.

One of the most popular variations on the theme is the traditional stomp-and-stick technique. This method is fairly self-explanatory, especially if you have ever had a good look at an elephant's feet and tusks. Recipients of this treatment are often difficult to repackage owing to the amount of topsoil that inadvertently gets mixed up with their tatters, making the whole remains a good deal heavier than the original hunter. In execution, the S & S system involves thorough kneading with the forefeet, followed by rolling with the knees, and judicious stirring of the whole mess with the tusks. Results are most impressive.

Other jumbos, outfielders at heart, have a marvelous time throwing their victims in graceful arcs above the trees, then running over to see if they can smash them with their trunks before they hit the ground. An imaginative, creative elephant can stave off boredom for hours with these games.

Although I doubt that personal consideration is a motive, it has often been recorded that elephants will "bury" their victims when the fun is over. The reason for such behavior is unknown, but apparently they will gather grass, leaves, and branches, piling them on the body until it is completely hidden. George Adamson recalled an elderly African woman who had fallen asleep beneath a tree being interred, unhurt, in this manner. This practice may be one reason for the circulation of strange tales of man-eating elephants, in that some victims of the animal are never found.

Elephants are, of course, supposed to be strict herbivores, but truth can be stranger than fiction. Many supposed cases of man-eating can be traced to the occasional playful habit of a frolicsome rogue carrying around a limb or torso of his last victim in his mouth. Perhaps he likes the salty taste of the blood. I have personally seen this "Yorick" syndrome in the species: a jumbo may take to wandering thoughtfully around with a bone from a dead relative or, in one case in Botswana, the twenty-pound tusk of a dead cow clenched in its teeth. I do not, however, believe that elephants are inclined to eat people or any other meat, for that matter. At least, I didn't until I came across the case of Bertha Walt. The incident is hardly representative of field conditions, yet conclusively proves that *one* elephant did eat *one* person.

Bertha was a typist at the zoo in Zurich, Switzerland in which sported a docile Asian elephant named Chang. We don't know much about Bertha, but it would seem that quite a rapport grew between the girl and the elephant, grew to the extent that Bertha was permitted to sleep in a room alongside Chang's stall. (I suspect that even *Playboy* would consider that something of a bizarre relationship.) One morning in 1944 Bertha didn't show up for work. The fact that the stall area was doused in blood and littered with sundry fingers and toes raised some eyebrows, but the stolid Swiss authorities didn't jump to any half-cocked conclusions until Bertha's frock, or half-digested pieces thereof, were fished out of Chang's droppings. Even they had to call *that* conclusive.

Although more man-biting than man-eating, another incident was reported some years back from the grounds of a Transvaal, South Africa, circus. A drunk had been showing off for the crowd, and, as a grand finale to his antics, he stuck his head into the mouth of a smallish jumbo who proceeded to chew it to the consistency of a second-hand plug of tobacco.

I have always enjoyed the tale of the Irishman who, upon seeing his first elephant in the Dublin Zoo, stared for a moment, shook his head, and stalked off muttering, "I don't believe it." It is not the object of this book to become bogged down in such technical considerations as gestation periods, parasite types, or vertebrae counts of any species, but anything as wonderfully weird looking as the elephant deserves more than a perfunctory physical exam.

One form or another of elephant has been scaring the bejeesus out of man since his debut on this earth. Jumbo's remote ancestors date back some 60 million years that we know of, infinitely predating the unwashed forebears we all share. Over this period there have been more than 300 different brands of elephant-related critters that have been distilled by natural selection factors such as climate, competition, and a hundred other pressures down to two basic remaining production models, the African and the Asian or Indian families. To spare you a lecture in comparative proboscidean anatomy, and since we are not concerned with hunting the Asian variety, let it suffice to say that the

Indian elephant is smaller in body height and weight, has a distinctive skull conformation, different numbers of toenails, a single-fingered trunk tip, and much smaller ears than his Afro cousin. The Asian species is largely employed as a work animal, particularly in the timber industry. If you think you have a boss that is less than considerate of your working conditions, ponder the fascinating fact that until very recent times and possibly even now, the value of a trained working elephant was so great that he would be permitted to kill up to five human handlers before being destroyed in the name of labor relations.

A common belief, because of its long use to man, is that the Asian elephant is more intelligent and tractable than the African. But contrary to general supposition, African elephants have been trained to work, or *inspanned*, to steal the old Boer term. The Belgian Congo in the 1930s carried out a plan that proved that African elephants could be handled with the same ease as the Asians.

You will find as many breakdowns of the African elephant by subspecies and race as you will find people who write books about elephants. No exception here. I am not a zoologist, nor do I want to tell you more about elephants than you wish to know. However, I believe that there are only two general classes of African elephants, albeit many family and race differences. The first is the largest, *Loxodonta Africana*, the bush or savanna elephant.

From a hunter's viewpoint the simplest method of subspecies segregation is that of general physical appearance, especially the tusk type, body proportions, size, and weight. Even a person who had never seen elephants before could, with little difficulty, determine that a bull elephant from Kenya's Tana River area, traditional home of many of the best tuskers, is quite different looking from a bull of the Botswana-Rhodesia-Angola regions. The eastern African race, loosely found north of the Zambezi, is not quite so bulky as a comparable member of the southern African tribe, has longer, less stumpy ivory, and, from my observations, is not so meaty and broad at the point where the massive trunk muscles meet the face. In body type the southerners are considerably heavier and taller, as much as several inches on the average height, and will sometimes weigh a ton more.

The body size of an elephant is measured by both body weight and shoulder height, both partially imprecise calculations for obvious reasons: bull elephants are rarely agreeable to stepping onto scales, and the taped distance from shoulder to foot of a dead specimen is not representative of live height since the compression of body weight is not present. The tallest and heaviest African elephant ever recorded was the whopper shot by J. J. Fenykovi in the Cuando River area of Angola in 1955. It is now a full mount in the Smithsonian Institution's Natural History Building in Washington, D.C., and scales an unbelievable thirteen feet, two inches at the shoulder. The scientifically accepted weight at death of the behemoth was twelve tons, or 24,000 pounds, although the ivory was only in the eighty-pound-per-tusk class. Figuring that the top of the bull's head had to be at least a couple of feet above the level of the shoulder, this means that the old boy would have had to duck to fit under an average highway overpass! A normal, large bull would weigh from five to seven tons and stand between ten feet, six inches and twelve feet at the shoulder, still quite a handful.

Loxodonta cyclotis, the so called forest elephant, is the second category of African jumbos. Smaller than the bush variety, the forest type is easily identified by its thinner, down-pointing tusks, smaller ears, and reduced bulk. The species is composed of a bewildering pseudoscientific hodgepodge of presumed subspecies and types. *Cyclotis* is generally found in equatorial regions, typically in the Congo, Niger, and the Guinea coast forest block. The subclasses include the "pygmy" elephant, "water" elephant, "dwarf" elephant, and so forth. Since most elephant hunting today is confined to the larger bush elephant, it is safe to leave the discussion of forest elephants there.

*   *   *

Ivory, from earliest times, has been one of man's most valued commodities. Historically, it is probably the oldest form of barter material besides food and female favors. Both sexes of African elephant grow tusks normally, although a few do not because of genetic mutation. Although rare, some elephants have grown multiple tusks sometimes numbering five or more. Elephant ivory is composed of dentine, the same material that lies beneath the enamel of human teeth, and varies widely in color from very white to dark amber, depending upon age and place of origin. The semitranslucent quality of the best ivory permits a fascinating play of light over and through the cross-laminations of the material found in no other mammal substance. As a commodity, elephant ivory was as much responsible for the exploration and opening of Africa as was slaving. For many years it was valued at the rate of 1 Sterling per pound although now, coveted as a hedge against inflation, its value has risen astronomically in recent years.

Elephant tusks rank among the most impressive trophies of the hunt. Elephants, like people, tend to be right or left handed (or tusked), favoring the use of one tooth over another for bark stripping and other food-gathering functions. Therefore, a pair of tusks from the same animal are almost never the same weight and length. Frequently, the "working" tusk will be shorter and more worn, although it can be thicker and heavier. This tusk usually has one or more smooth, shallow grooves worn into the ivory near the tip, where the animal beats grass and roots over the tusk to clean his food of dirt. Customarily, the size of an elephant in hunting jargon refers to the weight of his heaviest tusk. It follows, therefore, that a "fifty pounder" would have tusks of about fifty and forty-eight pounds respectively, if undamaged. A hundred pounder will cause your name to be forever enshrined in the musty tomes of Rowland Ward, Ltd., of London, keepers of the records of African trophies. It will count just the same if your bull has only one tusk, not rare in aging jumbos, since the weight of the heaviest is the only consideration besides length and circumferance.

72

These days, if you are prepared to take off for six months, walk a couple of thousand thirsty, hungry, footsore, tsetse-bitten miles, spend money like there's no next Tuesday, and pray yourself hoarse, then you might—just might—cut the spoor of a hundred pounder. In all my years of elephant hunting, I have only seen three tuskers outside of parks that surpassed this mark and have had just one client actually collect one.

What are the all-time world's record tusks? It is an interesting question but the answer depends upon the source you investigate.

It is generally accepted that the heaviest pair of tusks are those that now reside in the British Museum of Natural History in London, weighing, at the present time, according to recent information obtained through the courtesy of Carey Yeates of Holland & Holland Ltd., the prestigious arms manufacturers, in the region of 210 pounds each. This is a rough estimate, considerably lower than the original weights of 214 and 226 pounds each at the time they were acquired separately from cutlery firms. They were reportedly killed by an Arab hunter on the slopes of Mt. Kilimanjaro, although other legends say that the Arab found the great bull dead or that the origin of the teeth is not known.

Part of the confusion about the weight of the tusks stems from the fact that ivory tends to dry out quite a bit, losing considerable weight with the passage of time. Different sources list the pair of tusks, acquired in Zanzibar in 1898, as, variously, 235 and 226 pounds, 236 and 225 pounds, and the generally accepted original weight of 226 and 214. They are not well-matched tusks, as are few, one clearly more worn, identifying it as the working tusk. They have, however, not shrunk visibly in length and are the amazing lengths of 10 feet, 2½ inches, and 10 feet, 4 inches, with girths of 24¼ inches and 23½ inches, as thick as a girl's waist. I have been privileged to inspect these greatest of all hunting trophies in their vault at the British Museum, and their very presence is awe-inspiring.

Although the traditional criterion for "size," because of the fact that ivory is commercially reckoned by weight, is heaviness, this is not necessarily the fairest way to rate the relative trophy value of elephant tusks. The longest recorded pair, those in the United States National Collection, measure 11 feet, 5½ inches and 11 feet even. They are, however, thin in relation to their length and average only about 140 pounds per tusk.

One of the most overdone aspects of the African elephant, as he appears in pulp magazines, is that of the madness or "musth" that overcomes bulls in the mating season. This phenomenon of musth is said to be the product of overactivity of the temple gland which produces instant rogues, insane with lust, trampling and goring every hero in sight. It may be that the Asian elephant suffers from this peculiarity, but I have never seen nor heard of such shenanigans on the part of an African elephant. The temple gland seems to be always slightly trickling, marking the sides of the upper face with damp blotches, yet we have no idea of the actual purpose of this gland. Some erudite elephant books tell of the small stick or stem of grass usually found embedded in the orifice of the gland, presumably placed there by the elephant for some odd reason. In actuality, this stick is usually a dried core of secretion moulded by the shape of the gland channel itself and is not present in every elephant.

Probably because we tend to associate wrinkles and rheumy eyes with extreme age in humans, it is assumed that elephants are very long lived. It's likely that the average person would venture a jumbo's lifespan as up to a century or more. I don't believe this to be true for two reasons.

First, the elephant has a system of tooth shedding and regeneration that permits a finite number of sets of nine-pound molars to wear down and be replaced from the rear of the jaw, pushed out much as a child loses his first teeth by the upward thrust of the permanents, although, in the instance of elephants, when a tooth is lost, the replacement is already in position. There has been some controversy as to how many sets of molars an elephant may produce in a lifetime, educated guesstimates running to between five and seven sets, not counting the two-inch milk tusks that are shed shortly after birth. When an elephant wears down his last set of chewers, he's really had it. Without the great, flat-iron, corrugated grinders to process his coarse food, he soon weakens and dies of starvation.

The second reason is based upon my experience while hunting in central Africa, both as a safari guide and an elephant cropper for the government. The lower mandibles of most elephants killed were turned in to the research team at Mfuwe, on the Luangwa River, for analysis. As I recall, the oldest elephant ever examined, out of literally thousands, was an ancient cow of fifty-four years, giving my memory a year's cushion either way. These specimens represented some very big and obviously old cows and bulls, yet through actual investigation, the conclusion was that it is the exceptional elephant that ever sees the far side of fifty.

A classic confirmation of the overestimation of elephant age came from the famous tusker, "Ahmed," who ranged through the Marsabit Park in Kenya carrying what was believed to be the longest and heaviest ivory of any living elephant. A glance at his deeply sunken temples showed that Ahmed was a very old bull when he died of natural causes in 1974, after four years of personal protection from poachers by his own bodyguard of rangers. At his death he was reported in the world press as having been 75 years old and carrying 200 pounds of ivory in each tusk. But since then scientific investigation has clearly established that Ahmed was only 55 and his tusks weighed just 148 pounds per side. Phenomenal ivory, make no invision, but hardly in the league of the Kilimanjaro elephant.

As in all big game hunting, the greatest risk to man comes from the unpredictable behavior of dangerous animals. An elephant that, on a given day, would turn tail at the first whiff of human scent might, the next day and for no obvious reason, carry through a deadly charge. It is there-fore not only inaccurate but suicidally perilous to regard elephant charges as the elemental bluffs that some armchair experts would have you believe. I would estimate that approximately 8 to 10 percent of all charges, including obvious, bluff-threat demonstrations, are genuine. It fol-lows that if you confront enough elephants with impunity, you are sure to have to kill some that would not have been necessary had you left them alone. That, or get yourself hammered as dead as free lunch.

Distance is the critical factor in judging the seriousness of charges. Just as every human has a "personal" area or territory about him which he considers inviolate by stran-gers, so do animals. If you permit a threatening elephant to get within ten yards of you, then the odds have quintupled that the threat will change from bluff to deadly earnest, the results of which you may not like. The best rule I know of is to stand your ground, wave your hands, and shout, trying to outbluff the animal. Pick a stick or rock about ten yards from you, and if the animal comes past that point, put him down—no questions asked.

Incredible as it may sound, contempt-bred familiarity is the factor that probably kills more good professionals than any other. The case of Johnny Uys, an ex-hunter and ex-chief game warden turned conductor of photographic safaris, is a pathetic example. Uys, who had spent much of his life with and around elephants, had some clients in a game reserve armed with nothing but their trusty 35mm Nikons. Uys walked them up to a cow elephant, which charged flat out, grinding Johnny's life out in a long, bloody furrow in the hard earth. I did not see the body, but from what I was told, it was a particularly thorough example of death by elephant.

Having shot between 750 and 800 jumbos, mostly for ecological reasons I'll explain later, I am always amazed at how anybody could ever lose their respect for elephants. If you are not afraid of elephants, then you've either had no experience with them or you're not especially bright. I have twice the respect for them I had when I started hunting, probably because I have seen what they can do. In the everyday life of an African hunter there are just too many potential close calls for me to fathom how a man without a *kamikaze* complex could ever be lulled into a sense of security around the big, gray mountains of mayhem.

One of the most interesting and widespread legends about elephants is that of their supposed graveyard, a vast, hidden storehouse of ivory somewhere in the deep bush. The tale probably got its kickoff from the observations of early travelers, who reasoned that since the plains were not littered with the skeletons of expired jumbos, then they must surely go to some secret place to die. Actually, a fair amount of ivory is picked up each year lying around the bush, provided it hasn't lain there too long. Porcupines, mice, and other small rodents eat ivory for its minerals. The great African sanitary squad of hyenas, vultures, maribou storks, kites, jackals, and ants do an admirable job on the rest of the carcass, and before too long even the largest bones are gone. Additionally, when an elephant is ill, old, or weak, he frequently will bog down in soft river or pond bottoms that he could normally free himself of and drowns. I have three times found decomposing elephant corpses in water.

Genuine, certifiable "rogues" are fairly rare items in Africa. There are many areas, though, that harbor *kali* herds (from the KiSwahili meaning "fierce") that will charge on sight or scent of man. Their extreme aggressive behavior is usually caused by constant harassment by poachers and they are definitely elephants to avoid.

Over the years, a bull with decent ivory can collect an amazing amount of scrap metal in his body, particularly if he lives around an area of heavy tribal poaching activity. Most of this junk is from the muzzles of muskets which shoot a variety of missiles, ranging from chopped wire, nails, melted bottle caps, and iron pyrite to chunks of reinforcing rod and cold-rolled lead slugs. In many parts of Africa, it is impossible to leave an empty fifty-five-gallon oil drum lying about because of the lead alloy or solder used to make the cap and seal the seams. I don't know how many African poachers meet their makers trying to melt the lead from the joints of a gasoline vapor-filled drum, but I have heard of two cases, both spectacular. One old Masarwa Bushman I knew in Botswana, who had apparently mastered the process, had killed six buffalo, all with the same bullet, which he would dig out and reroll into rough shape between small sheets of flat iron.

Most nonvital wounds inflicted by poachers, other than with wire snares, will heal in the almost bacteria-free dry air of the southern African winter. But, if a slug becomes lodged in the huge root of the tusk, a conical cavity extending about a third of the length into the tusk from the jaw, that elephant may well become, in his constant and terrible pain, a rogue in the classic sense. Some of these jumbos have killed over thirty people before being hunted down and destroyed.

A condition often mistaken for that of true roguehood may occur when elephants, especially bulls, become rip-roaring drunk on the fermenting fruit of several trees, particularly *marula*, which is somewhat plumlike. Because of the vastness of the elephantine digestive system, even grain like millet may ferment in the digestive process, causing the elephant to become quite out of hand, quarrelsome, staggering—and, if crossed, deadly dangerous, unlike other animals that become fumbling, good-natured oafs. I once had to follow up a quartet of bulls, out of their skulls on *marula* fruit, after they had raided a village in Zambia in which they killed three people. It was quite an adventure that ended with a multiple charge in thick cover, although I was able to drop all four bulls before they reached me. Later, when the local people were butchering the tons of meat, the pervading odor of alcohol was enough to make a man giddy.

Ever since the first of our hairy-chested ancestors pit-trapped a mammoth, elephant hunting has been an apogee of dangerous sport. Shaka, the mighty Zulu conqueror who placed most of southern Africa under his heel in the nineteenth century, frequently amused himself by ambushing and hamstringing elephants on narrow mountain paths. From what we know he personally chopped away at quite a few of these monsters with nothing but a special axe made for the purpose. Farther north some Arab tribes used to practice the same sort of suicidal madness a few hundred years ago, hunting on horseback in two-man teams. One man would drop off his partner with a long sword behind the elephant while he rode to the front to distract the animal. When, and if, the hamstringer did his work, his pal would pick him up and ride out of danger. Theoretically, that is. Having been within waltzing distance of a couple of thousand elephants myself, I have no doubt that quite a few Arab sports made it to Paradise a hair ahead of schedule.

Africa, to a great degree, was opened up by the professional elephant hunters, as colorful and independent a group as ever entered a wilderness. In the last century and early in this one, a man with a good rifle, some capital for a safari, and an overabundance of guts could make his fortune in a few seasons—provided, of course, he didn't die of disease, crocs, snakebite, cannibals, treachery from his own bearers, heat, cold, starvation, thirst, or boredom, to mention a few specialties of the house awaiting the unlucky or unwary in early Africa. However, despite the long list of more exotic ends that an ivory hunter could achieve, he was more likely to fall victim to an overdose of elephant than anything else.

A very few, like the supertough little Scot, W. D. M. "Karamoja" Bell, named after the Karamajong region of Uganda where he hunted, killed a couple of trainloads of ivory with rifles even lighter than many used today for deer in America, never getting so much as a hangnail in the *bundu*. Nonetheless, old jumbo caught up with most. In reading the old journals, the most amazing aspect of the profession was not how many practitioners were killed, but how many lived through maulings that would make a survivor of Custer's Indiscretion look like a piker.

Arthur Neumann, one of the fraternity, was pounded and gored for an incredible fifteen minutes by a wounded bull that, among other substantial modifications to Neumann's person, actually shoved a tusk through his upper arm, between the bicep and the bone. If you consider that this was forty years before penicillin and that he was several hundred miles into unexplored bush with only his native mule drivers, you get the flavor of what kind of fix Neumann was in. Heaven only knows how or why he lived, but he did—at least long enough to retire a wealthy man in England. Dozens of other hunters were gored, stamped, and tossed, tramped and hammered by bulls that didn't die on schedule, pointing up the high cost of ivory. One, George Rushby, the same fellow that eliminated the Njombe man-eating lions, was thrown fifty feet—five stories—through the air by a wounded elephant. Picking himself up, he limped back to his rifle and killed the bull with one shot. That takes a sense of humor.

Every year during the rains ivory hunters used to have little get-togethers that have been compared to the rendezvous of the American Mountain Men. The object of those hoedowns was to share the news and find out how many of the brethren had gone west during the past season. It has been said that it was possible to get stinking, motherless drunk at such affairs by having just one belt to the memory of each hunter who had zigged when he should have zagged during the past few months.

The strain of elephant hunting in the heavy bush and long grass was enough to wear down even the gutsiest of the pros after a while. Many good ivory hunters lost their lives along with their nerves when just one *tembo* too many came thundering down on them. A typical case was that of Billy Pickering, who shot one of the best tuskers on record, almost 200 pounds of ivory on each side. The very next day after his triumph, he drew a bead on another bull, which charged him after a shift in the wind. His gunbearer later

reported that although Pickering raised and aimed the rifle, he seemed paralyzed and did not fire as the elephant barreled down on him. Pickering must have known what fate had up her sleeve for him since he never even tried to run. For openers, the bull literally ripped Billy's head from his body, pitching it quite a respectable distance away in the bush, where it was later found by a fellow hunter named Clarke, sent to scoop up the remains. Strangely, Clarke, who was an old hand himself, had a similar thing happen to him a short while later. He was about to ventilate a nice bull from a canoe, a relatively safe position, but he could not force his finger to press the trigger. Although the bull never saw him and did not charge, that afternoon wrapped up Clarke's hunting career. He never fired another shot.

I have often pondered, on a time-elapsed basis, if I have spent more time running from or after elephants. In an area as thickly populated with jumbo as Zambia's Luangwa Valley, chance encounters at close quarters with elephants are an everyday affair, and getting chased is one of the greatest and most frequent hazards of safari life. Although elephants do not see well, they can hear you clear your throat at half a mile and sniff you from twice that far. I know their powers of scent for a fact, having once been more than a mile from three tuskers drinking at the river, with the wind at my back. Roughly calculating how long it would take for my scent to drift that far, I sat down and waited. Sure enough, right on schedule all three bulls stopped drinking, lifted their trunks, and lit out. The only way to avoid groups of angry or disturbed elephants is to "cut the wind" on them, always keeping the prevalent breeze blowing from them to you. This is not as simple as it sounds, especially when the wind is eddying and shifting, and a protracted game of hide and seek with a large, displeased herd is not the sort of experience that fades with the passage of years.

I particularly recall a single day in the Luawata area of the Luangwa Valley in 1969 that is as fresh in my mind as if it had happened this morning. I was hunting with Dr. Marco Ugoletti, an Italian physician from Bologna, who had brought along a reporter from one of the Italian "slick" magazines for a series of articles on African hunting and safari life. A local tribesman had come into camp and reported to me that there was a good bull in a large herd some ten miles from camp, along the Munyamadzi River. Normally, I would disregard such information because Africans, if you ask them, will tell you there is a huge bull with teeth like telephone poles just over the next hill. Their reasoning is that, who knows, there just might *be* a tusker, and if a crazy white man kills it, then they are in for a reward for the information. Really good ivory is rarely found in herds, which are mostly composed of cows and calves (the former always acting as leaders). Still, I had gotten reliable information from this man before and decided to investigate.

Because of the terrain, we left the hunting car about five miles from the last reported position and approached on foot, arriving at the Munyamadzi about midday. To my astonishment there were two herds of elephant on a wide plain along the river, totaling perhaps a hundred animals, a very substantial gathering for that part of Africa. Glassing them carefully, I spotted a single big bull mixed in with the rest, a fine tusker with a left tooth that had to go eighty pounds. The right was broken off a foot shorter than its mate but would still probably weigh seventy pounds or so. I have no idea to this day what he was doing in a herd like that, but times being what they are, if a bull with eighty pounds on one side can be found, you had better forget the shopping list and take him while you can.

It was an interesting and tricky tactical situation. The herd was a quarter-mile away across completely open ground, quite the opposite of normal shooting conditions. Our approach would have to be very cute, or we would become the center of attention of a lot of angry elephants. The problem was compounded by the pockmarked character of the ground, typical of the dry-season condition of the area. During the rains herds of elephants coming to water along the riverine zone sink two feet or more into the gummy, black soil with each step, creating a terrain like a lunar landscape. When the dry, cool winter comes, these depressions harden to rocklike consistency until they are almost impossible to walk over, balanced on the rims, without breaking an ankle.

I lit a cigarette to check the wind. Then, after I instructed my six other men to head for cover—they never had to be told twice—Marco, Paolo, Silent, and I huddled closely together in a sort of rugby scrum to give the appearance of a single large animal and started toward the herd. We stopped often to check the position of the big bull since he appeared to be drifting through the loafing herd. At thirty-five yards an old cow swung our way, studying our composite form suspiciously, her trunk waving like the rope trick performed with a steamship hawser. We froze long minutes before she turned away, satisfied that we were a rhino. At that moment the bull appeared at the edge of the herd, offering an open shoulder shot. I patted my own side to signify that Marco should take him in the heart with his .458 Winchester caliber over/under Austrian double rifle. I saw his hair fly with the kick, the 500-grain slugs thumping just over the animal's heart, certain to take out the big plumbing over the organ.

There was a silence of a half-second of stunned disbelief from the herd, and the world literally went mad. There's not much point in describing the scene because the typewriter hasn't been invented that can adequately portray what it's like to be next to a hundred furious elephants at close range with no place to hide. Shoving Marco, whose rifle had frozen its action, and Paolo at Silent, I suggested that they begin the process of placing at least two zip codes between themselves and the elephants while I brought up the rear at flank speed. I was about to wheeze a breath of relief upon completing a hundred yards through the pockmarks when the naiad airs pulled a switch on us. The wind changed abruptly 180 degrees and here came the elephants, two by two. With a communal grace that would make the Bolshoi ballerinas blush, we took off crosswind, hopping over those craters in a state of classic motivation, like O. J. Simpson taking the tire drill.

We got away with it. Almost. At the edge of the plain, after 300 more yards of wind-sprint, lateral Arabesques, we collapsed and looked back at the herd, which was howling in frustration at losing our scent. At that point a very interesting thing happened. They all bunched up for a minute or more, making whatever you would like to call elephant conversation, then began to fan out from a central position. It was, I am convinced, a mutually agreed-upon decision to hunt us down in organized fashion, despite the wind. I may save a lot of printer's ink telling you that they very nearly did just that, forcing us to dodge and run for an hour and a half before we lost them completely. From a treetop I could see that the old bull was down, surrounded by his retinue who hung around until two o'clock. When they were well gone, we sneaked back out and inspected the ivory, which, if anything, was even better than I had hoped.

Reasoning that the clients were hot and thirsty as well as a touch jumpy from the experience, I gave them my driver to guide them to the car and take them back to camp while I covered my skinners and trackers as they began the long, precise business of chopping out the ivory. After five or six days of warm weather tusks may be pulled free without chopping, but I was apprehensive about leaving a pair of beauties like this for someone to stumble upon. Wolfing a strip of biltong, I instructed the driver to return, after dropping off the clients, to a point close to the carcass to pick us up.

It was nearly dark when we finished the task and I realized that there was still no sign of my car. At last light I saw Teapot, the driver, loping across the plain from the other side, a bedraggled, thorn-torn man if I had ever seen one. Shuffling his big, bare feet in the dirt, he told me he had run into the herd again, outrun them despite hot pursuit, only to hang the car up by the chasis in a gully in such a manner that none of the wheels would touch the ground. He tried his best to free it, but the increasing sound of the approaching herd had forced him to run for his life. I debated whether to wait for morning to see about the car but decided that we had better go straight away and hope for the best.

Twilight was just a golden smear in the west when we started off, plotting a course around a pair of large bush fires that are common in the dry season. These are fast, spectacular blazes that, although some would disagree, I believe generally benefit the bush and grasses by removing the dead matter and fertilizing the new with ashes, yet not doing serious damage to living trees and game. The world, as seen upwind of a burning peninsula, was eerie, blood red from the glow of the flames, and the air was punctuated by the popping of exploding grass stems that sounded like a distant fire fight. I was wandering casually along when I felt Silent's hand grab my shoulder and shove me to the right. Surprised, I swung around and looked straight up at a group of elephants bursting from cover mere yards away, headed right at us, black hulks against the glow. More by instinct than anything else, we ran almost at them, passing only a few feet from their right flanks, close enough so that I easily could have touched the last one with my hand. In a second the night swallowed them up, spooky in their awful silence. Whether because of the smoke in the air preventing them from catching wind of us or just the masking darkness, they had missed us. That's just as well because at that range, had they noticed us, I doubt that I would be writing this now.

The hunting car was in a magnificent state of uselessness. Deeply wedged into a sandy draw, it had been tusked completely through the radiator as well as penetrated through the body metal five times. I wondered why it wasn't worse, then realized that in its awkward position, the elephants couldn't crush it with their feet. By the signs only two cows had found it and attacked the human scent, then retreated. Still, it was a long walk back to camp and a week before it could be repaired.

Elephants do not like cars, especially at close quarters. In most parts of south-central Africa, a man gets from one hunting area to another over a series of tracks cut before the season, sometimes by hand, sometimes by tractor. Most of these permit the dizzy speed of about six miles per hour for reasonable comfort; at ten miles per hour, the ride is not unlike one in a paint mixer. Since the least rocky terrain is usually near the rivers, at least in Zambia, of necessity these tracks run through huge patches of chokingly thick bush that permit little visibility forward and to the sides. One chum of mine, in a hurry at dusk, actually hit a cow elephant across the back of her hind legs, which forced her to sit down on the bonnet of the car. Fortunately for my friend, she was as surprised as he was, and, after blowing both front tires and crushing the forward body work and suspension, she took off through the darkness.

Another morning, the late Peter Hankin and I were riding together with his safari crew as he showed me around a new area I would be taking over. As we bounced along an especially bad stretch of track, across a streamlet, the men in back of his pickup Land Rover began shouting and pounding us on the back. We looked around and were horrified to see a one-tusk bull jumbo bearing down on us like we were standing still. He was about thirty yards behind the car and rolling along at nearly twenty miles per hour, while we were forced to crawl along at eight. Obviously, it would not be long before we met. Hankin downshifted and yelled for the men to hang on, then slammed the accelerator to the floor. I was almost thrown out twice before we had covered a few car lengths over the pot-holed path, despite a death grip on the dashboard "Jesus" bar. Two of Peter's men were not so lucky. When we hit the edge of an antbearhole, the Rover disappeared from beneath them and they landed in the road, smack in front of the bull.

There was no way we could help; both guns were cased and there was no time to get them out and loaded. As we watched helplessly, both men sprang up and dashed in opposite directions just as the elephant was almost on them. The bull pulled up in confusion, uncertain whether to take after one of them or keep chasing the car. The blacks were gone in a twinkling and we had gained a few precious yards to a smoother part of the road. When we were sure we had enough room to maneuver, we began to shout and blow the horn until the animal took after us again and we were able to lose him. Both men turned up, stark naked, a few hours later, having shed their clothes to slip through the bush easier. I never saw that elephant again, although we went back to look for him and lost his spoor in a rocky area. An animal matching the description of this one tusker was later killed in the game reserve after being labeled a chronic car chaser, considered a very negative reaction to the public by the Tourist Board.

Unquestionably, the most controversial single issue ever raised about African hunting is the question of which animal is the most dangerous game besides the over-excited client. The choice is usually made from an individual's personal experience with the species that came closest to helping him cash in his chips. As a personal sentiment I am very democratic, being scared blue of anything that bites, even though I have probably come as close to the Big Tax Shelter in the Sky with elephants as with any other animal because so much of my hunting experience centered around them. In any case the matter has never been settled (and probably never will be) because there are so many factors to be considered. Take terrain. Lion hunting as it was done in the old days on Kenya's Athi Plains, wide-open, low-grass tableland, is nothing like tiptoeing through the high grass after a gut-shot feline in Botswana's Okavango Swamp. The contour of the terrain affects all hunting of dangerous game, the degree of danger being dependent upon individual circumstances. The thing to remember is that all big game are very good at killing you if you give them even a fraction of a chance.

But many of the "Great" hunters (meaning any hunter who is either dead or retired and not competing with you for safari clients) considered the elephant *numero uno* for solving all of life's problems. Certainly, there are enough lonely little rock-piled bush graves, with inscriptions stating simply that the occupant was guilty of indiscretion with jumbo, to give plenty of credence to their opinion. This came home to me recently when I ran into a friend from Zambia while hunting in Rhodesia last year. Over a couple of tall ones at the Vic Falls Hotel, he told me that six people I had known and hunted with had been killed by elephants since I had left the country five years before.

Dangerous as they are, elephants sometimes produce the most unlikely stories. One young man, for several years a professional hunter in the Luangwa (until he mistook the parked car of a high government official for that of a poacher and sabotaged it), had a client who shot an elephant one day with a frontal brain shot. The animal collapsed convincingly and the white hunter leaned his rifle against a tree, cut off the elephant's tail and was sitting on the carcass. The next he knew, he was flying through the air into a thorn bush, his men disappearing in all directions. The elephant got up as if unhurt and roared away through the bush before anybody could do anything about it. The hunter kept the tail as a souvenir and was a good enough sport to tell the story on himself. I've had clients shoot two tailless elephants, the healed wounds seemingly made by a knife, which may point up the fact that stunned elephants are often mistaken for dead, especially with brain shots which pass close enough to that organ to stun but not kill.

The current ecological status of the African elephant, as well as his eventual fate, is, like that of most of the Pleistocene leftovers of that great continent, lost some-where in between the teary, oversimplified emotionalism of the preservationist foreigners and the stupid if-it's-meat-then-kill-it attitude of many Africans, black and white. In a place as unbelievably vast as Africa, it's impossible to slap a valid label on a species as widely distributed as the elephant and decree it in danger or not. Whereas there may be, by way of example, extreme poaching pressure on jumbos in Kenya's Tsavo District, this has little to do with other areas of the animal's range, which might be dangerously overpopulated.

The greatest professional compliment of my hunting life came when I was offered a position as a full cropping officer in the Luangwa Command under Bob Langeveldt, who ran the herd reduction "scheme" for the Zambian government. It was a compliment because elephant herd cropping or reducing was considered very dangerous work and was usually offered only to men who had achieved some reputation in skill at arms and reliability in a touchy situation. Obviously, in my case there had been some mistake, yet it was nonetheless flattering. As things turned out, I spent quite a lot of time cropping but eventually turned down the job as it required a three-year contract, which other obligations would not let me fulfill. Also, I decided I would rather live.

I was no stranger to the biggest wildlife problem in Africa today: elephant overpopulation. Since the 1950s each year had worsened the conditions that were crowding the great herds off their ranges and into the national parks from eastern to southern Africa. Each season had seen more and more land that was once available as elephant habitat fall to the ploughs and cattle of the tribes, and now the reserves were so overcrowded with elephants that they were literally eating themselves—and other species—into destruction. It wasn't so much that there were a hell of a lot more jumbo than there used to be; rather, they had become so compressed and jammed into the only habitat left for them that there was no way for the land to support them.

The basic cause of the problem is the vastness of the elephant's stomach and the methods he uses to fill it daily with the average 600 pounds of forage necessary to keep his bulk going. Principally existing on bark and leaf shoots, elephants destroy trees in unbelievable numbers to reach the higher branches by simply smashing them flat or by stripping away long ribbons of bark for the soft, inner lining, leaving the tree to die. The situation is very uncomplicated if you face it head on: overpopulations and over-concentrations of elephants kill trees faster than they can grow back, knocking the entire ecosystem of a huge national park into a cocked hat. Shade is lost, which affects grass and predator-prey relationships. The symbiosis of many species is destroyed. Great amounts of soil are lost in the rains. If permitted to continue, elephant concentrations would destroy whole areas, turning them to deserts and effecting a death sentence on the elephants themselves. The situation resembles the tragic starving winters of deer and elk in America produced by overpopulation because game control has been blocked by sincere, genuinely concerned, but hopelessly misguided "preservationists."

The problem of elephant control has long been handled by a good man with a big rifle, but in the past, control was largely a matter of removing a few troublesome animals from the area where they might be raiding crops or just generally being difficult. Not so today. With the reserves being overrun, whole new concepts and techniques of population control have had to be developed by trial and error.

One of the finest places in Africa for number and variety of game, the Luangwa Valley National Park, had been losing hundreds of square miles of game-supporting habitat each year to the depredations of the estimated 30,000 elephants that had drifted in from as far away as East Africa. After several years of study by the Game Department and numerous international wildlife agencies, a "scheme" was developed to reduce the herds to safer limits as well as to benefit both the park and the protein-starved local people. At considerable expense an ultramodern abattoir and meat-processing plant was built at Mfuwe, across

94

the Luangwa from the well-known tourist lodge of the same name. The plant has a capacity of completely processing 2,000 jumbo per year and wastes no part of the animals that are culled. The meat, inspected by a team of veterinarians, is canned or dried into biltong for consumption by laborers in the copper belt farther north; the skins, stripped off and thinned on special machines, are sold to leather companies in Britain and the United States. The ivory is auctioned internationally, and Mfuwe has its own bone meal plant. The offal goes into fertilizer; the feet end up as bar stools and umbrella racks, while even the lowly tail hairs are knotted into bracelets for the tourist trade.

In Zambia there's a pretty good case to be made that without the cropping scheme at Luangwa, there wouldn't be a national park there today. The park had been used as a political crowbar for some factions who advocated turning the land over to the tribes for agriculture. However, the profits from cropping and the cheap protein thereby provided to the local tribes without poaching have proved that a park is probably the highest and best use for the thousands of square miles it occupies. Zambia is proving that game can pay its own way.

Perhaps we had best get one thing straight right off: elephant cropping or herd culling has absolutely, unequivocally *nothing* to do with sport hunting. It is as different in purpose and practice from sport hunting as slaughtering steers for meat is from formal bullfighting. Certainly, nobody becomes a cropping officer for fun; it's bloody, disgusting, depressing, and insanely dangerous work. The cropper usually lives in less than elegant quarters, often grass huts, and spends his rainy seasons on foot safaris after poachers who will cheerfully give him a half-dozen extra navels anytime they have the chance. Between bouts with almost certain malaria, he can count on lousy food, sore feet, thorn infections, and, if he's the slightest bit unlucky, maybe a nice, fatal dose of bilharzia, that homey little snail fluke that may only quit living in your system when you do. Oh, yes, and then there are the elephants.

Why would anybody do it? Certainly not for the money; the pay was equivalent to $320 per month, paid in Zambian *kwatcha*, which is worthless outside the country. Glory? Hardly. What glory is there in slaughtering mostly cow and calf elephants? Adventure? There's not much adventure in amebic dysentery and athlete's foot. So, why does a man like Langeveldt do it? The crazy thing is that Bob absolutely loved elephants, which seems a little incongruous if you remember that he's killed well over 1,000 of them. I doubt even he would have been able to tell you exactly why. I think it is nothing but the only possible life for a man who is happy only in the bush with danger at his elbow. A lot more of Africa gets into your blood than the malaria, you know.

My reasons for cropping were not nearly so complicated; in fact, they were downright selfish. I wanted to go home to the States some day and write a book about elephant cropping and the men who do it. A good, hairy, gut-pulling novel à la Ruark, out of Hemingway. After shooting something like 700 elephant, I came to the conclusion that (1) nobody would believe how scary it is, and (2) if I didn't get the hell out of there, one fine morning I would make one of those teensy, tiny errors that elephant cropping does not permit. I went back to nice, safe white hunting in Botswana.

In the early days of the culling scheme cropping was done with dart syringes loaded with deadly poison for fear that rifle fire would have a bad effect on the rest of the park's game. It was quickly discovered, however, that darting was actually a greater disturbance to all species because of the death throes of the stricken, panicked animals. The crash of an express rifle, oddly, didn't disturb animals in the least; perhaps they thought it was thunder. But panicked flight by elephant or other animals sent a shock wave of nervousness through the reserve that could last for days. It was an odd phenomenon that I had noticed several times when a client would kill one of several bulls, even from close range, with an instant brain shot. The dead animal would slump quietly and his fellows would pay absolutely no attention to the shot. Often, if they did not move off, I would have to fire several shots over them and shout to force them to scram. But merely wounding an elephant causes the others to act like fleas in a frying pan, running madly in any direction in which they happened to be pointed. Because of this behavior, rules for cropping strategy were developed.

Capsulized, the format for attacking the herds was based upon selecting family groups of up to sixteen or so members, well separated from other elephants. If a group had a good bull among them, they were spared. Elephants have a distinct matriarchal society, and the herd leader is always an old cow. Upon selecting an isolated group of animals, the inviolate rule was to sneak up on the herd and actually charge the leader, which brought an immediate return charge. When she was knocked down, the rest of the herd would mill in confusion for the few seconds it took to systematically kill every one. The object was that under no circumstances could a survivor be permitted. One escapee inevitably spread panic through other herds, which could result in such behavior as attacking tourist vehicles in other parts of the park. Perhaps you would get the picture better if you came along on a typical morning of cropping with Langeveldt and me.

The short wheelbase hunting car ground to a muffled stop, a cloud of reddish dust enveloping its bush-battered, doorless body. The engine windmilled in the afternoon heat for a few seconds, then gargled to a reluctant death. Digging the small binoculars from the breast pocket of his camouflaged bush jacket, Bob Langeveldt climbed from the right-hand driver's seat over the dash and onto the bonnet, sweeping the gray, winter bushveldt of the valley for the movement that had caught his eye. He grunted, trained the dusty lenses for a long time on the clump of *Brachystegia* trees across a wide, open *dambo*, then stooped and passed me the glasses. I took them, stepped up alongside him, and placed the hot, black rubber of the eyepieces against the bones under my brows. I stared for several seconds, seeing nothing but the labyrinth of shadows and broken angles of elephant-damaged bush. Then a small, regular movement flagged from the thin shade of the stand and, as I stared, resolved itself into an ear—a great, dirty-gray mainsail of an ear that could only belong to an elephant dozing away the torpid midday hours. As if by magic another massive, putty-colored form materialized from the bush-striped shadows, then another, until I counted fourteen in all. I nodded to Bob and passed back the glasses.

"I make it fourteen," he said quietly. "Just about right." Langeveldt glanced at the fine stream of thin, loose earth pouring from the scarred fist of Ricetime, his hawk-faced Senga gunbearer. It drifted smokelike away from the herd in the warm breeze. "*Kipa mbumbulu*," muttered Bob as Ricetime lifted the flat, leather case, unsnapped the brass catches, and swung open the lid with its gold-embossed stampings. Sunlight gleamed on the amber and ebony grain of the Rigby's Circassian walnut stock and on the obsidian bluing of the barrels, nested like twin, black cobras in their lair of faded, green plush. Expertly, the Senga hooked the softly scrolled action to the barrels and closed them with a glass-smooth snap. He clicked on the forepiece, rebroke the rifle, and handed it to Langeveldt.

"*Eeeh, na lo gamina*," I motioned to Silent. He unzipped the soft case and slipped out the silver-worn, Game Department issue .458 Magnum, a Winchester Model 70 African. I shook the cartridges from a box and dumped them into a pocket, then stuck another of the familiar yellow packages into the waistband of my shorts. Opening the bolt, I clicked three of the sinister, blunt, full-metal-jacket rounds into the magazine and, depressing the uppermost, chambered a fourth of the thick, steel-reinforced shells. Langeveldt emptied a supply of .470 Nitro express fodder into his pockets, the long, 500-grain solids clinking softly through the cotton fabric. I checked the safety, in the full ON position, and passed the rifle to Silent. Taking the flax-fiber water bag from him, I had a long swig, trying to wash away that slight, coppery aftertaste of fear from the back of my tongue. It didn't work; fear doesn't wash away. It's hard to think about walking into a herd of elephants—on purpose—without considering the possible consequences.

We walked slowly across the *dambo* toward the trees for 300 yards, impala and zebra watching us curiously but keeping their distance. A lion-scarred, old bull wildebeeste called at us with his comical cry of *Woiink!* and bounced a few yards, stopping to stare at us again. The brown grass crushed softly under our sockless hunting shoes, sending a dry, dusty smell into our nostrils. I ambushed a tsetse, his abdomen bulbous with blood from the white welt on my wrist, and crushed him between my fingernails. Clouds of *mopane* flies, as small as gnats, swarmed the sweat-moist places around our eyes and mouths. I wondered idly how Langeveldt could stand the little bastards crawling in his full, chestnut beard when he was in the field. At seventy yards from the still-unsuspecting herd, he held up a dust-frosted hand and we squatted down for a last smoke to study the herd's position and plan our assault.

"Watch out for that big bitch on the right, hey?" said Bob, exhaling a deep drag. He picked at an imaginary piece of tobacco on his lip and gestured at a huge, tuskless cow at the group's perimeter, undoubtedly the herd leader. He didn't have to tell me about *tondos*, tuskless elephants, or how they would sucker you in as close as possible before that shocking, surprise charge, tossing head held so high that you had to drive the bullet into the brain up through the top of the trunk, a very difficult angle. *Tondos* didn't bluff. If they came for you, they always carried the charge through and would do everything possible to recycle you into a frothy little puddle of hairy bouillabaise. *Tondos*, I knew, were aggressive because of their very way of life. Lacking tusks to peel bark from trees for food, they had to wait until another elephant had a juicy strip almost free, then they would bull in and shove the other elephant away, taking the food for themselves. Usually, they were so threatening that their victims didn't feel that a dispute was worth the trouble. Consequently, the tougher *tondos* grew even bigger than the normal elephants and were about three times more dangerous. Oddly, there are more and more *tondos* around these days because no hunter wants to waste an expensive license on an animal with no ivory. Therefore, they live to breed and pass on their genetic propensity for tusklessness.

I sat smoking and watching the herd, mentally going over our plan of attack. In the dry, hot breeze that blew into our faces, we could hear their mutterings and smell the acrid-sweet waft of their droppings. I waved an airy diagram, and Langeveldt nodded that he and Ricetime would come in from the left while Silent and I took the right flank in a short pincer movement. If possible, I would fire the first shot. Although we would normally provoke a charge from the herd leader and kill her immediately so the rest of the bunch would mill around while we executed them, I wanted to take no chance with the *tondo* and would try to drop her unawares with a side brain shot. I slipped the safety to the middle position for instant action, partially withdrew the bolt to check the chamber, and closed it again. I unsnapped the sling swivels and handed the leather strap to Silent. This was no place to get your rifle hung up on a piece of bush. We field-stripped the smokes and rose into a crouch, Bob and Ricetime moving silently off to the left, the white man flicking a quick thumbs-up sign for luck. I counted sixty seconds for them to get into position, then slid the safety to FIRE. As I began to move toward the herd, the giant *Tondo* loomed larger with each step.

At fifteen yards I had a good angle on her, a clear shot at the line between eye and ear, slightly lower and closer to the ear. I had the front sight mated to the rear, perfectly lined up. The trigger crept slightly as I squeezed, and then suddenly all hell broke loose. She swung toward me with a bellow like a ruptured boiler, ears spread like billboards, her head waving high. As she charged, still trumpeting like a fury, I lowered the muzzle and touched off below her eyes, the slug impacting in a wallop of dried mud at the base

100

of her trunk. She halted as if hitting a wall, and before she finished sinking in a rising mountain of dirt and dust, I ran up to her and paid the insurance with two more rounds in the chest. Instantly reloading the magazine, I started running into the herd as it erupted, jostling and shrieking, thick trunks high and twisting like immense, gray pythons in the choking dust. Over the thunder of pile driver feet and the terrified trumpeting, I could hear Langeveldt firing the .470—cool, spaced shots almost lost in the chaos of the slaughter.

I was jolted from the fantastic scene by giant movement right in front of me. I swung ahead of the earhole of a big cow as she raced past in confusion, not six yards away, and fired. She fell toward me, blood pouring from her ears, stone dead. I piled up another animal a few steps into her charge as she spotted me and bore in, the slug taking her perfectly above the eyes in the frontal brain shot. She dropped as if pole-axed, dead as charity on her knees, and remained balanced there, her head swinging back and forth, held up by her neck muscles and tendons. Without looking down, I reloaded and shoulder shot a smallish bull as he tried to break away into heavy cover. At the second round, he fell in a welter of lung blood blowing from his trunk. Fire. Reload. Ignore the searing barrel. Never let the magazine get empty. Blood. Dust. Urine. Fresh dung. The smell of smokeless powder mixed with Bob's cordite and the incredible sound of the terrified herd washed over me. I killed another running elephant with a rear brain shot as it angled away, then swung on an immense cow that dropped at my shot from a shallow angle. Not satisfied that she might only be stunned, I ran up and shot her again in the back of the neck as she lay on her side. Down to one cartridge in the magazine, I pushed my hand into my pocket for ammunition and heard Silent shout over the elephant noise, "*Basopa! Basopa! Lapa kohlo! Nyalubwe!*"—"Watch out! On your left, Nyalubwe (my African name)!" I looked up and saw a broken-tusked bull break away from the far side of the group Langeveldt was destroying, headed right at me from twenty-five yards. No time to reload. I slapped the bolt over on the last round and waited for him to close on me. At ten yards I lined him up for a prefrontal lobotomy and squeezed off. Immediately, from the heavy recoil and deafening report, I knew that there was something damned strange about that shot. I saw the dirt blossom on his forehead in just the right spot, but instead of dropping the way they always do for Stewart Granger and Clark Gable, he didn't even break stride!

How about that, I thought. He's actually going to kill me. Me! I stood, rooted with panic, trying to get another cartridge out of my pocket and into the Winchester. At the last instant, as his trunk was reaching for me, I threw myself off to the right, rolling to escape the smokestack-diameter feet and groping trunk.

Suddenly, he turned away as something flickered through the air and hit him smack in the face. He swung around and began to beat the earth with his trunk, squealing and squalling like a six-ton puppy. Silent, probably because I owed him a month's back wages, had thrown the fiber water bag into the bull's face and, distracted from me, the elephant was methodically tusking and stamping the bag's human scent into oblivion. I fished out a fresh cartridge and sent it through his brain, not daring to get up. That wasn't too clever a move since he almost fell on me. Refilling the magazine, I realized that all was quiet. I know the term "deathly quiet" is a bit overdone, but there are few things more quiet than fourteen dead elephants.

I leaned up against a termite heap and managed to get a cigarette lit. Silent accepted one in the polite two-handed manner of his tribe and lit it off my coal. I had almost gotten over the shakes when Bob and Ricetime came over.

"What happened, Old Boy," he said looking at my face. "Have a hairy, did you?" I pointed to the dead bull and told him about the freak first shot and how Silent saved me from the statistic books. He shook his head, shrugged, and walked around among the seven dead jumbos in my section, popping each one a couple of times with his Browning

9mm. pistol to be extra sure. The week before, a big, head-shot cow had suddenly come to life on the flatbed of a recovery truck from the abattoir. Nobody among the recovery crew was killed, but I'm sure I don't know why.

Cutting a stiff grass stem, I went over to the bull and tried to probe the wound channel from the first shot. The stem entered about two inches and stopped. "What the hell. . . ." I wondered out loud. Where could the slug have gone? Bob provided the answer with his sheath knife at the back of the bull's head, from the skin of which he recovered the errant bullet. Somehow, instead of driving through to the brain, it had just penetrated slightly, then pulled an unauthorized right-flank move, traveling between the skull and the skin until it ran out of steam at the back of the head. It had not given the bull so much as neuralgia. Later, I recreated the incident and found out the reason for the freak performance. That particular cartridge had been in the bottom of the magazine for something like twelve shots, kept in reserve while fresh ones were loaded over it. Gradually, from the recoil of the previous shots, the bullet had been driven down in the cartridge case until it had created a compressed load, a dangerous condition that may produce extremely high pressures and velocities. When I had to fire it in the emergency, it had been going so fast as to be unstable and, instead of boring through bone, it turned on an erratic course. A small technicality, but more than enough to cost a hunter his life.

We walked over to the hunting car, which Ricetime had pulled up near the site of the massacre, and Bob got on the squawker to tell the recovery crew where we were and how many passengers they had. In a few minutes I could see the big trucks crawling up the firebrake like metal hyenas on a spoor. I glanced around. They didn't resemble elephants now, just so much meat lying in their own glazing blood and slop. Fat, shiny, green flies began to whine in the ovenlike air, while above, king vultures slid lower down spiraling columns of sky. Bob started the engine and engaged the clutch, shifting smoothly to second as we bounced along the firebreak in the eye of a plume of pink dust, looking for the other sixteen elephants who would die this afternoon before the quota of thirty was reached.

I thought about it as the greenish dun of thorn and scrub flashed by the open door. Maybe it was just the law of nature in its purest form: the few must die that the many may live. At least here the dead weren't wasted. In fact, their dying kept thousands of square miles of virgin gameland from the hands of man and his bloody crops and cattle. I have never been proud of having been a cropping officer, have never felt anything but revulsion for the slaughter that has been necessary for the survival of the parks and the animals in them, small and large; and slaughter, after all, is the only way to describe the cropping process. Sometimes, late at night, I think back on those days of gore and mayhem, and an interesting little idea comes to mind. Maybe we're going about this whole thing wrong. Might it not make a lot more sense if we were to crop a few excess people—for their own good, of course—and give the elephants a bit more room?

3

Leopard

The palest shard of Kalahari moon was just rising over the broken stand of *maroula* trees when the old man, July, placed another short log on the fire. The bright, blue tongues of flame licked hungrily at the dry wood, and he hunched closer, his one good eye squinting as he scraped with the small knife at the tiny bits of fat and flesh still adhering to the kudu's headskin. He had worked for many hours now, and most of the hide lay across his lap, as clean as parchment. He would finish it in the morning, he decided, knowing that the cool, dry Botswana evening would not let the hair begin to slip. Placing his hands at the small of his back, he stretched his old muscles and took a long swallow from the calabash of *tshwala* at his side. The fires around the safari staff compound had lapsed into round, red pools, like crocodiles' eyes on the powdery *gussu* sand, he thought as he took out one of the cheap OK cigarettes the client, a Texan, had given him for cleaning the ivory yesterday. He was a good man, the *Mlungu*, July had calculated. He had not run like a woman from the elephant's charge, and more importantly, he had plenty of tobacco.

As the half-breed Masarwa Bushman sat over his cigarette and beer, he saw a movement from his own hut. Across the shadowy compound came his son, seven years old, his only living child. There had been others, he remembered, but they had all died, and his wives had grown old. Not until he took the tall Masarwa girl, the last, had he fathered a man child who had lived for more than a few months. The boy would not have a proper name, of course, until he was circumcised, but old July called him Xleo, Little Fish, in the smacks and clacks that formed the vertibrae of the Bushman tongue. Sleepily, the boy walked past the old man to relieve himself at the edge of the bush, and July watched him pass. Neither knew that death waited only feet away.

The big, male leopard had lain flat against the cool sand for more than two hours, watching the camp from the thick bush just past the first ring of deep, black shadows. He had seen the strange, hairless baboons feeding around their fires then, with much chattering, going into the grass caves where they slept. Only one old male had stayed in the open, and the leopard sized up the best approach through the dense bush to slaughter him from behind. Then, the young one had come out of the cave and was walking directly, stupidly, right at him. Without the smallest sound, he bellied to the edge of the winter-dry bush near the opening of the compound. His seven feet of steely muscles rippled hard beneath the rosettes of his glossy, dappled hide, his hind claws digging into the sandy earth to grip for his charge. At the very edge of the light's halo, the child stopped, fumbling with his loin apron, and, at that instant, the leopard burst forward from the murk, a silent, hurtling streak of death.

Quicker than thought, he was on the boy, feeling the hooked scalpels claws grip deep as he wrenched the body for the bite that would crush the spine at the base of the neck. The impact drove the child backward into the circle of light where, with the leopard on him, he turned open-mouthed to his father, paralyzed with shock and pain. Ignoring the hoarse, screaming shout from July, the big cat executed the boy with a single, crushing bite at the base of the head and, grabbing him with long fangs across the middle, leaped back into the bush and the blackness.

Awakened by the shouts and screams fifty yards from my tent, just across the safari camp, I arrived wrapped only in a *kikoy* seconds later. July was being held down by Debalo, my tracker, and Simone, my gunbearer, the old man's lips flecked with foam and a *panga*, or bush knife, locked in his right fist. I twisted the knife away and shook him, demanding to know what was the matter. His good eye shone insanely in the firelight as he tried to break loose, finally almost collapsing. Over and over he muttered one word: "*Ingwe*"—"Leopard."

I took a flaming branch from the fire and flipped off the safety of the Evans .470 Nitro. At the edge of the bush that formed the perimeter of my camp, there were big, wet gouts of dark blood over the pug marks of a leopard and the small, flat footprints of the boy. The blood, black in the torchlight, led into the cover, overstepped by the pads of the big cat, now splayed with the weight of the boy. I sent Simone running back for my electric torch and shotgun and, shivering in just the loin wrap, followed the spoor into the dark scrub. It took only a few hundred feet, with pauses at each step for some sound of either the man-eater or the child, to realize that there was no hope. I had picked up enough patch-work in my years of pro hunting to realize that the only thing I was likely to get out of this adventure was some radical redecoration, maybe worse. I retraced my steps to the fire and went over to Simone and Debalo, both of whom were inspecting smears of the boy's blood between their fingers. "*Quedile*," clicked Debalo, shaking his head slowly. "*Eeeehh*," agreed Simone, "*file*." "Dead," said I, and we were all quite correct.

I led July up to the big, hissing pressure lamp the cook had hung from a tent pole outside the gun tent, where the first-aid kit was kept. An injection quieted him down enough to be led off by two of his wives, tears streaking down his wild face. My client, a manufacturer from Dallas, Texas, was looking on, trying to figure out the mixture of Fanagalo and Tswana I used to communicate with my staff. I explained to him what had happened and he paled, an understandable reaction, since he had been sleeping in a canvas tent sixty yards from where a man-eating leopard had struck. I asked him to give me the time from his safari to take off after the man-eater in the morning, saying that I would make it up at the end of the trip or refund what time I spent on my own. He wanted to go with me but understood that I would lose my license if the Game Department got wind of my exposing a client to such an escapade. Dead or injured paying customers are very, very poor for the safari business and tourist promotion. He took it gracefully, though, and told me to take as much time as I needed. Following the washed-out beam of the flashlight through the *tshani* grass, I went back to my tent and climbed into bed, staring at the black canvas above me, thinking about leopards in general and man-eaters in particular.

The leopard was once described by a man who spent a lifetime studying them as "the perfect killing machine." With the exception of man, he is the most effective and successful mammal predator in the world, a fact borne out by his presence from South Africa to China, in every possible terrain and climate condition from high, icy mountains to steaming swamps, to open grassland to rain forest, bushveldt scrub, and the *miombo* of most of south-central Africa's safari hunting areas. He does very nicely in Iran and parts of southern Russia as well as in Ceylon and Java, where the tiger gave up the ghost long ago. As we will explore in a few minutes, contrary to popular opinion, leopards are anything but in trouble as a species, and huge areas of Africa today still have large populations of them.

Pound for pound, *Chui,* as he is called in KiSwahili-speaking East Africa, *Nyalubwe* in Zambia, and *Ingwe* farther south, is one of the most powerful, elusive, clever, bold, and dangerous animals in the world today. The secret of his success is his adaptability together with his fantastic natural equipment. He can and does live on fish, insects, birds, offal, carrion, other scavengers, garbage, smaller antelopes, pigs and wart hogs, monkeys and baboons, domestic stock, and, all too often, man himself. A big leopard is anything over 115 pounds and 6½ feet long, of which a couple of feet is tail. Yet a cat of this size can, and normally does, kill and carry off prey three times his weight, usually stashing the body thirty or more feet up a tree to keep it safe from other predators and scavengers. The leopard is the smallest animal that consistently kills and eats man—the ultimate evolution of the carnivore.

Besides his incredible strength the leopard moves at blinding speed from close quarters and is noted for his patience, calculating intelligence, hair-raising ferocity, and boldness wrapped in the best camouflage in nature beside a fashion model. Many natural history books claim that he is

110

afraid of men, but I don't know a professional hunter or game officer who would agree with that. He's shy, secretive, yes, but he's afraid of damned near nothing. Leopards frequently live very close to man's habitations, eating garbage that would gag a vulture, picking off a stray cow or goat, even taking a man or child if they think they can get away with it; and they usually do. One pair, if you can believe it, was trapped in the Johannesburg, South Africa, soccer stadium a while back, where they had been living very successfully on stray dogs, pigeons, rats, and such for what may have been a long time.

One of the most difficult factors in hunting down man-eating leopards is that they tend, in many instances, to be "casual" killers. Whereas a man-eating lion or tiger will return to a kill or even stay on it, leopards frequently will not. Their depredations form no pattern because they usually take men when the opportunity arises along with hunting their "natural" prey. Our old pal, George Rushby, one of Africa's greatest hunters of man-eaters of all species, felt strongly that leopards in particular eat people as part of their normal diets, citing the fact that even hard-core killers continue to eat monkeys and baboons right along with their forays against Homo sapiens. It's likely that leopards consider men just another form of monkey or ape.

The old theory that man-eaters only pick up their odd culinary preferences through the ravages of old age, broken teeth, injury through porcupine quills, and other disabilities that preclude their successfully hunting their natural prey was shot down during a recent study of seventy-eight man-eating leopards after they had been killed. Nine out of ten of these central and south African confirmed man-eaters were males in the bloom of health and carrying on their activities in areas of good to excellent populations of game. Of the entire seventy-eight animals, only one fell under the category of "aged and in poor health."

Despite the fact that so many leopards are casual about their people-eating, there have been some individuals that have made the great lion and tiger man-eaters look like bush leaguers. The idea that the *dedicated* man-eating leopard may be the most dangerous animal on earth seems to hold some water when viewed in the light of the box-scores of cats such as the Panar leopard, who reduced northern India's population problems by 400 souls before the late, great Colonel Jim Corbett corrected its table manners. In part of 1959 and 1960 a pair of leopards operating in Bihar State, India, killed and ate more than 300 assorted men, women, and children. A potentially great contender for the Mixed-Sex-and-Age-High-Overall People-Eater had his career tragically cut short at the sixty-seven mark in the Chambesi area, north of my Zambian activities, when he goofed one late afternoon, attacking a man from the rear who happened to be carrying a fishing spear over his shoulder. As the big cat sprang, the steel point entered its eye, pierced to the brain and killed it instantly. The Mirso leopard, also a central African, ran his tally a bit over one hundred tribesmen a few years ago before being trapped and destroyed.

African and Asian leopards are absolutely identical animals, subject to the same family variations on both continents. As a very rough rule, the paler pelts seem to come from grassland animals, whereas the darker, more striking markings are usually from leopards who live in shadow-mottled foliage. The leopard is sometimes called a "panther," especially in India, but this is an overgeneralization of the word. Technically, a panther is any member of the *Panthera* genus of cats, which are distinguished by having a hyoid bone in the throat that permits roaring. These include the lion, tiger, leopard, and jaguar and exclude the snow leopard, puma, ocelot, and similar cats that cannot roar but "scream." The "black panther," seen in zoos and rarely in the wild, is, despite the American Heritage Dictionary's observations, not without spots; the animal is really a deep, semisweet chocolate color, produced by recessive genes through an overabundance of melanin in the pigmentation of the fur. These variants are more common in

112

Asia, although I have inspected a skin from the Simien Mountains of Ethiopia. Black leopards are born of both mixed and normally spotted parents and the litter may be shared by both "black" and normally marked offspring. In strong daylight the underlying rosette patterns are clearly visible, as they are on the pelt of a huge, black or melanistic jaguar I killed in Brazil in 1968, one of my few personal trophies.

Since the African and Asian leopards are identical, one sometimes wonders why the Asians seem to have run up bigger scores of killed or maimed humans than the Africans. I suspect that the answer lies in several factors, including the fact that the human population concentration is lighter in Africa coupled with the fact that most Africans are habitually armed in game country. Also, Africa is broken up without the common government found in Asian areas; therefore, and also because of remoteness, a substantial proportion of successful man-eating attacks is not recorded.

Some leopards, especially consistent man-eaters, become as stuck on human flesh as do lions, although this is not normally the case. A classic example of the horror these animals can create is well woven through the history of one of the worst, the Rudraprayag leopard. In the 1920s, when Jim Corbett was hunting in the Himalayan foothills of his beloved Kumaon in northern India, this leopard actually interrupted and terrified 50,000 Indians who were on pilgrimage in the area. That it preferred human meat to any other was horribly demonstrated in the events of a single dark night in Uttar Pradesh State.

An orphaned goatherd boy (shades of the Little Match Girl!) was sleeping with his animals in a hovel in a small mountain village. To keep his charges from stepping on him as he slept huddled on the dirt floor, he had erected a flimsy barrier across the hut. The leopard, passing outside, caught the boy's scent mixed with that of the goats and, with incredible strength, tore the door from its hinges. With complete singleness of purpose he climbed over and through the terrified goats to reach the boy, whom he killed and partially ate on the spot. Of course, it would have been much simpler to just grab one of the goats, but he clearly preferred the boy.

This same Rudraprayag leopard again demonstrated his sweet tooth for Homo sapiens, this time with Jim Corbett himself. The hunter had lashed thick bundles of thorn around the base of a tree in which he was waiting at night for the cat to come for a bait he had placed for it. Corbett was standing on the bases of the bundles, about fifteen feet up the tree in the pitch dark when the tree began to shake. The leopard was trying to knock Corbett from his precarious perch, completely ignoring the goat staked out for him. Despite the several unfruitful shots that the colonel fired, the leopard, with remarkable boldness, returned many times during the night, determined to get the man, but was unable to clear the thorn barrier. Corbett lived to settle accounts with the cat several months and many lives later. In all, the Rudraprayag leopard was credited with 125 human kills.

That leopards love to kill, often for the sheer hell of it, has been shown with crystal clarity on several bloody occasions. The weasel-in-the-henhouse syndrome surfaced in one case on the Ruvuma River near Masaguru, Tanzania, where a big Tom slaughtered, over a short period of time, twenty-six women and children, none of whom was missing an ounce of flesh. George Rushby, who killed it, reckoned it must have developed some weird Translyvanian craving for human blood. In the 1940s, when Zambia was still Northern Rhodesia, fifteen tribesmen were bitten to death through the throat by a leopard who simply slaughtered them, then walked away. Nobody ever caught up with that one.

Dawn was a tangerine hint somewhere over the great Makarikari salt pan to the east when I tossed off the dregs of the tea, stuck some biltong into my pockets, and began to thumb the dull, brass cases of the British SSG buckshot loads into the Winchester Model 12 pump gun. I have always favored shotguns for close work with thin-skinned, light-boned, dangerous game like leopards. Close charges are so unbelievably fast and unexpected that a rifle could be less than useless. With the plug out of the magazine and one shell up the spout, the old tooth-scarred scatter gun could spew as much lead as a submachine gun if I held the trigger back and fired it from the hip like a trombone player gone mad, slamming the firing pin into the primer on the return stroke of the pump. In case I had a shot out of range for the shotgun, I decided to take along the .470 Nitro, whose twin barrels held more than 10,000 pounds of muzzle-energy persuasion. Carrying my twelve-pound rifle balanced across my shoulder by the barrels, I picked up the dry blood spoor and, with Debalo and Simone, eased into the enveloping bush.

Debalo is a Bushman—at least mostly so. Simone also has some of the blood, but he is much darker and closer to civilization than Debalo. Of all the fascinating ethno-racial groups of Africa, I find none so exotic and interesting as these people of the most remote areas. Probably the oldest racial group in Africa, if not the world, Bushmen once roamed in small, nomadic bands over most of the continent until the conquering Bantu advanced from the forest regions of the equator and drove them slowly into the vastness of their desert retreat, real estate so worthless that even their enemies didn't want it. Living today in small family and clan groups in the desert and part of the Okavango Swamp—not a swamp at all but an immense delta of crystal lakes and channels formed by the only major river in the world that doesn't flow to the sea—they are on the decline through interbreeding with the Bantu and continued encroachment on their territory by black and white alike.

In appearance Bushmen at first give an Oriental impression, with slanted, almond eyes and a yellowish, apricot skin tone. They are usually short, around five feet for the men, with tight, peppercorn hair and flattish faces. Yet, there are other characteristics that set them completely apart from any other of the earth's peoples. The men maintain a semierection all their lives, and it is said that many of the women are born with a natural skin flap or apron that covers their genitals. The women are also subject, in times of plenty, to a unique condition called steatopygia, which is an ability to store fat in the buttocks until they reach the point where they resemble the afterdeck of the *Andrea Doria*. The Bushman language is one of the most difficult, having been mastered by only a very few whites, although the *tsks*, clicks, pops, smacks, and clacks are alive and doing fine in most Nguni-based tongues such as Zulu and Xhosa and are a basis of Fanagalo, the lingua franca of southern Africa.

Despite stories of the feared Bushman featherless, jointed arrows, poisoned with a concoction of beetle grubs, these little people are mostly very shy and inoffensive. In fact, a rough translation of the name of one of the desert tribes, the *Kung*, means "It's Only Me." Usually, in a family group, there will be one or two men who are responsible for hunting, and they are among the finest trackers imaginable. Civilized man has credited all Bushmen with great hunting skills, but, in truth, most are merely gatherers and scavengers, unable to track a wounded hippo through a fresh snowbank. I have usually had problems hiring pure Bushmen as trackers because, living so close to the land, they would only work long enough to earn some beloved tobacco and, after a few days, be gone without warning.

If you think there is racism in southern Africa between black and white, you ain't seen nuthin' until you watch the attitude of a Bantu toward a full or half-bred Bushman. Despised and hated as an inferior, the Bushman has one of the hardest lots in Africa today. In Botswana, it is cause for justifiable homicide to call another man a Bushman, and it is actually against the law! Incredibly, many Bushmen were murdered like animals for sport by early whites with rifles. I have been told by old-timers that some of this still went on into the 1930s when a strict law was passed that, in effect, classified them as certifiably human.

The Okavango Bushmen belong to a group known locally as Masarwa. They are not as pure as the desert tribes to the south, having intermarried to some extent with the black Batawana tribesmen of the area, which has resulted in a wide variety of skin tones and facial features. The most unusual-looking Masarwa I ever saw was Debalo. An odd, pale orange in color, he had the pronounced Oriental eyes of his mother, yet the height of his Batawana grandfather. A slender man, he had a reputation as a great hunter and runner. This became apparent one day, the same day I hired him. I was off looking for a wildebeeste for my staff rations and saw him trotting alone along a grassy plain. As I watched him through the glasses, he flushed a fleet serval cat, which he immediately began chasing with a short axe. Running like a cheetah, he overhauled the cat and brained it with one deadly short throw, a feat I would never have believed possible. When I found that he could speak some Tswana, the local language, I hired him on the spot as a tracker, a move I was never to regret.

As we entered the chest-high tangles of bushveldt, I stopped to study the pug marks of the cat where he had sneaked up before his charge. He was a very big Tom, Debalo and I judged by the spoor, perhaps as much as 160 pounds and seven feet, three inches of velvet-sheathed murder that could take a man apart faster than you could pull off a sock. Debalo went ahead of me in his characteristic, low crouch, eyes strictly on the track while I covered the front, over his back, and the sides. In case of a charge he would fall flat, clearing my field of fire, a technique that had worked quite well on wounded lions twice that season already. Simone, a powerful and bush-wise young Batawana-Masarwa who had been one of the rising stars in the local poaching industry until he spent a year in the *Kingi Georgi Hoteli*, or whatever they called the local slammer in Gaberones, brought up the rear, his anthracite skin an odd contrast to Debalo's. I watched the early sun glittering on the fresh, spiderweb hone marks of his spearhead.

The Bushman had tracked for more than two miles,

stopping three times to point with a stem of grass to where the leopard had put the boy down to shift his fanghold, then lifted him again like a house cat with a dead mole. Except for a few tiny smears on the grass and the dry, gray bushes, the blood had stopped, only Debalo's hooded, primitive eyes and intuition picking out the trail through the barbwire entanglements of thorn and scrub. Then, he stopped, pointing at a splash of fluffy green 1,000 yards ahead that was floating in the growing heat mirage over the silvery toupee of bushveldt, a deeply-shaded grove of sausage trees. "*Kaha, Morena*," he whispered in Tswana. "He will be over there, Lord." The lizards racing around in my guts made me believe he was right. When Debalo tracked leopard, he didn't think like one, he *was* a leopard.

Softly, we crept to within 300 yards of the grove. At the edge of a tall termite heap I carefully glassed each tree with the little eight-by-thirty binoculars, looking through the gaps in the thin bush ahead. I probed each dark cranny of shadowy limbs for the giveaway of a lolling tail tip, but there seemed to be no sign of life at all, which further convinced me that the man-eater was, indeed, lying up in the trees. There should have been birds and monkeys. He had to be there, I thought; his trail had led directly to the place. Rifle ready, I inched forward a few more yards and my heart fell as a flowing dapple of ebony and amber drifted down the trunk of a big tree in an oily-smooth movement, then disappeared into the high grass like ground fog. "Christ," I said between clenched teeth, "Blew it." Our chance for a shot at the killer unawares as he lay up, digesting his ghoulish meal, was gone, but in spades. Yet, we might not have spooked him too badly; he might not have even associated us with the dead child. We moved closer, glassing the trees until I caught the flash of sunlight on a drop of dark blood, falling slowly to splat on the ground under the tree. Finally, I picked out the boy's body, wedged tightly in an upper crotch, well obscured by foliage. Most of his buttocks and part of his side had been eaten away, I noted, trying to keep my breakfast from rising above my throat. Motioning the men back, we retreated to consider the situation.

The only chance now, we all agreed over a short smoke, was for me to wait in ambush for the big bastard to show up to finish his meal. There was an off chance that it might be before dark. He had seen us, I was pretty sure, but if he had had the boldness to kill the child right in our encampment, it probably meant he hadn't been hunted and had very little wariness of man. In this remote part of Botswana, Ngami-land, he may never have even seen a person before last night. Quietly, hoping the leopard was still in the thick stuff and could not see us, we went back toward the tree until I noticed a small depression at the base of an old termite heap, probably an abandoned ant-bear hole that had caved in. Lying flat in it, I could see the dead boy about fifty yards away. I didn't dare to disturb the area with the construction of a proper blind or hide, so this would have to do. Taking the light jacket of camouflage netting from my shooting bag over Simone's shoulder, I put it on and pulled the hood over my head. There was also a flap of mosquito netting material that hung down and effectively covered my face from shine. Crushing a few lumps of termite earth, my men smeared it all over my bare legs and shorts until I looked just the color of the heap. I lay down in what I fervently hoped wouldn't prove to be a shallow grave, and the men covered me over with a light layer of branches and dead grass, just leaving a wide hole for frontal vision. I took a last, deep swig at the water bottle, checked the rifle and shotgun, and instructed the men to make plenty of chatter leaving. Leopards don't count too well, and I hoped he might get the idea we had all left together. Talking loudly, they walked back down the spoor the way we had come, leaving me with an odd, hollow feeling of loneliness.

The long, hot, afternoon hours crawled by like centuries as I scanned the tree and grass line for movement. Sweat sheeted into my eyes like battery acid, but I dared not move to wipe my face or shift away from the pain that was growing like twin, glowing logs along the spine of my lower back. At least, my mind wandered, the tsetse aren't bad. Attracted by motion, they hadn't noticed my camouflaged lump lying in the hole. I tried not to look at the face of the boy, his body now aswarm with irridescent green bottleflies. My body as stiff as a *sjambok* whip, I watched the sun start to slide down the slice of cobalt sky toward the treetops, the lengthening shadows reaching out to me across the hot, sandy scrub like an incoming tide. I stared at the bush, the grass, the trees, the patches of open ground until my eyes ached like hot, gritty marbles. I had left my wristwatch with Debalo, having found out the hard way how far away the bugging devices that are a leopard's ears could pull in the tiny, metallic ticking, but decided it was nearly five o'clock. I started involuntarily as a troop of white-faced Verbit monkeys scampered into the grove, then erupted into shrieking, howling chaos as they saw the leopard's kill. Minutes later, a sextet of red-necked francolin toddled their way by like bob-white quail, pecking only a few feet from my face, frozen into granite. If I flushed them, I might as well have blown a whistle and fired a couple of flares to let the man-eater know I was there. With a low sigh of relief I watched them move off into the grass twenty yards away and vanish.

The sun was at the edge of the trees, now, flashing copper and crimson spears through the leaves. I cursed myself for not having drunk more water and was fighting down my starvation for a cigarette when, suddenly, I *knew* he was there. I felt my hackles rise like a fighting cock's, and the blood began to pound in my ears as I held my breath, listening. It was the tiniest, dry, snakelike rasp on my im-mediate left, the most minute trickle of dirt slithering down the side of the dead termite heap into the branches that covered me. Adrenalin pumped through my arteries as I caught the lapping of a shadow across the dirt in front of me. It was the head and shoulders of a tremendous leopard, actually standing on *my* ant hill, in front of and above me to the left. I felt the smooth steel of the .470 under my hand and the shotgun paralleling it under the layer of dead grass.

No way. Too close. He was within six or seven feet at the most. With my slightest movement or breath he would chop me into Cat Chow before I could ever cover him with one of the guns. He stood there for perhaps thirty years before I realized he was probably looking for me! He had completely faked me out by circling the whole grove and coming in from behind me, where the long grass covered him, instead of the far side, where I had expected. Only luck placed me just downwind so he didn't scent me, although I must have smelled like a locker room in Yankee Stadium after a doubleheader on the Fourth of July after the hours I had spent in that hole. Basically, I felt like a gift-wrapped salami at the zoo. Then the shadow disappeared like an undernourished wraith, as silent as a puff of smoke as it moved across the ground in a short leap. I realized that if I was going to have a chance at him while it was still light, it would have to be now or never. Infinitely preferring never, I decided on now.

In an explosion of flying branches and grass, I rolled stiffly to my feet, screaming the first thing that came to mind, certainly unprintable, counting on the shock effect of my voice to confuse the man-eater for the second I would need to round the termite hill and dust him off with the shotgun. As I cleared it, I was astonished to find the ground empty, not a trace of the big cat. Safety off, the gun pushed well back on my hip so *Ingwe* couldn't come between me and the muzzle, I ran forward into the grass, trying to head him off. I have never been noted for my intelligence.

Fifteen yards away there was a streak of movement as something flitted between two thick clumps of thorn bush. Instantly I fired twice, the shots blending almost into one as the big pellets sleeted through the cover in a shower of clipped debris. Silence. Before the second, smoking hull pinged on the ground, I had the bush covered, finger on the trigger, slipping forward with something less than confidence. Was there a small swish of grass, or was that just the crash of the shots still ringing in my ears? I took another step toward the grayish, yellow clump and he erupted, catching me in midstride, a hurtling, gold and black blur of whitish claws longer than shark hooks and long, very long, yellow teeth floating straight at the bridge of my nose. He was six feet from me when the shotgun went off and I saw the concentrated charge of buckshot smash into his out-stretched right leg near the shoulder. He actually swung in the air from the impact of the shot charge as I tried to work the pump; but I was too slow, as his side and pelvis caromed into the muzzle of the gun and caught me across the hips. I went down, scared fit to wet my pants, the shotgun twisting painfully in my hand, the trigger guard dislocating my right forefinger as I tried to shove at the cat with my left hand. On my knees, I finished pushing the pump forward, and, for the longest half-second on record, we stared into each other's eyes across three feet of Kalahari *gussu* sand. He started to snake his hind legs under him, the pellet holes where I had clipped him with my first two shots bloody and covered with wet dirt. The shotgun fired again, the burst of lead like a solid chain ripping into his upper chest at the base of his neck. He looked at me, made a low, guttural sound, and sank down, his head resting on his forepaws like some Great Hound on a sabbatical straight from hell. The lights went out of his amber, dilated eyes, and he was dead. I drew the pump slowly back, ejected the shell, and clicked it shut. A final shot blew a fist-sized hole just under the last. That was one son of a bitch I wasn't about to let get up.

It took three matches to get the cigarette lit, my hands and fingers doing the samba on their own. I walked over to the hide and finished the water bottle, popping the finger back into place just like Steve McQueen would have done it. It didn't hurt then, but two hours later it felt as if six Gestapo men were amputating it with a dull tack hammer. In fifteen minutes most of the camp was there, including the Texan who, Lord save his soul forever, had brought along a bottle of bonded Kentucky Drain Opener.

Debalo climbed the tree with Simone and maneuvered the pathetic little corpse of Xleo into a plastic fertilizer bag, lowering it to July. Nobody said anything when the old man, tears streaming down his dusty face, went over to the leopard and, kicking him onto his back, castrated him with one sweeping slash of his knife. Blood for blood has been Africa's way for a very long time and I was just as pleased that, for once, none of mine was involved.

I had always thought of myself as a fairly average Joe until a few years ago. I never put razor blades in the Halloween apples. I was nowhere near My Lai. I hardly knew Martin Bormann. I have a large mortgage and a writer's income. What's more, I *did* give at the office and only beat my wife occasionally. But, there is something in my past that lurks like the shrunken mummy of the milkman in the cedar closet, a character defect so horrendous that I have been blackballed from spaghetti dinners at the ASPCA and socially snubbed by the recording secretary of the local Audubon chapter. The newsboy knows; he doesn't bring the paper to the door anymore, just throws it into the densest part of the rosebed. I doubt that even Cleveland Amory could grant me salvation for, you see, I dearly love to hunt leopards.

If there is a more misunderstood big game animal than the leopard, then you and I haven't been seeing the same cocktail crowd. Women who wouldn't know a paradox from two waterfowl will screech with indignation when they find I am a leopard hunter, apparently one of the worst social offenses this side of necrophilia. Well-meaning local conservationists, who wouldn't know *The African Queen* from a gay tribesman, expound mightily and indignantly to me of the fate of the poor leopard, apparently suspended by rotting dental floss over the yawning abyss of extinction.

Not that anybody seems particularly interested in the injection of any facts into the hysteria we have long been fed about leopards, but, just for the record, the African leopard is in better shape as a species than just about anything you can think of up to the Norwegian rat. The United States does not permit the importation of skins of *any* spotted cats, regardless of how they were obtained, no matter how legally the pelt was obtained in its country of origin. It would seem another example of our Big Brother Knows Best international attitude.

Our great, grinding bureaucracy takes its advice, I was recently advised by the United States Fish and Wildlife Service, from such organizations as the Survival Service Commission of the International Union for Conservation of Nature and Natural Resources (IUCN), the World Wildlife Fund (WWF), and other such covens of experts. You can imagine my surprise when, a short while ago, a slender report crossed my desk on a joint project conducted by the IUCN and the WWF stating the conclusions reached in a study of "Leopard Status South of the Sahara," which says with bald-faced candor that *the joint is crawling with leopards* and even offers the tentative suggestion that they might be *commercially* hunted under close control! Good Lord! This from the organizations responsible for placing the leopard on the endangered list? Practically giddy, I sat back to read the report carefully.

"The leopard enjoys better distribution and numbers than the lion, cheetah, spotted hyena, wild dog, hippo, crocodile, sable and roan antelopes, white and black rhinoceros and several other major wildlife species. More pertinent still for long-term conservation, the leopard enjoys adequate prospects in the face of extensive and intensive disturbance of wildlife environments due to man's expanding populations and expanding aspirations."

Don't go away, there's more:

"The leopard's present status is better than that of many wildlife species in Africa which are not usually considered as endangered. . . . The species can be expected to survive with acceptable numbers and tolerable distribution into the foreseeable future."

The author of the report, Dr. Norman Myers, declares that the leopard population in many parts of the African range numbers as high as "*one per square mile and higher*"; moreover, conservatively estimated, there are as many as 500,000 alone in the Zaire Basin and another minimum 100,000 and "perhaps many more" in the *miombo* belt further south through Zambia, Botswana, Rhodesia, and Mozambique. This didn't sound very much like an endangered or extinction-threatened species to me.

It took twenty minutes to find the right man at the Fish and Wildlife Service, long-distance all the way. He seemed a reasonable guy, a sportsman himself, who agreed to level with me if I didn't use his name. He had a clear, concise answer to my query of when—in the light of this new evidence from the same people who had shut the door on leopards—he thought sport-hunted, legally licensed leopards might again be permissible to import.

"Never," he said.

"Just how do you mean, 'never'?" I asked him, somewhat taken aback.

"Do you have any idea of the pressure that antihunting organizations exert on legislation of this type?" he asked me back. "Unbelievable. You think you can't import your leopard trophy because the cat's supposed to be about to fold up as a species. Wrong. The preservationists found they couldn't really prevent hunting on a moral basis so they used the threat of extinction to accomplish the same ends. This law may have been instituted to save endangered species from commercial exploitation, but there is no provision at all for animals taken under license for sport."

"But," I asked incredulously, "isn't there just a mite of difference between a bale of poached hides and a legally documented trophy?"

"Not as far as the pressure groups are concerned," he said. "What you have to remember, Mr. Capstick, is that in the eyes of these people, the killing of anything is morally wrong, and believe me, they've got the muscle to keep that law on the books unaltered. If you think it's tough to get a law passed, just try to get one rescinded, particularly with some animal like the leopard. People aren't interested in any facts that are going to let you start bringing leopards back into this country. So forget it."

I thanked the man from Fish & Wildlife for putting it so straight and hung up. It was incredible. The so called

authorities report after considerable research—two years—
that the leopard is anything but endangered, with heavy
populations in much of its range. They may be legally
hunted throughout most of black Africa, yet, through our
wisdom at 6,000 miles range, you can't bring one through
United States Customs. It's not just a matter of leopards,
either chum. If you treasure your right to hunt under the
law and want your kids to be able to do so also, there's a
message in this state of affairs that you should heed.

I might also point out that, while any sportsman under-
stands and loathes poaching, it is also the sportsman's dol-
lars that support game departments and fight against commercial exploitation of game through the payment of very
stiff license fees that are not redeemable if you do not shoot
a leopard on your safari. Obviously, not many people want
to pay the high fees to hunt leopard if they may not keep the
skin as a trophy, and therefore, a great deal of revenue is
lost that would go directly to preserve leopard habitats and
reduce poaching. So, ironically, by not permitting properly
documented trophies to enter the country, we actually do
more to harm the leopard as a species than we do to help it.
Of course we should implement and enforce every law or
deterrent possible to stop poached, commercially obtained
hides from entering this country or the world market. If we
can stamp out demand, we will cut off the need for supply.
But nobody ever made a coat from one legally killed, very
expensive leopard hide, and certified trophies should be
permitted to enter the United States if for nobody's sake
other than the leopard's.

It is the very will o' the wisp character of the leopard
that gives the impression that he is rare. One does not go to
a game reserve and see old *Chui* standing around like the
elephants and zebras. One sees lions, wasting their time in
classic fashion, as well as cheetahs. But a glimpse of a
leopard is extremely rare, especially in hunting areas.
Leopard hunting offers a dramatic contrast to the techniques used for the rest of African game, most of which

amount to spooring or tracking down game. The leopard presents the exact opposite situation. Here's your problem: to make an immensely shy, mostly nocturnal, dangerous animal come to you in disregard of his normal habits, you must bring him within forty or so yards without his detecting you with his predator's ears, eyes, and cunning, place him in the open area of a tree which he generally shuns, and kill him with a single shot so he doesn't escape, sick and savage, into cover thicker than clam chowder where he will get somebody—maybe you—hurt or dead before he can be stopped.

That the leopard can exist in amazing numbers all around man without being detected was well demonstrated on my first safari in Botswana with the firm of Ker, Downey, and Selby Safaris, Ltd., a famous Kenyan company. My clients, Dr. John R. "Bob" Welch and family of El Cajon, California, wanted leopards very badly. Unfortunately, the Khwai Concession, an Okavango Swamp region where we were to hunt, was reputed to have very, very few leopards due to heavy poaching when the country had been Bechuanaland. In fact, after a few days of scouting before the Welches' arrival, I had to agree that there was no fresh leopard sign to be found anywhere. Although I explained that the time we would have to spend trying to dig up one, let alone two, might seriously cut into hunting other game, Bob still insisted that we give it a try.

At this time, none of the other professionals conducting safaris in the area were even bothering to try for leopards, and the sight of me with a Land Rover festooned with bait wire evoked some substantial ribbing. Nonetheless, we spent an afternoon hanging wart hog and impala quarters in four different places about five miles apart. The next morning, to my complete astonishment, all four baits had been fed upon by different leopards and two had been completely torn free and stolen.

Impressed by the size of the tracks of one particular Tom, who was feeding with a female about two miles from camp, I picked this location to build a blind in the heat of

the day when the cats would be lying up away from the spot. When we returned late that afternoon, I found that the leopards had actually been using the blind to lie in, keeping an eye on their larder! Nevertheless, we settled in and weren't in hiding for twenty minutes before a huge male appeared in the tree next to the bait. Bob swatted him cold into the record book.

Two days later, hunting in the area for buffalo, I sent one of my men, Debalo, over to the tree to see if the female was still feeding on the remains of the bait. He came back wide-eyed, saying that he had flushed another big male out of the same tree along with the female. Apparently, this gal had some Indian Love Call to whip up another oversized bachelor within forty-eight hours! Sure enough, when we returned that dusk, the pair were back on the bait with all the abandon of pussycats. With a very careful stalk, we were able to get into range for Bob's son, also with a single shot, to add his record-book Tom to the collection. As the safari continued, I hung some bait on my own, just to see how many leopards actually were in the area. Within ten days I had eighteen different leopards feeding in an area ten by ten miles. This, in a place where perhaps one or two leopards were shot through an accidental sighting each year among perhaps a hundred clients hunting a month each.

Unfortunately, this result did not overly endear me to some of the other professional hunters whose clients started asking pointed questions as to why they hadn't had a shot at a leopard. Professional hunting is about twice as jealous a livelihood as opera singing or ballet dancing, and the usual catty comments started passing around that I had either trapped or bought the pelts, which made me do a bit of a slow burn. Fortunately, I had taken a series of photographs of the whole process, which tended to dampen some of the nastier observations on my professional integrity.

The easiest shot you will have on safari—if your professional knows his apples with *Ingwe*—will be at your leopard.

It is also the shot you will be most likely to blow. Leopards do strange things to the nicest folks. Look at it this way: any damned fool can sink a two-foot putt for a nickel. But, let that two feet represent the United States Open Championship and a hefty stack of thousand dollar bills, and you have a different proposition. People who can shoot the eye out of a downwind tsetse offhand at 500 yards far too often completely miss or, worse, wound stationary leopards at 40 yards.

You have been sitting for two hours in a cramped blind watching the flies you cannot swat as you peer blearily through the tiny peephole above the gun port at the half-eaten remains of a wart hog or impala. Your mouth is raw from chain smoking. (The professional says it's okay as long as you don't scratch a match because if the leopard can smell your smoke he can smell you too.) You are suddenly aware of looking into two golden-green eyes as evil as poison gas, while a hulking male leopard changes to solid form. Log-thick forearms flex as he drifts further up the tree, the dull-white talons in his great pads cutting into the bark and flesh of the tree—and you can imagine them doing the same to your face and hooking deep into your guts to spill the eland filet you had for lunch all over the tops of your nice, new Clark's Desert Boots.

You try to remember what your hunter told you, to pick out a particular rosette on the point of his shoulder and break him down with the 300-grain .375 Silvertip from which the tip has been carefully pried to facilitate quick expansion; blow those lovely chips of bone through his chest cavity like grenade fragments, smash him in the engine room.

Your breath catches in your throat as you ease—ever so slowly—down to the rifle resting in the Vee-sticks, the safety softly gliding under your sweating thumb. Through the scope, he looks bigger than a tiger, 150 pounds of nitroglycerine poured into a gold, amber, and ebony sheath of the most perfect camouflage as he sticks his head into the hole he has eaten out of the carcass the night before. The post and cross hairs bounce and shift as your pulse hammers in your ears, your breath short as you inhale, then let half out. You start to squeeze. *Wait*! He pulls his head back and shakes his muzzle, a horror of black gore, shifts his weight then inserts his face back into the bait. Wham! The rifle surprises you as it fires. The leopard is leaping—a high, impossibly beautiful arc as he hangs in the sunset, his body extended and angling like a muscular javelin—only to disappear thirty feet from the tree into the snarl of head-high grass. Fear and despair wash over you like you've just been told you have cancer. You've screwed it up, created the most dangerous situation in African hunting, put a wounded leopard in the long grass. Then you are aware of being pummeled on the back, your hunter grinning like a mad man.

As if from a great distance, over the ringing of the shot in your ears, you hear a voice saying: "Right through the pump! Never jump like that unless it's a heart shot, right on the button! Nicely done, you old bastard!" You are still in a fog as the bwana thrusts a fresh butt into your face and lights it for you. You hear him say he will wait five minutes for the other eight lives to flow out of him before he goes to collect him. Then, snuffing out the cigarette, he checks the loads in the scatter gun, wraps his heavy sweater around his neck and knots it, and walks out of the blind, the lion-scarred gunbearer a pace behind with his stabbing spear. Slowly, as if wading, they enter the cover until it closes over and around them like a great, yellow fog. Time oozes by like slugs on a cold log. You light yet another smoke, trying to see something, anything, in the darkening field of grass. Then you hear them, the finest words you have ever heard, words you will remember for the rest of your life.

"Here's your pussycat, Bwana, dead as fair play. Helluva big blighter, too!" You bull through the grass until you see the faint outline of the men, the hunter bent over the body of a superb male leopard, spread flat on his stomach, dead in full stride. It is like opening your eyes at the first Christmas you can remember. He does not look shabby, like the lion you busted last week, tick-infested and filthy; he doesn't look simply dead like your elephant or the record-book buffalo with the scabby, five-o'clock-shadow hide. He looks fresh, perfect, bigger than he did even when he was looming against the afterglow in the tree. Except for the ridiculously tiny white-edged hole almost hidden in his lower chest, he looks as if he's been invited to this odd little gathering in the thick *tshani*, just one of the gang. You bend down, smoothing the hard silkiness of the long guard hairs, and decide not to mention that your bullet is six inches from where you intended.

A wounded leopard in the thick bush is the most dangerous animal in the world. Some will tell you buffalo, others lion, even others opting for elephant or tiger. Yet, if you want to form your own opinion, go hang around Riley's Bar in Maun, Botswana, or the New Stanley Long Bar in Nairobi, or plunk down on one of the caned stools along the big, split *mukwa* log that serves at Mfuwe Lodge in Zambia. Ask where those funny, puckered fang marks and long, raised scars on the bodies and faces of the off-safari pro hunters came from and four out of five will tell you leopard. They don't kill as many people as lions do; one good bite in the chest from *Simba* and that, old boy, is *that*. Still, more professionals and other hunters as well as native staff are injured by leopards than by any other game animal in Africa.

Perhaps the great classic of wounded leopard tales, told to me by John Dugmore, who had the camp next to mine in the Okavango, happened a few years ago in Kenya. John used to hunt in both Botswana and Kenya, safariing in one when the other had rains. A hunting party was on safari in, as I recall, Block 53, where one gentleman was indiscreet enough to stick a small bullet, a .243, into a big leopard with inconclusive results, the cat vanishing into a horror of thick thorn bush and grass. The professional said his prayers, loaded his shotgun, and went in after it as both the law and hunting morality demanded he do. Ten minutes later he reappeared at the edge of the bush looking like a tattered khaki bagfull of corned beef hash. The client and gunbearers got most of the major holes plugged and carried him back to camp, where they were able to raise Nairobi on the safari radio, ordering up a rescue plane, posthaste.

When it arrived, another hunter, quite a well-known one at that, stepped off to take over the safari for the mauled man. First order of business: settle the leopard.

It was too bad the plane had already left because, an hour later, he, too, had a lovely collection of spanking new scars-to-be, guaranteed to get you any amount of free grog from the tourists at any of Nairobi's bars. The third professional arrived the same day, in the late afternoon. He packed Number Two on the rescue plane, dropped off his kit at the hunter's tent, and took off for the patch of bush and the leopard. Yup. You guessed it. The big cat nailed him from behind and ripped off enough of his nevermind to make a meatloaf for six and then before anybody could do anything, savaged not one, but two gunbearers, merging back into the grass before a shot could be fired. Halftime ended: Leopard 5, Visitors 0.

Getting a bit panicky at the attrition of its staff, who were occupying most of a wing at the Nairobi Hospital—not to mention the air charter fares—the safari firm sent in John early the next morning. I don't know what was running through Dugmore's mind when he stepped up to that thicket, but it's more than even money he wasn't being careless. He had covered no more than fifty feet in a half-hour when the spotted blur was hanging in the air right in front of him, colliding nicely with the charge of buckshot from John's right barrel. But not quite nicely enough, because John found himself flat on his back, the barrels of the gun sideways in *Chui*'s choppers, very occupied with trying to keep the cat's long, hooked dewclaws from pulling his insides outside, an unpleasant sensation before one's first cup of tea. His boys, however, were able to insert the muzzles of a second shotgun into the leopard's ear, touching off both with definitive results. It wasn't a very big cat, either,

John told me—only about six feet, six inches over the curves.

I have a sinking suspicion that it is beyond the descriptive ability of any man to really tell you what it feels like, that last thirty seconds before you enter the long grass after a gut-shot leopard. I have never participated in a bayonet charge across open ground into fortified machinegun positions, but I can't but believe that the sensation is similar. It's getting dark fast; night in the equatorial regions doesn't fall, it positively plummets. Because of your client's shot all the natural bush noise is hushed, but the whisper of the grass in the rising *moya ga busuku*, the night wind, is enough to mask the cat's movement in the murk. Standing well back from the cover, you can think of 650 good reasons why you should wait until morning, but you reject them all; even though your professional experience screams that you have a better than even chance of being horribly disfigured or disemboweled, your professional pride and your self-respect force you to open the separate shooting bag, the leopard *katundu*.

In itself, my leopard bag is not inclined to load one with confidence. Even a few years ago most professionals would rather have taken a cobra bite than a lacing from a leopard because of the deadly risk of septicemia caused by the layer of rotting meat film under the cat's claws that, before modern antiseptics, could mean almost sure death. Contained in this specialized piece of equipment, assigned to one of my men to carry full-time, are the following items: a leather jacket with vertical strips of thick linoleum attached to limit claw wounds; fifteen rounds of SSG buckshot, 12-gauge; three five-packs of Brenneke 12-gauge rifled slugs; a quart of the best wound disinfectant my doctor clients can steal for me; an old, leather United States Marine neck guard to prevent saber cuts to which I have had strips of light sheet steel riveted; six styrettes of morphine; four buckle-strap tourniquets; tape, bandages, and a six-cell electric torch with extra bulbs taped to the butt. I used to carry a 9mm. Browning high-power 14-shot pistol, but the authorities looked upon that dimly. Now I can use my thumbs to poke in a wounded leopard's eyes without threatening their national security. Charming.

When you get all this paraphernalia hung about your person and stoke up the shotgun, you still take a few more seconds to think about your little spotted friend with the off-center hole. He is very, very clever. He's not like a lion who will test your bowels with a bone-chilling roar as he charges, at least giving you some idea he's coming. Oh, no. Not *Ingwe*. He'll stay pat, even if you bounce rocks off his skull and pepper him with probing birdshot. He only wants one thing. Guess what. He'll snuggle up behind some cover, flatter than a half-dollar after inflation, his claws dug firmly for the charge, his floating collarbones letting him hunch almost even with the ground. As soon as you are close enough, as soon as he's positive he can't miss, he'll take you. Maybe from the front, maybe the side or behind. But as long as he's alive, he'll drag himself out for a piece of you. It's almost impossible he won't have some success before you stamp him canceled—he's that fast.

If he catches you, you're in for a very interesting time. He will usually lead trump, fastening his teeth in your arm, shoulder, or face, itself a finesse since he's really interested in unzipping you from adenoids to appendix. To manage this he uses his hind legs and the curved knives of his dewclaws. He is so good at doing what comes naturally that there are records of a single wounded leopard mauling five armed humans in one charge and melting back into the grass before sustaining so much as indigestion. If things reach this point, my best advice is to get your knees up against your chest to protect your guts and feed him an arm or two until somebody peels him off you. This is where good gunbearers earn their wages. It's very difficult to find somebody stupid enough not to run while a leopard is sorting out his bwana.

Most accompanying gunbearers, if permitted to be armed, have a disconcerting tendency to empty their guns into the leopard and the hunter, too, which doesn't exactly solve the problem. Therefore, I eminently prefer my men to have spears, which, even in their enthusiasm, are less easy to stick through the cat as well as the boss. Other hunters tell me never to pay one's gunbearer until after the leopard of the trip has been taken. It makes them a bit more careful in such situations.

I have personally been incredibly cautious around leopards, especially perforated ones, and have enjoyed supernatural luck in not having gotten the chop. At least not yet. A lot of associates have not shared my good fortune. Brian Smith, whom I shared a camp with on several Zambian safaris, got caught twice, once by a wounded leopard and again by following an unwounded one into cover for some reason he was never able to make clear to me. He does not recommend the experience. More seriously, Heinz Pullon, a good friend and fellow hunter in Luangwa, a talented off-season ivory carver from southwest Africa, was horribly mauled by a wounded leopard he went into the crud after. The incident occurred shortly after I left Zambia to work in Botswana, and I was told that the cat just about pulled his face off. I think it left him when he passed out from shock and pain, or it might have been that somebody pried it off him; I'm not certain. From what I understand, they just about lost him before they could get him to Chipata Hospital, about 150 miles away. Strangely, last season I had a party of Germans from Southwest Africa for buffalo hunting in Rhodesia, and they all knew Heinz well. From their description he is still undergoing plastic surgery for the wound, and that was after five years.

Unlikely as it would seem, there is a very elite little fraternity of men who have killed leopards with their bare hands. Most of them accomplished this with small or very badly injured cats, or both, as in the case of Carl Ackeley, the naturalist-taxidermist who collected and mounted many of the animals in the African Hall of the Museum of Natural History in New York. Attacked by a seventy-pounder, he managed to get the leopard onto its back and crush in its ribs with his knees, puncturing the injured cat's

139

lungs and killing it. Akeley, however, looked like he'd been gone over by a rogue power mower.

The title for leopard fighting in the heavyweight class unquestionably goes to an American hunter named Cottar, an ancestor of my friend Glenn Cottar who operates in the Tsavo District of Kenya today as a professional. A huge Oklahoman, "Bwana" Cottar, as he was called, came to Kenya early in this century to be a white hunter and on one occasion choked *two* leopards to death at the same time, one in each hand! The story goes that one of the small leopards had been chewed up in a tussle with the other when Cottar happened along, and they decided to take out their differences on the Bwana. Considering that the Oklahoman used to like to do his leopard wrestling after a few belts, his success is even more fantastic.

Cottar was a man who took his hunting seriously. Around dusk one night he wounded a leopard on his farm and followed it into the bush. As might be expected, he got the hell bitten out of him, and the cat ran off into the gathering darkness. Wrapping the tatters of his shirt around his wounds, Cottar repaired to the farmhouse and broke out a bottle of 100-proof cure-all. In a couple of hours he had drunk most of it and, fuming over the failure of having lost the cat, cracked open another quart. About halfway through this one he finally decided to blazes with it, picked up his rifle and a kerosene lantern, and went crashing out into the stormy, black night. Stamping around the thick bush, commenting on the ancestry of the leopard while suggesting physical impossibilities, he found it. Or, more likely, it found him. Again, it showed no hesitancy to shred Cottar, but this time he managed to shove the muzzle against its chest and finish it off. Cottar picked up the big leopard, slung it over his shoulder, and went back to polish off the booze in, presumably, a better frame of mind.

A few years later the Bwana had another meeting with Spots that cost him the use of his right arm through terrible injuries by the leopard. Undaunted to the end, Cottar learned to shoot with his left until gored in the heart by a rhino in later life.

Over the length of my career I have had to root six wounded leopards out of heavy cover. Perhaps it would be better said that there were six leopards I had to shoot after being wounded, many, many more that had been mortally hit and died before I found them. Although several of these experiences were hirsute, to say the least, I probably came closer to the long, long trail awinding with a dead leopard than any live one.

You will remember Armando Bassi as the Spanish client who killed the lion that was trying to bite Paul Nielssen's leg off near his camp at Luawata. After Paul was sent to the hospital in Chipata, I took over the safari for the Bassis from the camp adjoining Paul's, Nyampala. Although Armando had been on safari several times with Paul and with Tony Sánchez Ariño, another Spanish professional employed by the company, he had never seen a leopard and wanted one in the very worst way. In the last few days of my previous safari my clients and I had often heard what sounded like a very big leopard calling from a tremendous thicket of riverine bush and grass on the far shore of the Munyamadzi River, not 300 yards from camp. As a courtesy we never invaded other hunters' territories and had gotten two good leopards elsewhere, but since Paul was in traction and his concession unused, it seemed reasonable that Armando and I should try to nail the lovesick tabby.

The same day I got the Bassis' kit moved across from Luawata, Armando and I, after firing into the water to discourage crocs, waded across to the far side of the river and shot a puku, a chunky, deer-sized antelope of about 150 pounds, and made a "reccy" for a leopard setup.

A lot has been written about leopard hunting, an especially good job having been done by Robert Ruark. Yet, I don't think even he realized how fantastically precise a business it is. I would rather hunt leopard than any other species because of the challenge of it—the lack of luck as an element as compared with most types of shooting. I am a fanatic about my leopard setups. If they're not perfect, they usually don't work. That I lavish great care on them is borne out by the fact that I never had a client with a leopard license who did not have at least two open shots at stationary leopards over a full safari, and over 80 percent of my clients' leopards have qualified for the record book. Yes, I did have one man miss not one, but two literal sitting ducks. I can get them there, but I can't hit 'em for them.

The first step of the process is the selection of a tree for the bait, the most crucial element. Since the concept is to get the cat to come back to the bait while there is still daylight, there absolutely *must* be very heavy cover all around the tree for him to be able to approach unseen. You can have the best-looking leopard tree in the world, but if the big cat has to cross open ground, he won't use it until after dark. Leopards hate to have any other wildlife see them because of the alarms they set up ruining *Ingwe*'s hunting. This cover, of course, is innately part of the problem: if you give him the cover to approach to feed, you also give him the same cover to disappear into if wounded.

Bait trees should be somewhat slanted because a leopard is basically lazy and the easier you make it for him to investigate the bait, even if he has a full stomach, the more likely he will return to feed. The branches of the tree should be sturdy and wide enough for a leopard to comfortably lie on. Of equal importance is the fact that the situation of the tree must be such that the spot to which the bait is attached has open sky directly west of it so that the cat can be silhouetted against the afterglow of sunset. Every second of light counts.

Zambia is perfect for bait trees because the prevailing winds in the winter always blow west to east, more or less. I do not believe that leopards have much of a sense of smell for airborne odors, although hunters are far better off with the wind in their favor. In Rhodesia, however, in the Matet-si region, the wind is always just opposite, making one choose between wind and light.

Leopard baits are also a matter of preference between hunters. Since that gruesome set of faked pictures of a leopard killing a baboon (they were taken in an enclosure) appeared years ago in *Life*, most people think that baboons are the best possible leopard bait. Although leopards do, indeed, eat baboons when they can catch them, they are too small to hold a leopard at a bait site because he'll finish the whole animal at one sitting and not return. It's also a common misconception that rotting meat is a leopard's favorite fare. Leopards are scavengers of the first order and will eat decaying flesh of the most revolting kind, but the value of a decaying bait is that of creating enough stink for the cat to find it in the first place. If you "top-up" a leopard bait that has been fed upon with fresh meat, the cat will invariably, in my experience, abandon the rotting bait for the fresh.

Ideally, I prefer wart hog as the perfect initial bait for drawing leopards for several reasons. In the incredibly dry winter season, much meat tends to mummify rather than rot, leaving almost no invitation of scent to blow around and draw cats. For whatever reason wart hog tends to rot quite quickly, especially if speared to allow flies to lay their eggs in the wounds. Leopards seem to place wart hog high on their list of prey, and the animal is sturdy enough to resist the cat tearing it loose from its anchorage and escaping with it. Once a leopard has found the bait, practically anything will hold him there, particularly when he has established a feeding habit at the spot.

It's very important that after the bait is attached the cat not be able to remove it and carry it off because, obviously, if he has hidden the bait somewhere else, he won't be looking for food at your tree, and you will have to wait several days for him to finish it before he goes on the prowl again. Usually a leopard will lie up somewhere nearby to keep an eye on his chow, and some risk is entailed in inspecting baits lest one bump into the cat in the grass, an interruption to which they do not take kindly. Some of my leopards have been killed while I was bait inspecting; if they are in a nearby tree, they can be stalked close enough for a shot, although with their senses, it's unusual to surprise a leopard and be able to stalk him. If you manage it, you've pulled off one of the classic feats of hunting. In all my hunting years, I've only been able to catch five this way.

Sometimes, you will come up against a leopard that has been hunted before, and perhaps missed. These cats simply won't show unless it's pitch dark and, therefore, illegal to shoot; not that you could see them, anyway. A ploy that has worked for me a couple of times with these sharpies is to try to track the cat to the spot where he hides to watch things during the day. Usually, he'll pick the same spot. Then, rather than using the bait as the focal point, you can make a small blind when you're sure he's not around and wait for him at this point. It usually works.

Baits should be wired in such a manner that the cat cannot freely feed upon them, but can only reach part of the meat. I use the underside of the branch, wiring the bait at both ends and the middle. On the theory that stolen grapes are sweeter, the cat frustrates himself most of the night and only partially feeds. The next day he may become impatient and hit the bait while it's still light enough to have a shot. That, in a nutshell, is the theory and practice of leopard hunting.

It only took a half-hour of poking around the thicket to find where the cat had been doing most of his housekeeping. It was a perfect tree, the sloping trunk a mass of claw scars and some white belly hairs. In a lower branch the bleaching skull of a young impala was caught, showing that the leopard used this spot as a regular place to eat his own kills. Sekala, a skinner, scampered up the tree and squatted casually twenty feet up while Invisible threw him a rope's end. I knotted the braided, buffalo hide line about the horns of the puku and, with Sekala hauling from above and the rest of my men pulling, we hoisted the antelope to the branch. Under Silent's and my direction they triple-wired it fast in position. Silent flipped his knife to Sekala, who opened the paunch, tossing down offal to sprinkle on the trunk to mask the human scent.

I walked some forty paces away, lining up the bait and open sky behind it with the base of an elephant-killed fallen tree, a super spot for the blind. The tangle of roots still left would provide a solid, natural-looking support for the structure. "*Mushy, Bwana*," nodded Silent in approval. "*Lo Ingwe hayiazi bona tina lapa.*"

"Silent says it's a good place," I answered Armando's questioning look. "He reckons the leopard'll never see us here." Collecting their hatchets and knives, my men disappeared into the bush behind us. I explained to Armando that in order to make the site look absolutely natural, all the grass and foliage had to be brought from out of the area. Leopards just aren't that stupid. When they find a nice neat package of goodies, they tend to look a gift antelope in the mouth, but anything out of place will keep them away like the plague. In two hours the blind was perfect, a blob of meticulously woven grass and dead bush that blended exactly with the jumble of the thicket. I went back to the bait tree and had Silent move around inside the hide. Satisfied I could see nothing except a flash of white axe scar on one of the supports—quickly corrected with spit-dampened dirt— I told Invisible to cut two wrist-thick Vee-sticks for the gun supports.

"Hell's bells, Pedro, I could hit him from this distance with my eyes shut," commented Armando. "Why all the rests?"

"First off, *amigo*, unless you have him within your sight from the word go, he'll disappear the second he spots your muzzle movement through the gun port. Second, you're using my rifle." His eyebrows went up. "Again for two reasons. Your 7mm. won't put as big a hole in him as my .375, and I would rather stitch up his hide than mine; second, you only have cross hairs in your scope. In the bad light the post in my scope will be much easier to pick out." He shrugged and watched with interest as Silent removed the blade from his fighting hatchet and stuck it vertically into a split *mopane* stick as a digging tool. Carefully, he placed the gun rests in front of the small hole in the blind and marked where their bases touched the earth. Little by little he chopped away at the dirt, measuring the depth until satisfied. I took the .375 Magnum and rested it on the sticks, lining it up on the rough center of the bait. At my grunt Silent packed earth around the sticks until they were as solid as if concreted. Tomorrow, or whenever the leopard hit, I could just replace the rifle and, with a bare minimum of movement, be right on target. After a final inspection from all angles we recrossed the river and, taking only Silent, Invisible, and Armando, drove a pair of miles away to check the scope on the .375. I have always shaken my head with wonderment at people who have other men shoot in their guns for them. Almost no two men shoot to the same point of impact with a telescopic sight because of vast differences in facial structure, the way they hold the rifle, and how they squeeze the trigger. A man can only zero in a scope for himself.

Selecting a dead *muSassa* tree standing in front of a termite heap to absorb the slugs, I had Silent cut a two-inch-square white blaze. I carefully paced off forty-seven yards, the same distance as from the bait to the blind, and pulled up the Land Rover. Armando lay the rifle across a folded blanket over the bonnet and dry-fired with the rifle empty to get a feel for the trigger. With the tip of my Randall knife, I carefully pried off the alloy tips of six Winchester Silvertip slugs, exposing the bright, soft lead beneath. It is hard to get 300-grain soft-point ammo in American loadings for the .375, and the Silvertip bullets are manufactured with an aluminum alloy tip to prevent expansion on big game until penetration has been achieved, not my aim with the light-boned, thin-skinned leopard. I wanted as big a hole as possible on the way out for free bleeding and a clear spoor in the poor light. I didn't know it then, but that little trick might just have saved my life with this particular leopard.

I saw Armando's hair fly at the recoil of the first shot, the muzzle blast leaving a score on the hood paint that would go unnoticed among the numerous bashes sustained by bush. A splash of bark spurted two inches high and three inches left of center of the blaze, a shower of powdered wood exploding from the back of the tree as the slug whumped into the termite heap. With the rim of a .470 cartridge, I clicked the scope adjustments down and right, rapping the mount to settle it. His second shot tore smack into the mathematical center of the blaze, a ragged, black puncture that swayed the tree. A third, just-to-be-sure round doubled the last. "There goes your last excuse," I told the Spaniard, who made me an attractive offer on the rifle. I'd sooner have sold him a couple of fingers.

Back in camp, the fire crackling away the evening chill as we digested the fish course of fresh tilapia bream followed by Manyemba's breast of francolin in cream sauce with a bright Stellenbosch '64, Armando and I got down to cases. "Okay, *viejo*," I launched into the lecture. "Here are the rules. First, no moving around in the blind. At all. Do all your scratching, sneezing, and coughing now, and obviously, all your talking. If a tsetse starts chewing you, don't slap. Push him away. This probably sounds silly, but you can chain smoke up 'til twilight if you want to, just blow the smoke down, not up or out of the blind. Most of this bush is smouldering from grassfires this time of year anyway. Once you've put a smoke out, it's got to be your last. These cats can hear a match or a lighter wheel a half-mile away. Understand?"

"Just where and when do I pop our pal, anyway?" Armando took another pull at the *Fundador*.

"Good point," I said. "Leopard hunting is a little like quail shooting. Don't yield to the temptation of just shooting at the shoulder or chest—pick your spot exactly. Just as you would choose a single *perdiz* from a flock of your Spanish partridge, pick a particular rosette and put your slug right through the middle of it. Choose one in the middle of the shoulder and try to break bone. Then you'll probably get lung and arteries, too. Leopards are easy to kill if you hit 'em right. It's when you wing 'em they get tough and I wouldn't want any nasty marks in my lovely complexion."

I topped off Armando's and my snifter as a nightcap, careful to cover the glasses so the stream of flying ants at the bar pressure lamp didn't fall in. "Now, this is really important," I warned him. "Do not, under any circumstances, fire until I signal you. Unless the cat is actually feeding on the bait, he could get jittery and move at any second. Let him settle down. If he jumps as you shoot, it means a miss or worse, much worse, a wounded cat. If you do that to me, I'll take away your brandy or shoot you, whichever is worse."

"*Dios*," said Armando in awe, "shoot me."

We were shooting ducks the next morning on a nearby lagoon when I noticed Silent trotting down the track that ran from the Munyamadzi toward us. I waved him over and he squatted down, formally clapping his hands softly for an audience. "*Yena buyile lo Ingwe?*" I asked him, aware that he had crossed the river earlier to inspect the bait.

"*Eeeh*," he nodded, "*ena buyile.*" I winked at Bassi.

"There's service for you, pal. Twenty-four-hour delivery at Pedro's Pantry. The gentleman here says you're in business."

I questioned Silent about the size of the spoor and how much bait had been eaten. He replied that the cat was a real *Induna*, a chief or general, and that although he had nearly severed the bait wires, he hadn't eaten more than about six pounds of the puku. Spot on! If everything went properly, we should have a very nice *Ingwe* pegged out by cocktail time, I thought.

It was about four o'clock when we bellied up to the blind and sneaked in. Silent set up a pair of camp chairs as I put the .375 into its supports and had Armando adjust it so that the sight picture was just over the bait. Wrapping the barrel in leafy vines so that there would be no reflection from the blued steel, I fished out my small binoculars and focused them on the bait. I could easily see the flies crawling around the spear punctures and the big gaps in the claw-marked hams where the cat had fed, ripping out chunks of meat.

We settled back, listening to the sounds of the bush-veldt, watching the little black *drongos* chandelle and split-S over the grasstops. Around us roosting doves began to gurgle their sorrow at the fading day as the sun changed from incandescent white to crimson to carmine, sliding soundlessly behind the acacias. I probed with the binocu-lars, but there was no movement. *Come on, come on,* I thought. Another twenty minutes and it'll be too dark to shoot.

A tiny, scraping sound suddenly froze me. I edged the glasses back to my eyes. In the first crotch of the tree, silhouetted against the western sky, crouched a tremendous leopard. There had been no warning at all, only the dry whisper of razor claws cutting into bark as he came to the top of his ten-foot bound into the tree. I softly nudged Bassi, watching his face contort with amazement.

The muscles in my forearm tightened as I dug in my fingers for absolute silence. He flashed a sideways look at me, which I answered by holding my palm flat and down. Wait. Thirty seconds hobbled arithritically by as the cat cast his green-eyed stare around him. Once more, I was certain that nothing in the world of hunting dangerous game could compare with the magical appearance of a huge leopard in the tortured magnificence of a sunset-lighted tree; this was the moment that made all the aches, sweat, and risks worth it.

One moment the cat was in the crotch, the next he was gone like ectoplasm. He had simply dissolved before our eyes. My heart stopped until I found him again, ten feet higher, standing on the bait branch. Again he studied every leaf around him as we sat frozen in the blind. Then satis-fied, he slashed with his paws at the bait with blurring speed, sparring with the carcass. Lying on his stomach, he stretched around to reach the bait on the underside of the branch, scissoring off a slab of flesh with the edge of his face. I squeezed Armando's arm twice more and let it go.

He looked at me and I nodded. Carefully, he worked up to the rifle stock and settled it in his shoulder hollow.

I waited for the crash of the big rifle, holding my breath unconsciously. The cat was perfectly still, gnawing at the bait, exposing a big chunk of his right shoulder. An eternity passed. Why didn't he shoot? I knew the safety was off, I had checked it when I settled in the gun. What the hell was wrong? If he doesn't shoot soon, the bastard will . . . BOOM! I saw a flash of movement beyond the muzzle flame as the leopard flickered down the tree head first. Then he was gone.

I was furious with the anger of frustration and fear. "What the bloody hell happened?" I snapped at him. "It was a perfect setup!"

"He moved," Armando said in horror, "just as I touched off. I saw the post of the sight on his stomach just as it fired. Couldn't stop the trigger squeeze in time." He looked so miserable I regretted my outburst.

"Well, don't sweat it, *amigo*," I said. "He'll probably be dead as a rock right over there," I lied in my teeth. Silent brought over the leopard bag, and I got into my armor.

The old, cold feeling settled as a lump in my stomach as Silent and I started to go into the grass. I hadn't liked the mobility with which *Ingwe* had poured down that tree, nor did I like the greasy look of his dark blood. Stomach wound. The worst. It makes him the most savage but does nothing to slow him down. As we penetrated the murk, I could feel drops of gore being wiped off the grass stems and onto my bare shins. When we had made five yards, I motioned Silent to forget tracking and cover our rear, which he did, back to back with me. Darkness was a badly woven shroud by the time we were ten yards into the vegetable morass. I slowly swung the shotgun back and forth from the hip; no chance in this stuff to shoulder-shoot in case of a charge. In case of? There'd be a charge, all right.

The growl sounded low, vicious, rising to a threatening snarl. In a heartbeat, I covered the spot in the grass it came from, every nerve tight as a bicycle spoke, crouched in readiness. Nothing. No charge, no leopard. I was dumb-founded. I had never heard one betray a charge with a single sound before, yet here was this one, threatening unseen a few paces away. I waited for ten seconds, my brain whirling. What the hell was going on? Why didn't he come for us? I dared not waste a shell in a blind shot.

Silent tugged at my bush jacket, pulling me away. Cautiously we backed away into the open, still covering the spot. "*Yinindaba*?" I asked him. "What gives?"

"*Ingwe gula*, Bwana, too much," he said thoughtfully. "The leopard is dying, Bwana. He is too sick to charge. If we wait, he will die in that place. His blood flows like water." He spat for emphasis and thumbed the edge of his spear.

"Maybe you are right, *Medalla*," I answered him in Fanagalo after some thought. It had to be that the cat was almost gone, or he would have attacked and not just threatened. Sure, that was it. We'll just wait a couple more minutes, then go in and find him with the flashlights. Sure we will.

It was full, inky, stygian, sable dark. Black, no-moon night. We had sat with Armando smoking while he begged us to wait until morning. Nothing could have pleased me more, but if we left the body, hyenas would find and eat it before dawn. We'd gone to enough trouble to prevent that, and besides, what kind of a fate was that for a beautiful cat? Carrying the fingers of light, we went back into the grass.

As we approached the place where the growl had come from, I gave Silent both torches and covered the spot, slipping the muzzle of the gun through the stems of grass as a probe. In the light nothing was there but a slick pool of drying blood, damp smears, and splotches leading off toward the river. Oh, boy. Still with us.

It took twenty minutes for us to follow the spoor across a break in the thicket into a choked grove of yellow acacias. I worked my light as far ahead as it could reach, searching for eyes, while Silent caressed the thin blood trail with his. As we entered the grove, the spoor ran beneath a twisted, giant tree, straight into a stand of scrub *mopane*. Eyes riveted on it, I double-checked the shotgun and went forward.

The drop of blood splocked squarely onto my head, warm as it ran through my hair to my scalp. In a high-voltage bolt of panic, I threw myself back, swinging the shotgun up into the blackness above. Before I could aim it, there was a small sound and a hurtling splotch of spots rushing through the beam, thudding at my feet, motion-less. It was the dead leopard.

The next morning Silent and I put it together. When the cat had left the place where it growled, it had deliberate-ly left its blood trail under the big tree and clearly into the thicket beyond. Then, with the cunning only a leopard could call upon, it had doubled back, gotten up the tree, and waited for us over its own spoor, using its own gore trail for bait. He had really won, clearly outmaneuvering us. The only thing he hadn't counted on was our waiting before taking up the hunt again. In the interim he had bled to death from the big slug, which had nicked an artery. If we hadn't stopped for those smokes, he would have had us completely unawares.

Who says smoking isn't good for your health?

4

Cape Buffalo

The man who was about to die padded softly along the narrow trail, tiny puffs of reddish dust spurting from beneath his crude, auto-tire sandals. He carried his spear easily across his right shoulder as he walked, the honed edges of the iron head flickering with the golden light of late afternoon. Wiping the sheeting sweat from his scar-welted forehead, he thought about the pot of sorghum beer that would be in the shade of his hut, another two miles down the path, and licked his leathery lips. He thought he could almost taste the sharp flavor on the back of his tongue as he passed the deep, *conbretum* thicket, its waxy, green leaves masking deep caverns of shade.

Terror grabbed his chest with the first grunt, short and hard from the tangle to his right. It was close, too close, the man knew as he froze, watching the branches shake as the snorts came nearer. He found his legs in a burst of adrenalin panic as the buffalo broke cover, black, hooked head up, pale gray eyes locked on his. Too frightened to shriek, the man dropped his spear and ran for his life, the thunder of flatiron hooves hammering just over his shoulder. Thirty yards ahead a large *muSassa* tree overhung the path with fluffy, green arms, and hope flooded into the terrified man. He was only two paces from the leap that would save him when the flats of massive horns smashed into the small of his back, driving him against the base of the tree with terrible power. Instantly, the bull hit him again, crushing his upper chest against the rough bark, splintering ribs and clavicles like a lizard under a heavy boot. The man was probably dead before his shattered form could fall over. That was just as well.

Foam blowing over his boiler-tank chest, the buffalo sprang back for a moment, then charged, hooking the cadaver on an icepick horn and dragging it back onto the path. For long minutes he chopped the man like chicken liver with axe-edged hooves the diameter of salad plates. Then, the way a dog will act with a dead snake, he methodically ground what was left of the corpse into the earth by rolling his ton of weight upon it again and again. Satisfied, the gory hulk grunted again and backed off a few paces, watching to see that his victim did not move. Ten minutes passed before he turned and made his way back into the thicket where he lay down, pondering the maggot-crawling, festering wound on his hip.

An hour later, returning from a successful kudu hunt with two clients and four of my native staff, we found the body lying in the trail. We had come from the opposite direction, dry and tired after long hours of tracking, and it wasn't until I had stared at the remains for several seconds that I was even able to recognize what it was. You will see better-looking bodies in plane crashes. The spoor told the story as clearly as if in neon lights and, gagging down the dry heaves, I dunked a pair of 500-grain solids in the .470 and unfastened the sling for quick handling. Waving back my clients and the rest of my men, I advanced a few yards up the trail and spotted the buff's track leading into the thicket. Silent swiftly scampered up a tree for a look around. He glanced about for several seconds, then stiffened with a slow nod and pointed into the heavy bush about thirty yards off to my left front. He raised his arm, palm down, parallel to the ground, to indicate that the bull had stood up and was listening for us. I held stock still, then moved a little to give myself an open shooting space in front of the thicket. I must have made a sound. Instantly, there was one hell of a bawl and heavy crashing as the buffalo charged, bulling through the thick bush like it was so much popcorn. He caught the first bullet at fifteen yards, just as his outline became visible. It took him in the center of the chest, just below his tree-trunk neck, and staggered him slightly. The bull was too close for comfort now, so I snapped off a brain shot and saw an eruption of horn boss fly like heavy bark where the big slug clipped him, almost knocking him down as 5,000 foot-pounds shocked his brain. To my definite consternation he was back up again in a flash, like a big, black tennis ball bounding off concrete, bawling and bellowing like a bass banshee. Instinctively, I thumbed the lever and broke the double rifle, the empties pinging in smoky streaks over my shoulder, and loaded the two asparagus-sized cartridges from between the fingers of my left hand. He was almost on me when I belted him with both barrels right in the face. Except for the dim sensation of meeting a bright red, speeding locomotive in a dark tunnel, that was all I remembered for quite a while.

When I came around, I wasn't sure what to rub first. A gash and lump the size of a teenage cannonball was growing over my blood-filled left eye and I had enough assorted contusions, abrasions, and bruises to supply a rugby team for the season. I felt like I'd done fifteen rounds with King Kong, but closer inspection proved that I was still relatively functional and that the majority of the blood belonged to the late buffalo. Silent, who had witnessed the charge from the tree, explained that the bull had been just about dead when he piled into me, but had made a reflex toss with his horns, which caught the muzzle of my rifle hard enough to smash it back up into my face, where the rib between the barrels had clouted me over the eye, knocking me cold. Both the last two shots had been winners, right through the lights, but his ton of forward motion hadn't given a damn. The clients and gunbearers had levered him off my lower body, and why my legs weren't broken still puzzles me today.

Invisible, my Number Two, came over and dropped something wet and smelly into my hand—a .577 lead ball he had cut from the buff's thigh. Shot there by a poacher with a wire-bound muzzle loader, it had lain festering along the bone, which it had lacked the power to break. The pain must have been frightful, slowly driving the bull to the point where he would charge anything that crossed his path. I sent Quiza back to the hunting car for a tarpaulin and my camera and, when he returned, took a roll of film for the authorities to accompany the report I would have to write. A short while later I got a note saying that it would not be necessary to appear to give evidence at the inquest. The condition of the tribesman's body was ample evidence as to the cause of death.

* * *

The African Cape buffalo, *Syncerus caffer* (not "water buffalo," NBC), has enjoyed a Jack the Ripper reputation since the first European thwacked one with a muzzle loader more than 300 years ago. He has always been considered a top contender as the Dangerous Continent's most dangerous animal, and there is no question that the sheer physical characteristics of *Mbogo, Njati, Inyati*, or *Narri*, depending upon what dialect you hunt him in, give him a very unique package of aggregate attributes that in their total are unequaled by any other member of the "Big Five": lion, leopard, elephant, or rhino.

The most impressive fact about the buffalo is that he has virtually no weak points. Jumbo and rhino are myopic in the extreme, but a bull buffalo could read the want ads in dim light across Times Square. The talent of his big, scruffy, thorn-torn ears is incredible, fully the equal of both lion and leopard, either of which he outweighs by many times at no apparent cost in blinding speed and maneuverability. His sense of smell is practically supernatural when he sticks that big, black nose like a #10 jam tin into the wind—as good as elephant or rhino and much better in ambient air than any of the cats. He is a living arsenal of weaponry for use against jerkwater hunters or preoccupied Africans, offering a Chinese menu choice on your shortcut to Glory of horns that can disembowel a locomotive, hooves like split mattock-heads, and up to a ton of bulk that can roll you into a fair resemblance of shaggy tollhouse cookie mix. What's more, if you cross him and get caught, he will display a singular lack of reluctance, regardless of race, color, or creed, to give you a nice, home demonstration of his talents. If you are planning on hunting the mighty buff, you had best give some thought to putting your affairs in order. In the thick stuff, where he loves to loaf away the fly-filled, hot afternoons, *he* has the edge, not you.

How *really* dangerous is the Cape buffalo? In a thoughtful word, plenty. Of course, as would be the case with any dangerous animal that looks as purely malevolent as a buff (Ruark distilled it well when he said that they look at you as if you owe them money), there has been no shortage of "sea stories" to help along his reputation as an advanced felon, charging on sight, an unstoppable mountain bouncing .600 Nitro Express slugs off his horn boss like soggy lima beans. Actually, with properly constructed, nonexpanding bullets of reasonable caliber, buffalo fall quite easily to brain shots *if* a proper angle can be used for the shot. I once won $50 in a bet with another pro by driving a 7 × 57mm. bullet completely through the skull of a big bull.

I have tried to follow up on the legend that buffalo regularly lick the meat off the legs of treed humans with their wood rasp tongues but have found no reliable report that this is so. I can't imagine anybody sitting still while a buffalo licked away his flesh like soft pistachio ice-cream, although it does make a juicy tale!

As is consistent with the current trend to debunk the idea that there is *any* dangerous game at all, some preservationist writers have tried to paint the buffalo as just another of Mother Nature's sweeties, absolutely harmless unless hounded by those awful hunters, a pox on them. In a way, this may not be unfounded from their viewpoint and exposure. The "Run, Bambi, it's Man" and "Don't Shoot Him Mister He's a Sheepdog" mentalities rarely waste their time in the thick bush of a hunting concession when they can sit in a zebra-striped minibus at a game preserve and photograph buff that are used to people. They will tell you that they've photographed thousands of buffalo without any incident whatever, and I'm sure they have. What they don't realize is that park buffalo behave entirely differently from "wild" ones, acting more like dairy cattle than anything else, drinking and grazing in daylight, while normal buff lie up in heavy cover during daylight and only come to water at night. When I say heavy cover, I refer to thorn and scrub thatched with grass until the end result is thicker than boiler plate, and about as translucent. To spend a few days tiptoeing around this vegetable morass looking for a good

159

bull at tag-you're-it distance is possibly the most tense, ner-ve-wracking hunting in the world. The first thing you will notice in this pastime is the absence of lady photographers in fake leopard hatbands.

I don't know if buffalo take their lead from elephants, but they don't seem to like automobiles much, either. Short-ly before I joined him, Bob Langeveldt was driving home from an elephant cropping expedition late one afternoon when a lone bull buffalo came boiling out of some cover along the track and slammed into the passenger-side fen-der, driving one horn through the metal of the body and lifting the car's front clear off the ground. By all appear-ances pleased with his work, he backed off and charged again, doing about as much damage to the radiator as a well-placed hand grenade might have accomplished. Each time Bob would try to get his rifle uncased, the bull would wallop the Land Rover again, flattening Bob. Finally, he got the rifle out, loaded it, and broke the buffalo's neck as it tried to untangle its horns from the car's gall bladder. He said it was a long walk home.

In Botswana in 1970 I had another bull come roaring out of the thorn and give the tail of my big Toyota a stunning thump, but he did nothing beyond cosmetic dam-age, and I was able to outrun him. In Rhodesia in 1975 I lived in the house of a man who had been killed by a buffalo in the backyard three years before. His tombstone nearby was always a handy reminder not to take *Inyati* frivolously. Geoff Broom, who owned the safari firm I worked for in the Matetsi region, was riding with his young son and a dog to inspect a stretch of new track for the coming safari season when a buff blew out of the shadows and stuck a horn through the metal just above and aft the driver's (right-hand) door, creating a three-foot tear that would accommo-date a prize watermelon as he ripped free. Geoff was un-armed at the time and damned lucky to get away without more serious damage. He always thought that the bull had either been fighting with another or had been in a tussle with a lion. Point is, dear friend in Disney, would you like to tell me that if a man had been walking past any of these points, rather than riding in a car, he would not have been charged? I didn't think you would.

I have heard hunters, back from their first foray in Africa, usually in Kenya where the buff limit is one per customer, opine that killing their bull was like pole-axing Elsie the Cow. And so it can be . . . *sometimes*. If you are lucky enough to find a good bull in the open and swat him where it counts with a big slug, he'll probably roll over and give up the ghost. But, if you flinch and pull your shot from even the heaviest rifle, you had better make sure the disaster insurance is all paid up because you have now got yourself a problem. A big one. There is a definite cause-and-effect factor in the fact that hunters tend to get the New Look from wounded buffalo because they tend to wound so many of them.

The problem is adrenalin. Although it's true that adrenalin and other high-performance additives are a factor with any large animal when wounded or excited, the Cape buffalo is clearly the champ in the overdrive department. If you don't drop him stone dead or mortally wounded with the first shot, he will completely lose his sense of humor and may get the idea he's invulnerable to bullets, a point he may prove to you over the next few minutes. If he makes you or your hunter follow him into the thick stuff, don't forget that you're likely in for a scrape that won't end until you collect his headskin . . . or he yours. You can shoot him practically to pieces, if he gives you the chance, but he'll keep coming despite wounds that would disable a tyrannosaurus. Blow his heart into tatters, literally, and he'll have enough oxygen stored in his brain to go a hundred yards and still have the moxie to take you apart with his tent-peg horns and mix you up with enough topsoil to start a modest tomato farm.

A buffalo whose attention you have gotten with a badly placed shot is really something to behold. For sheer, un-veering ferocity, he will make a range bull look like Fer-dinand. When he has you nicely in range and comes gal-lumphing over to chastise you, he keeps his head very high

until a few inches before contact—probably so he can watch
your expression—making it about as easy to slip a bullet
through the armor of his horns into the brain as to complete
a triple carom shot on a warped pool table after seven
martinis. Either you stick a big slug up his nose and hopefully catch his brain or upper vertebrae, or remember the
words to the "Hail Mary" in a hurry. I had a fascinating, if
somewhat gory, chance to see practical examples of the
physiological effect of adrenalin on a wounded buffalo last
year in Rhodesia.

I was hunting with a South African doctor client on a
short safari, just for buffalo at Matetsi, and we had found
the spoor of a herd of twenty-odd. Unlike most areas I have
hunted, this region was unusual because often the herds
would contain shootable bulls, whereas over most of Africa
the old bulls are strictly small bachelor herds from singles
up to eight or so. From the track, Amos, my Kalanga-
Bushman gunbearer, and I agreed that there were at least
two large males in the group. We tracked them into a
narrow valley between the basalt hills, where a small creek
flowed, the Bembe. There was plenty of cover along the
water and we were able to sneak to within forty yards of the
herd as they grazed across our front, a perfect setup. After
a good inspection with the binoculars, I picked out a nice
bull with a close boss and about forty-four inches of spread,
standing three-quarters facing us. The doctor fired from a
tree rest and, on hearing the .458 Magnum soft-point *whock*
home, the bull staggered and sat down on his haunches. He
got up and wobbled fifteen yards, then collapsed again. As
the rest of the herd thundered off into cover, I hurtled the
stream, anxious to get in an insurance shot before he got
back up. As I came up to him, he was still alive but clearly
unable to rise. Keeping a tree between us, I opened my eyes
in amazement at what I was seeing. The bullet had caught
him just at the base of the neck where it meets the chest and
severed the main artery before penetrating to do God knew
what inside. The incredible thing was that there was a
thumb-thick stream of blood pumping out of the bullet hole

that was hitting the ground at a later-measured thirty-six feet away! God's Honest, fellas. Can you imagine the power of a heart strong enough to produce that kind of pressure through a half-inch hole? It's no wonder a wounded buffalo can carry around more lead than an ore cart!

In Zambia I was hunting with George Lenher, a client from New York, and shot a mediocre bull for lion bait one afternoon with a .375. Since trophy quality was of no importance, I killed the buff myself and took it on my "pot" license, which gave every professional a dozen buffalo and some wildebeeste and impala for rations each season. As it happened my bullet was deflected by a piece of brush and did not kill the bull immediately, although he wasn't going anywhere. Following him up, I saw him standing broadside to us about thirty yards away. Not wanting to disturb the area, which had quite a lot of lion spoor, I got the bright idea of killing the bull with Silent's spear. Keeping my rifle handy in my left hand, I threw the spear and, to my complete astonishment, hit him smack dead center in the heart. After about thirty seconds he fell over, and, with George's 8mm. camera still rolling, lay for many minutes with the spear embedded in the center of his heart, *which kept beating*. I have seen the film run back in the States, and it bears out better than anything I have ever witnessed the incredible resiliency of the Cape buffalo.

Back in the Khwai Concession in Ngamiland, northwestern Botswana, on the same safari with Dr. "Bob" Welch that produced the pair of record-book Tom leopards, there occurred another typical example of the refusal of a buff to die.

Although most of the cover in the area is scrub and sand, there are many *dambos*, or open plains, favored by immense herds of buffalo. It was early in the season, my staff of twenty-three men were grumbling for some red meat, and I was anxious to start some biltong drying for snacks. Because of this, and as a chance for Bob to try out his new .460 Weatherby Magnum, the most powerful shoulder-fired commercial sporting rifle in the world, with over 8,000 foot-pounds of muzzle energy, we decided to convert a youngish bull at the tail of the herd to table fare. While I covered him with my .375, Bob snuggled up to a termite heap and probably wiped out most of the nest with the muzzle-blast concussion of his first shot. The 500-grain soft-point hit like a sumo wrestler beating a rug, throwing up a small explosion of dried wallow mud a touch high on the withers.

"Belt him again, Professor," I whispered as the bull took off across the plain. Clearly, the buffalo had not read the energy charts for the .460 and was blissfully ignorant that he should have collapsed like a dynamited bridge from the "shock" alone. Wham! Whock! The bull kept running along although I could see the second shot strike like a shell on a concrete bunker. Five shots later and the bull was *still* on his feet, moving toward cover despite the fact that I could *watch* the big slugs going into the chest cavity. From Bob's bloody nose, I knew he was taking a horrible pummeling from recoil, but he kept pouring on the lead. After another two hits the beast stopped and stood, legs splayed, until Bob's last and tenth round mercifully (for both of them) broke its spine. An awed cheer went up from the gunbearers as if I'd just announced a beer ration. We walked up and inspected the bull and found that Bob's shooting certainly wasn't at fault, nor was bullet performance. The chest cavity was absolutely devastated—heart, lungs, and everything else in sight. That buffalo had just gotten the notion he wasn't going to fall down, and by God, he didn't. At an average range of about 100 yards, he had absorbed better than 60,000 foot-pounds of bullet energy before the spine shot scuttled him. I'm glad he wasn't chasing me all that time!

There has been a good deal of what I consider pap written over the years about the "diabolical" cunning of the buffalo when wounded, purposely doubling back on his trail in a fishhook maneuver to ambush the pursuing hunter. I have had to dig out enough buffalo from heavy bush to respect them second only to a live, sixteen-inch shell with a smoking fuse, but I have never experienced an obvious trap-laying ambush. By nature, when hurt they head for the nastiest, thickest tangle of crud they can find, where their sense of smell, keen eyesight, and hearing work to their advantage to locate you before you can find them. True, they will permit you to walk past them if they think you haven't seen them and it looks as if they will have a "freebie" from the rear, but usually, they will wait until you are in range of a short, decisive charge, then come boiling out of the thorns and shadows in a black streak of high-brass murder. At that point, brother, they couldn't care less about your bank balance or your Rotary attendance. Unless you are fast and fortunate, you had better delegate somebody to give your regards to Broadway, 'cause you may not be seeing it again. You will be entering a state of Terminal Meditation.

Today, the great wild ox we call the Cape buffalo is the most prolific of the dangerous big game of Africa. In southern Africa there are truly huge herds, numbering into thousands of animals, itself a minor miracle because the vast majority of buffalo were wiped out around 1900 by a plague of rinderpest, the deadly cattle disease. Experts at the time thought they might even become extinct, forgetting that nature is pretty good at licking its own wounds.

A big bull buff is the second largest member of the *Bos* or cattle clan in the world today. The aurochs, which passed from this vale in the 1600s, was the wild ox of Europe, a formidable customer at six and one-half feet at the shoulder. Now, only the gaur of the dense bamboo thickets of tropical Asia has an edge on *Mbogo*, if you want to count the gaur's first cousins, the seladang and banteng, as the same tribe. These animals are, however, mostly solitary and do not have the blood-and-thunder reputation of the Cape buffalo. A walloping bull gaur will span about six feet from his cuticles to his shoulder top. The average buff, depending upon where he comes from, will weigh about 1,600 to 1,800 pounds, although I have seen several that I am certain would shade a ton considerably.

*   *   *

As a form of cattle, buffalo are good to eat. During the time I hunted in Africa, I would guess I ate buffalo in one form or another at least five days a week. It is tougher than beef, but with good flavor. The problem with buffalo as well as most African antelopes as a steady diet is that they have very little marbling or body fat and, after six months out in the blue, one dreams at night of a T-bone steak sizzling in great globules of yellow fat. The trick to shooting buff for the table is to make certain they can be dropped with a single shot. If they churn around for a few minutes, the adrenalin tends to toughen the meat and strengthen the flavor.

Lions also think buffalo are very good. Buffalo don't appreciate that very much. *Simba* and his friends don't kill as many buffalo as one might have the impression they do, although I believe that some lions specialize in the buffalo as food. Over the past few years, many people have come to believe that it is the female lion that does all the killing. This is by no stretch true. Many male lions do not live in prides and do their own hunting. Being bigger than the ladies, often it is they that will take on buffalo, sometimes working in teams of two. Even they are not successful on most occasions, and it is the relatively rare old bull that does not bear lion scars somewhere on his half-to-full-inch-thick hide.

I have noticed some variation in the methods lions use to actually kill buffalo in comparison to other game. Usually, the victim, once pulled down, dies of suffocation as the lion crushes the windpipe and holds it shut with his jaws. A buffalo is just too big to sit still for such goings on unless several lions are involved in the coercion. Most lion-killed buffalo I have examined have died of broken necks and bites to the back of the neck as well as throat wounds. I have been told by those who have witnessed the event that a lion will snag the buff's nose with a forepaw and wrench his head so he falls in such a manner as to dislocate the neck by the buffalo's own weight or momentum. I've seen lions try

this but have never seen a successful attack in this manner.

That lions are by no means infallible in attacking buffalo was illustrated to me from a grandstand seat in the rocky hills of Matetsi last season. In the western areas of the concession there are three valleys separated by ridges; small streams and relatively lush vegetation abound in each low area. We had cut the spoor of a herd of fifty buff, guessed they were headed for the thickets in the second valley, and decided to check them out from the heights. As we nestled up to the lip of the hill, I saw the herd in grass and scrub, like fat black beetles on a lawn. While I was figuring the swirling wind for an approach, Amos grunted and nudged me, pointed with his chin and said, "*Silwane, Nkos*"—"Lions over there, Chief." I shifted the glasses and finally caught a slip of movement downwind of the herd where three male lions, full-grown but not well maned, were stalking the herd. I did not relish sharing the high grass with a herd of buff *and* three lions and so settled back to watch with my client, cursing that I hadn't brought the long lens for my camera.

With the incredible, liquid caution of the hunting cat, I noticed them working to ambush the herd from a flank, taking advantage of some heavy patches of scrub *mopane*. From my view, they were as flat as cobras in the lion-colored grass, barely perceptible even with the binoculars, inching closer in short movements. It was a mixed herd, with ten calves and the rest mostly adult buff, including six mature bulls, of which two were real veterans, 2,000 pounders with worn, thick horns and scarred flanks. Whether they innately knew that any possible attack would come from the heaviest cover, I can only conjecture, but the two big boys and one of the others began feeding off to the side where the lions waited, stopping at intervals to glare around them. At the tip of the herd, downwind of the bulls, an old cow grunted and stiffened. Almost surely, the tricky wind had blown her a few molecules of lion odor. She whuffed again and cantered off high-headed, pushing a calf ahead. Instantly, all six bulls swarmed the edge of the herd and stood, heads thrust forward, drooling at the patch of bush, chopping the hard ground with tentative hooves like butchers sharpening their knives. In line abreast, they started to walk toward the lions. I held my breath as the spectacle unfolded through the lenses. At twenty feet one of the cats lost his nerve and, uttering a four-letter growl I could hear, started to stalk stiffly away. That did it. As one, the buffalo took after it, flushing the other two novice hunters practically from their feet. The rest of the herd poured after the bulls, even the calves. It was a maelstrom of dodging lions and hurtling buffalo dim within a rising pall of dust. I saw one lion stop to feint at a charging bull. That was a mistake. The bull hooked at him, missing, but smacking him with the flat of a horn hard enough to roll him over twice. Before he could recover, the buffalo was on him, so anxious that he was pushing the cat along with his nose in his excitement to gore it. It slipped under his face and he ran completely over the cat, which gave a roar of pain and scooted away into cover. Over the next ten minutes, the herd hunted the lions from one clump to the next until they forced them into the open stream area, at which point the cats decided to exit, frolicking, over the next ridge.

I really have no idea how many buffalo I have shot or been in on the shooting of under various circumstances over the years and different countries. Counting cropping, meat hunting, sport safaris, and destroying poacher-wounded animals, the total must be pushing 1,000 fairly hard. Certainly 800. I have personally killed over 400 in meat shooting on concession contracts and cropping alone. Nobody can be mixed up with that many *Inyatis* without a good portion being wounded ones of various severity, with the accompanying treat of following up on the spoor.

I have lost only one wounded buffalo that I am aware of, and that was under circumstances which convinced me that the animal was hardly hurt at all. In Zambia, Monty Toothacher, an American from Maine, and I were scouring the hills for something or other in the Mwangwalala area of the Luangwa when Misteke, a substitute gunbearer, noticed a good buffalo bull seemingly asleep in the middle of a thicket. I looked it over closely with the glasses, to be sure it was not a lion kill dragged there, and saw an ear move. Although Monty was carrying only a .300 Winchester Magnum that day, he was a very fine shot and I decided to let him take the bull. I whistled softly and he came to his feet, looking around him. Monty shot, and the bull swapped ends in a blink, disappearing even before I could stick a solid .375 up his backside in a raking shot, which is customary with wounded dangerous game if there is the slightest possibility of its escaping to turn rogue. Taking just the somewhat "windy" Misteke, I followed the spoor for more than a mile. Not once did the bull slow down, and the blood spoor stopped within a few hundred feet. Baffled, I returned to the spot where Monty had shot him and found that the light bullet at such high velocity had hit a thick stick and broken up into tiny fragments, doing nothing more than shower the bull with stinging little shreds of lead and jacket that hadn't penetrated through the skin. Satisfied that the bull would be no menace, I let him go.

One of the biggest problems in following up wounded bulls is that, whereas most herd animals will separate from their kind when wounded, a buff who is a member of a small bachelor group will stay in the company of his pals. In thick bush, there can be great difficulty determining which animal is the wounded one, and more than one man has gotten the deep six from watching the wrong one while the wounded one charged unseen from close at hand. In addition, sometimes the unwounded buffalo will adopt the attitude of the hurt one and be as willing to charge as he is.

I was with the president of a well-known manufacturing company in Botswana a few years ago, the gentleman wanting to better a mediocre head he had shot on an East African safari previously. We found four old bulls in a hollow in the grass near water and stalked them quite close. I pointed out the best bull and he fired, hitting it in the chest with a .458 Winchester, which caused it to hunch up and follow its buddies off into the grass. As is usual, we backed off into a wooded glade and sat down for a smoke to let the buff stiffen up and, with any luck, sound the death bellow that they all seem to make when dying of a chest wound. I have to admit that I was semidaydreaming, sitting with my back up against a tree, well in the open in the warm sunshine. The client was perhaps ten yards away, nearer Simone and Debalo, standing with his foot on a log. I casually noticed him looking past me, his eyes growing wider and wider, his mouth open as if to say something. Before he did, a very deep, very impressive UR-RRUMPPHH sounded over my shoulder, draining my blood down into my toes. The client threw himself into high gear, racing up a sapling even faster than Simone and Debalo. I jumped to my feet and looked around the tree, knowing full bloody well what it was: a large, angry buffalo. He fastened his eyes on me from three yards and trundled over, smacking that tree as I jumped behind it into a shower of leaves and dead sticks. My rifle, leaning against the trunk, was shaken loose and fell on its side. Fortunately, it was a pretty substantial tree and after several go-arounds, keeping it between the bull and me, I ended up on the rifle side. Somehow, the bull had missed stepping on the stock and breaking it and the .470 was functional. With the greatest relief I fed him both barrels right in the chops.

When we got most of the party back to earth, Debalo had a good look at the buff, punctuating his muttered *eeeehhhs* with a sudden *ooop!* "*Yena hayikona fana, Morena*," he said, giving it an irreverent kick in the rump.

He was right. It wasn't the same buffalo the client had shot at earlier. Except for the two holes in his head, there was no other bullet mark, and I was certain the American hadn't missed. As if in answer, a low, inexpressibly sad sound wafted in from a couple of hundred yards away: Mmmmmmbaaaaawwww! The unmistakable death song of the Cape buffalo. He was dead just where we thought he would be. I doubt that his *compadre* had just blundered into us; he was fighting mad when he arrived. Goes to show what happens when you get emotionally involved.

The very existence of the African buffalo has been well intertwined with that of the tsetse fly, which, curiously, was responsible at one time for the almost complete reduction of the buff in parts of his range and now is likely the buffalo's best friend. This odd symbiosis is due to the disease carried by the tsetse generally called nagana, which is fatal to all domestic livestock and pets. This is not to be confused with the trypanosomiasis, or sleeping sickness, which may also be carried by tsetse that have become infected by biting a human carrier or sufferer of the disease and passing it on through trypanosomes in the saliva to other humans.

Through untold millennia of natural selection wild game has a natural immunity to nagana. Yet domestic cattle or horses cannot live more than, at the most, several weeks in tsetse country without dying. It was long thought that, especially in regions hoped to be brought under the plow, the buffalo was the main host of the tsetse; it followed that if one shot off the buffalo, the tsetse would disappear. In some parts of Rhodesia, especially Matabeleland, nearly every wild animal was slaughtered in the hope of removing tsetse—a hopeless plot doomed to failure.

As research in later years began to prove, tsetse are very catholic in their bloodsucking and if anything, the wart hog is a bigger host than the buffalo. Because of the presence of tsetse in many large regions, game there is still very populous and it is logical to presume that the nasty fly with a bite like a hot ice pick is to a great degree responsible for keeping out man and his animals and preserving habitat.

While we are on the subject, the relationship between tsetse and man is not generally understood outside of Africa, many people believing that the bite of a tsetse is usually fatal or a sure cause of sleeping sickness. If that were so, I would be dead several thousand times over. Zambia's

Luangwa Valley is alive with the little monsters, and tsetse bites are just a part of every hunting day. Although there is tsetse in the area, there is no sleeping sickness because there are no carriers. In Botswana, on the other hand, "SS," as it's called, or "tryps," is much more common because of the Bushmen who hang around camps and carry the disease. When I was there I had two clients get "bad" or infected bites, which look like small boils. The only recourse is a flight to Johannesburg, where a quick course of treatment is effective in the early stages. Last season, handling a few clients in Rhodesia who made short safaris there for sable antelope, after having been on Safari in Batswana another two had "bad" bites. In itself, tryps is not necessarily fatal or even debilitating if caught in the primary stages. The high rate of fatality is accounted for by the fact that cases are misdiagnosed because of the masking effect of malaria prophylaxis pills or by the fact that Bushmen are diagnosed only after becoming semicomatose. Unfortunately, I have lost several friends from the disease, including the well-known hunter, Johnny Blacklaws, and, I believe, one or both his clients.

Getting back to the buffalo, at the time I was cropping elephant with Bob Langeveldt, we also had a quota of other game to be taken. One of them, impala, was a cinch since they could be shot by night with .22 rim-fire Magnums and solid bullets in the heads. The other, buffalo, were something else.

Over a period of several weeks, we had shot only about fifty, and those in small groups that made recovery operations expensive and awkward. For many an evening we would sit over sun-downers trying to devise a practical method of culling reasonable numbers of the big animals at one swoop, but the problem was always the reluctance of the buffalo to stay put once we had opened fire. We could always knock down four or five, but sooner or later one would move, just as one of us squeezed off, and trundle away wounded, panicking the rest of the herd into flight.

One night, Bob came over, a sly grin on his furry face, and poured himself a healthy wallop of Haig. Wordlessly, he reached into his pocket and withdrew a modern variety of flare pistol, really a spring-loaded tube that fired a charge which launched a parachute-hung flare. I looked at him like he'd been hunting in the sun without his hat.

"Feel like a little field exercise tonight?" he asked, patting his new toy.

"What're you going after, bats?" I turned over one of the flares in my fingers.

"*Hayikona*, man, buffalo. We ought to be able to really mop 'em up with this rig." He noticed my raised eyebrow. "Know that pan out on the Chibembwe Road? The one where we saw the big kudu a couple of days ago?" I nodded. It was a small flowage about ten miles away, well into the bush from the tourist loop roads. "Well, by the look of it, there's a herd of 300 or more using it every night to drink and wallow . . ."

"Whoa!" I interrupted. "You mean you want to go buffalo hunting at *night*?" I shook my head in remembrance. "Seems to me we've got enough problems with those bastards in the daytime, let alone crawling around the boonies after dark."

"Listen, chum," he said, explaining it as if to a congenital idiot, "you've read the old stuff on how they used to do almost all their buff shooting at water holes at night, hey?" I allowed as I had, and that if he had read his Harris and Baldwin closely, the process entailed something of a health hazard. Moonlight buffalo shooting from a soggy hole in the ground was not my idea of the perfect evening.

"Moonlight, hell! We've got our own moonlight." He waved the flare gun. "All we have to do is work in close and, when I fire the flare, clean 'em up while they're dazzled by the light. Can't miss."

Langeveldt is very persuasive, I thought to myself climbing into the car next to him and stacking the boxes of .375s on the dash shelf. He eased the clutch out and we swished down the track, narrowly missing the nightjars that sprang up from the still-warm dust of the road in alarm. Small packs of foraging mongooses reared on their hind legs like underfed woodchucks, chittering at us as we passed, and the lights picked out the eyes of impala and zebra in the roadside bush. Once, a lioness lay in the road, waiting to move until Bob almost nudged her; then, with a sneer, she vaulted into the cover and haughtily padded away. At a quarter mile from the pan, he stopped the car and we loaded the guns, walking the rest of the way down the road, dully lit by a sinking sliver of moon.

The last 200 yards we picked our way very carefully through the bush to the edge of the opening of the pan, where the bush was beaten down and lighter. We had lucked out with the timing, for as I stared ahead, I could see the first of a stream of black blobs that were buffalo trickling out of the cover and across the beaten earth to the water. I nudged Bob and loosened the tension knurl that held the swing-off scope in place and dropped the sight in my pocket. In this situation only the open express sights would do the job properly. Because of its greater firepower over an extended period, Langeveldt had chosen his .404 Jeffery's magazine rifle rather than the double. Slowly, the herd wandered toward us at an oblique angle, about parallel-wind to our position at some trees, placing them between us and the water. At about thirty yards I lined up the rifle and snicked off the safety. Langeveldt raised the flare gun at a high angle over the herd and fired, the charge louder than I thought it would be. The payload arched like a firefly higher and higher and with a muted pop burst into a brilliant white light that swung beneath the tiny parachute with incredible penetration.

I involuntarily gasped at the tableau before us. There were hundreds of buffalo, seemingly close enough to touch, a black ocean of them frozen in the light of the flare. Snapping out of my shock, I fired my first shot just as Bob did, and a pair of big bulls collapsed without a twitch with smashed necks. Nothing happened, no animal moved, as we reloaded and began rapid but careful fire, dropping the animals as fast as possible. We each had five straight; although ten buffalo, were down, within eight or nine seconds, all with brain, neck, or spine shots, still they stood, dazzled by the light.

Reloading with the speed of long practice, we continued to thin the herd, long plumes of muzzle fire streaking the shadows, collapsing the buffalo with easy, deadly shots. We had eighteen down when it happened. As suddenly as the flare had burst, it died, smothering the pan in blackness but leaving us and the buffalo nightblind from the sudden brilliance. We hadn't thought about what would happen when the flare burnt out, let alone planned to have a second one ready to fire before the first one died. In a split second it was like being smack in the middle of a Merrill, Lynch advertisement, nothing but the earthquake tremble and thunder of hundreds of hooves all around us, the overwhelming bawls, moos, grunts, and gargles filling the suffocating night.

"Climb, for Chrissakes!" shouted Langeveldt from somewhere nearby. I felt panic grab at me and slung the rifle by the sling over my shoulder, making a blind jump for the tree I had used as a shooting rest. I missed the first time, but finally got a grip on a broken branch, hauling myself blindly higher with the power of fear. A few feet below my legs, buffalo were everywhere, jostling the tree with their horns and bodies in their mad rush to escape back into the thickness. I hung on like a lizard as the herd swirled and poured over our position, shouting to see if Langeveldt was still okay. If he heard me over the tumult, he didn't answer. Then the madness seemed to subside, the sound less urgent as the stream of animals drifted away. I could still see nothing but the remaining glare of the flare on my retina, but heard Langeveldt call from a few yards to my right. I answered him with relief, and we decided to stay put until we could see, which took another half-hour until we were satisfied that we were alone at the pan but for a pair of hyenas cautiously shuffling around the carcasses. I told them something rude, and they hunched off to watch us from the edge of the grass.

I was afraid to light another cigarette for fear of impairing my night vision once more. Dusting ourselves off from the gray pall that had settled on us, we cautiously checked the downed buffalo. One was missing, the one I had fired at just as the flare had quit, but we found his body twenty yards past my tree, pretty well pummeled by his friends' hooves. The bullet had been low for the spine but had done a decent job on the upper lungs. There were four big cows, the rest bulls, lying in the half-light like a field of black boulders. I don't like to consider what might have happened had Bob and I not been near those trees. As it was, most of the bark was off them from about four feet to the ground where the buffalo had blindly run into them with their horns and shoulders. That sort of thing could really ruin the press of a man's pants.

Any dangerous sport, including buffalo hunting, needs practice for any eventuality, so I have become a great believer in Charging Buffalo Drills for my safari clients. Upon arrival at camp, clients spend the first three days of their trip learning the basic elements of buffalo hunting: running, dodging, climbing, rapid reloading, and praying, with the major emphasis on invocation of the Deity. Actually, these skills, although they impart a good deal of self-confidence to the paying customers, are superfluous. As any experienced African hand will tell you if you stand him a drink, the *only* sure way to stop a charging buffalo is to take away his credit card.

5

Hippo

It was nearly ten o'clock under a brass-bright Zambian moon when the Texan stifled a yawn, tossed back his bourbon nightcap, and pushed the webbed camp stool out of the circle of firelight. His excitement over the magnificent black-maned lion he had shot that afternoon had taken that long to wind down. I couldn't blame him; it had been reasonably hairy. The bloody nose of the big cat had lain just five paces from us where it dropped from a .458 soft-point that opened the top of his head like a can of pork and beans. But, enough celebrating. Now we both needed some sleep. Elephant hunting starts early, and I had laid tea on for 4 A.M.

Walking past the gun rack, I said a good night and reached over for the .470 Evans Nitro Express double rifle. I plucked out the two long cartridges stoppering the muzzles and chambered them for the 200-yard walk along the banks of the Luangwa to my own *kaia*, a grass hut nestled against a huge baobab tree. I turned the valve of the pressure lamp and watched the incandescent mantle fade to a dull orange. In the darkness I felt the smooth, cool checkering of the big electric torch along the rack and slipped the toggle forward. A hard lance of light goosed the blackness as I shrugged the rifle sling over my shoulder and started off on the little path along the river. I didn't fancy that walk late at night, the grass and bush too high and visibility too low for comfort. The area was swarming with big game of all sorts, and bumping into something large enough to have Liberian registry wasn't my idea of a pleasure stroll. I had already jostled a lioness with, by the sound of it, cubs, a month ago. I am not overly fond of lionesses under the most social of circumstances, but when they have the chilluns in tow, I develop a positive allergy. Putting her out of mind, I lit a smoke and pushed through the grass, hearing the watery splash of crocs in the river and, on the far bank, the yapping of jackals blended with the horror-movie chortle of hyenas on a fresh kill.

I was halfway home when I heard it, a heavy, low grunting from the thick *tshani* off to the right, then the hollow, crashing rattle of something big moving fast in my direction. The beam swung wildly as I slipped out of the sling and lined up the light along the barrels with my left hand. I knew what it probably was, which didn't do anything constructive for my blood pressure. When the sound was almost atop me, I lunged ten feet back down the trail as two and a half tons of bull hippo bisected the spot where I had been standing. He looked bigger than a steam roller, his mouth like an open picture window with pink curtains, but I knew that the white gleam the torch picked up in his face wasn't bric-a-brac. With a grace that belied his bulbous bulk, he whipped around and started to eat up those ten feet like he'd been practicing wind sprints. From the hip I yanked off both barrels simultaneously, never noticing the recoil or hearing the shots. The kick broke the filament in the flashlight bulb, however, leaving me in complete darkness with one bull hippo bent on murder about six feet away.

Despite what you may have heard, the greatest skill of a seasoned professional hunter is not the H. Rider Haggard, Hollywood business of nerving out charges and placing bullets precisely at the last second. It is the ability to get the hell out of the way. I am legendary in this field. Over the next six seconds I shattered the world record for one-man heavy-grass crashing and hauled up with two thorn-studded feet at the door of my hut. I scrambled around by feel locating two more rounds for the Evans and even found my other flashlight. With caution that defies description, I ignored the shouting and general uproar back in camp and retraced the path of my recent withdrawal. Sure enough, up loomed a 5,000-pound lump of deflated hippo, a huge bull with long, deep, suppurating tusk lacerations on his back and flanks from a free-for-all with a rival. Waving the beam in the air, I called for my men, who appeared like dusky jinns from the grass.

After I explained a slightly more flattering version of what had happened, we took a good look at the *Imvubu* and found that one big slug had gone smack between his adenoids, blasting his spine and dropping him dead before he hit the ground. I have always wondered where the second shot went. Missing a hippo from six feet, despite the circumstances, is rather like missing a barn from the inside. But, somehow I pulled it off, no mean feat of riflery, to be sure.

Most people who have never had a difference of opinion with one tend to consider hippos some sort of pathetic, overweight travesties of nature. Cartoonists usually portray them in short ballet skirts with little, round, flat-topped teeth, further reinforcing the idea that the only way a hippo could be dangerous would be if he fell out of a window and landed on you. Unfortunately, for several hundred humans in Africa each year, this is a fatal underestimation. An insecure bull hippo, wounded or not, can be as dangerous as cancer; and it would seem that bull hippos spend most of their time in the depths of insecurity.

The greatest and most common cause of hippo attack is their welldefined territorial instinct. Tourists love to take pictures of hippos displaying that big yawn so characteristic of the species. Actually, they are just showing you and other bulls what they've got to work with—an animal form of saber rattling. If you come wandering into his bailiwick in a dugout or outboard, he may well interpret your craft to be an interloper with amorous intentions on his womenfolk. If so, you had better lock all the doors and windows and take a deep breath. He has a mouth big enough to accommodate a dining-room table and, in reality, his tusks are razor-edged, self-whetting ivory scalpels as thick as your wrist, which can crush a native canoe or fiberglass speedboat with equal facility. In fact, in the old days hippos commonly attacked paddle steamers, often with impressive results! To be caught by a hippo is a singularly nasty way to receive your overdose of Africa.

Dr. M. P. Kahl, the man who took so many of the pretty pictures for this book, came by my digs a while back with a newsletter he thought might interest me. It was from the famous nature photographer and film maker Alan Root, of Nairobi, Kenya. It had been sent from Nairobi Hospital and clearly proved that Root is as handy with words as he is with pictures. I'll let him tell his own story:

"We were diving in Mzima Springs together with cameraman Martin Bell to get a few more linking shots we needed in order to add some Mzima footage to a lengthened balloon film. All had been going well and the hippos were quite cooperative. On this morning, however, one bull was a bit uptight. He was a second-ranking bull and they are never as relaxed as the one at the top. You can see this particularly clearly in advertising agencies, but it happens in nature, too. Anyway, we met him in the water and he moved off rapidly, stirring up a lot of muck so that we could not see. Rather than swim through the murk and risk bumping into something we simply lay in the water waiting for it to clear. (We were wearing aqualungs.) We did not realize that the bull had stopped about twenty feet away and was now staring and snorting at the spot where our bubbles were coming to the surface. Also, occasionally one of our tanks would appear, and this obviously disturbed him. Had we been in clear water where he could have lowered his head and seen what we were, I have no doubt that he would have moved away, and certainly we would have been able to see his mounting tension and moved the other way. As it was, only the people watching from the bank were aware of what was building up." [There were tourists watching Root's party film the sequence.]

"When he charged he made the typical upwards and sideways scything motion, mouth wide open, and Joan was first in line. At the time she remembers nothing except that she was hit by a tremendous blow—but somehow a soft, slow-motion blow like being hit by an E-type marshmallow. It seems that the hippo got his nose under her and threw her up and out of the water. As she was in midflight one of the hippo's canines pierced the rubber of her face mask just below her right eye and smashed the glass. (To put her face mask on and stick your finger through that hole is as chilling a feeling as you could ever want.)

"Having flung Joan aside, he turned on me and took a bite at my backside. Here I should explain that he still could not really see us; he was just making great slashing sweeps of his jaws as he ran toward us. His canines made two neatly incised holes through my swim trunks, taking only a sliver of skin from my right buttock. (This nicely balances the leopard bites on the other side, but unfortunately, like them, it will be a small scar and hardly worth showing.) But the blow rolled me over onto my back and the next thing I knew he had my right leg in his mouth. And I really did *know* it. I was vividly aware of every detail of what was happening. No pain, just a numbness and dull feelings of tearing and crushing but no pain at all. He got my leg right into his mouth, so that the left-hand canines were slicing through the calf while my foot and ankle were between his right-hand molars. Fortunately, they do not chew as a cat would, but just open and close their jaws enough to get a nice scissoring action of the canines. So at least my foot and ankle were only cut and badly bruised. My calf was bitten right through and chomped three or four times, fortunately all more or less in the same place. The hippo then shook me like a rat. I apparently appeared above water a few times and I was certainly scraped along the bottom too as my trunks were full of sand and debris. My most vivid recollection here is deciding that my leg had had it and the feel of the hippo's whiskers on the back of my thigh as I was shaken about. He then dropped me and went off."

"I had lost my mouthpiece and had water in my mask, but I still had air in my lungs and I stayed down a while. I knew that if the hippo was still there and I surfaced, I would be attacked again. I had to surface, though, and the hippo was gone. Joan was standing about twenty feet away in waist-high water. She didn't know I had been bitten and I didn't know she had been thrown. Martin Bell's head appeared about fifteen feet behind me—all he knew was that there had been a hell of a commotion and that something was wrong. In dream-like slow motion I emptied the water from my goggles, found my demand valve, cleared it, and put it in my mouth. Somehow, though I knew I had been bitten, I could not come to grips with the reality of it. Then I reached down and felt the floating mush that was my leg and called, 'Christ, I've been bitten.' Joan gave a wail and came wading toward me, but I yelled at her to get out of the water and she turned back to the bank. I lowered myself to swim for the shore, but I was swimming through blood and not doing too well when something clamped onto my wrist. It was so fierce and tight I thought it was the hippo again, but it was Martin, and he towed me across that pool with all the power of a nuclear submarine."

"We were concerned now about a ten-foot crocodile who had spent a lot of time over the past week methodically stalking us as we worked. We had met him in the water and faced him down a couple of times, but he had been getting bolder every day. I knew that as his fear of us decreased, I would have to watch him carefully, but felt that for the moment we were O.K. as long as we behaved

186

properly. Thrashing about on the surface and bleeding like a stuck pig did not come under the heading of proper behavior, so it was a relief to get to the bank."

"There I was bound up by an Italian doctor, part of a tourist group who saw the whole thing, stuck in the Range Rover where I lay drinking whisky on the way to Kilaguni Lodge, where we were able to amicably hijack a tourist plane. In less than three hours from the attack I was in the familiar, homely surroundings of the casualty ward of the Nairobi Hospital."

"Getting there was all the fun. In the next twenty-four hours I developed gangrene and became so odoriferous that even some of my best friends told me. In fact, all my best friends told me. I had some spectacular fevers—Boy! I have had the sheets changed before when I was sweating, but never the mattress! And, in between the sweats I needed an electric blanket to keep warm. Three days, seventeen pints of saline, eight pints of blood, many million units of intravenous penicillin, and several cups of tea later I was declared O.K. and since then I have been on the mend.

"As my surgeon put it, 'That hippo was as good an anatomist as I am,' and I must say that for all the random savagery of the attack the hippo really did do a neat job. There was a hole through my calf large enough to push a Coke bottle through, and by the time the doctors had cut away the damaged tissue to clean the wound they had enough meat, as they put it, 'for a reasonable hamburger.' But the teeth smashed muscle only—no bones, no tendons, no arteries and no major nerves and veins. It's hard to conceive of passing through a bull hippo's jaws and having so little real damage. (They are still the leading herbivore in Africa when it comes to killing people—crocs lead the carnivore list.)"

"I have now been in the hospital for two weeks, the leg is much improved, and I am having a skin graft in a couple of days' time. If it takes, I should be out ten days after that, though not walking for another week or so. Joan had a few bad days when the shock of her near-miss was compounded by my gangrene, but is now well and comes in every day to photograph the wound for the surgeons who are interested in just how it closes over. So that's it—my bum is numb and I'm putting on too much weight but I'm going to be O.K."

"P.S. Perhaps the hippo was a *better* anatomist than my doctor, for an X-ray has just shown that my fibula—the smaller bone of the two—was broken and there are several chips floating about in there. Skin grafting will go ahead anyway."

To observe that Alan Root was an incredibly lucky person to live through his brush with *Kiboko*, the hippo's KiSwahili moniker, would be gilding the lily. If that bite had been in the body instead of the leg, you may rest assured that he would have sent no newsletter. Many others, of course, whose work brings them within the reach of hippos do not fare so well.

A well-known crocodile hide hunter, Bryan Dempster, was returning from a foray against the saurians on the Zambezi one dark night with two African assistants, Albaan, and a Zulu, Joseph. Crossing a smooth, silent pool that lay along heavily vegetated banks, the blackness exploded without warning as the boat was rocketed completely clear of the water, the outboard motor screaming as the prop went wild, then dying as the hull smashed back to the surface. Dempster hit the water in a shower of equipment

and rolled-up croc hides right alongside a tremendous bull hippo. In the thin moonlight, Dempster saw the gleam of ivory and white foam as the bull clamped the boat in his teeth and crushed it like a wormy rowing shell. Aware his only chance was to remain as quiet as possible, he steeled his nerve and watched the monster only a few feet away. Dempster's mind raced. If the hippo didn't do for him, there was a growing chance the crocs would.

Suddenly, there was a screeching as Albaan panicked, unable to swim, and began flailing the water. Dempster knew that the *muntu* was a dead man and that, unarmed and in the water himself, there was nothing he could do about it. Gritting his teeth to remain silent, Dempster watched the bull charge over, open his giant maw and slam it shut on Albaan's head and chest. The screaming stopped. While the bull was submerged tearing Albaan to tatters, Dempster and Joseph quietly paddled to shore and lived.

A South African native-affairs official named Steyn, operating in the then-Bechuanaland protectorate (now Botswana) in 1959, was ordered to destroy a rogue hippo who had been flipping boats with fatal consequences in the Okavango River. He got a whack at the big bull and killed it outright with a brain shot, but drew the attention of a huge cow who charged the boat and, despite Steyn's shots, slashed the craft, throwing the man clear. He disappeared in a burst of bloody foam as the cow grabbed him. Steyn was never seen again.

When I was a professional white hunter in Zambia, hippos were on the general game license. Since popping a hippo in the water while you stand on the bank is something less than the apogee of sportsmanship, although justifiable in the extenuating circumstance of needing bait for a man-eating crocodile, we developed a slightly more interesting method for those clients who wanted the beautiful hippo ivory. Ian Manning, a very experienced professional hunter and ex-elephant cropping officer with whom I led many safaris in the Luangwa, was the innovator of the technique, which gave some clients a scarier time than their wounded buffalo. Ian would find a shallow sand bar and, after firing into the water to spook any crocs with ideas of ambush, would wade out into the territory of a big bull, the client following in the certain knowledge that Ian had been into the vanilla extract during the lunch break. Although steadfastly threatening, the bull would usually permit them to approach to about twenty yards away. At that point there would be a full-blast, flat-out charge. More than one client who had already stood up to elephants would display excellent basic reflexes by dropping his rifle and taking to the hills as Ian would drop the beastie in a depth charge of spray with a brain shot from about as far away as his shoelaces. Ian never made any serious mistakes (besides inventing the Gin Nyampala) but one day I nearly did.

My client was Rudy Cabañas of Mexicali, who stood his ground like a veteran of the battle of Isandhlwana. At his shot the bull crumpled up like a piece of wet newspaper, the bullet taking him between the eyes. Rudy waded back to shore where one of my men was brewing up a kettle of tea for Mrs. Cabañas while the skinners took the tusks, filets, and large slabs of skin for coffee-table tops. I stood about knee deep at the edge of the sand bar along a deeper channel, covering the butchering operation from crocs and other hippos with my .375 H. & H. Mauser magazine rifle.

There was another bull, I had noticed, about forty yards away at the edge of the small herd of ten or so, but I paid him little attention, more worried about a croc sneaking in under cover of the muddy water. As he seemed at a safe distance and was doing little more than muttering at me, I didn't notice it when he submerged. I smoked a couple of butts, started to turn around to see how things were coming along with my men, and just happened to catch a dark shadow in the water only a couple of yards in front of me. Like the Loch Ness monster putting on a one-man show, the second bull lurched out of the channel under a full head of steam right next to me as the water bulged and blew into a flurry. His mouth looked as if it could hold a pair of locomotives. My muzzle blast actually

194

scorched him as I got off a round where he looked biggest and his bow wave knocked me off balance in the water. To tell the truth, I wasn't scared—I was paralyzed! In all the near nasties I have come across in a business not noted for its security, that one was about the closest of all. I was so spooked that it took an hour before the shakes even started. I do not spend any more time standing around in rivers underestimating hippos.

Although most deaths by hippo are the result of unthinking intrusion by boat, a lot of souls have taken wing after meeting up with hippos on dry land. Hippos don't feed in the water, as you would suppose, but graze at night on grass and such at considerable distances from rivers and lakes. Around the Queen Elizabeth National Park, in pre-Amin Uganda, the hippo population was so overgrown that they had leveled the vegetation along the rivers to amazing distances, incurring official wrath that resulted in large numbers of them being cropped. The problem with feeding hippos is that they consider water to be their safety zone and become intensely unpleasant about the whole thing should you happen to blunder between them and their aquatic security blanket. River banks at night are marvelous places to avoid, especially along hippo paths. When a hippo is disturbed on land, he will charge back down his path to the security of the river despite any obstacle, including you.

A few years ago along the Pafuri River in South Africa's Transvaal, a tribesman and his wife were walking, the woman carrying a child on her back in the traditional manner. (Incidentally, after you have spent some time in Africa, you will notice that a black African will nearly always wear his shoes out along the outside edges of the soles first. All people who are carried in this manner, with their legs straddling their mother's waist, are slightly bowlegged and walk on the outsides of their soles.) Spotting a bull hippo ahead, the man yelled at it to scare it back into the water where he figured it belonged. Apparently the bull didn't see things quite that way. He charged, took the woman's leg off at the hip, bit away most of her side and wandered back into the river. The woman, of course, died on the spot, but somehow the child was unharmed.

It would seem that the Pafuri is noted for its savage hippos. About ten years ago another official named Steynberg was surprised while standing on the river bank. A hippo charged from the water and bit him just once. Once, however, was ample. His heart and lungs were exposed and he died in agony on a tortuous drive to the hospital. In 1966 on the Limpopo, the Great, Greasy River that forms the border between South Africa and Rhodesia, a single hippo cleaned house at an African beer bust, biting a man through the chest and killing him instantly. It had been the third fatality that year alone by hippos on the Limpopo.

The hunter and naturalist James Clarke reports witnessing an attack on a hunter named Barnard on the Olifants River in Transvaal. A young bull, weighing about a ton (quite small), charged Barnard, turning its head sideway for the first bite. Somehow, perhaps because the animal was inexperienced at disemboweling people, its first go resulted in its teeth bouncing off the man's hipbone, leaving just a whopping red welt across his stomach. (I'll bet!) However, with practice and perseverance, the young bull soon got the hang of it and crushed Barnard's elbow on its next try. Warming to the task, the bull encored the performance by driving a tusk deeply into the armpit but failed to sever the arm. A pal of Barnard's was then able to cancel the arrangement through the judicious application of two .505 Gibbs slugs to the brain. Barnard survived, but it is unlikely that the encounter did much for his bowling average.

I, for one, have never been able to figure out how a hippo, with his widely separated tusks, can manage to bite another animal in half. Yet there have been many reliable reports of just this happening, in one case the bitee being a child in Zululand who was described as neatly severed. I cannot imagine anything in the world tougher to bite in two than a ten-foot crocodile, but one of those unsociable Pafuri hippos did just that. The hippo has almost no natural enemies as an adult with the possible exception of man.

Whereas young hippos may sometimes be taken by crocs if the mother is lax, adults enjoy the distinction of being too big and tough for any other animal to molest. A lion could not possibly bite deeply enough to reach vitals even if it got up the nerve to try in the first place.

One of the major causes of rampaging hippos, such as the one who jumped me in the grass that night on the Luangwa, is the damage inflicted by other bulls in territorial and mating battles. These contests, unlike the relatively harmless tests of strength between the males of most species before mating, are bloodbaths that often result in the crippling and death of the loser and sometimes the winner, too. Every mature bull hippo has terrible scars over much of his body from the tusk bites of rivals, the acquisition of which must be a most unpleasant experience. I have seen several of these battles in closeup and assure you that they are hair-raising, incredibly bloody encounters, normally fought in the water. Both the winner and the loser are sure killers of anything crossing them in their agony and murderous temperament. I'd sooner try to push around a hungover gorilla than look sideway at one of those bulls after a Dating Game tussle.

The Greeks were not as inaccurate as the appearance of a hippo would indicate when they named the animal "hippopotamus" or "river horse." He may have a figure like a gourd, yet it's not fat but muscle under that leathery hide. Hippos are startlingly fast, both on land and in the water, where they may swim or walk along the bottom. Their dung, which is spread through the water by vibration of the tail, is seemingly very important to many of the smaller fish species, including the Tilapia bream, possibly the most delicious of the fresh-water food-fishes. In places like Botswana's Okavango, it has been found out the hard way how important the animal is to the shifting water system that varies from season to season, flooding roughly from north to south and back again. Many of the channels that had historically been kept clear of vegetable debris by hippo movement have become seriously clogged and water movement has been impeded because of pressure of poaching on Okavango hippos. They are now closely controlled in that area.

It is my personal opinion that hippo meat is one of the finest of game foods. I had a safari chef who could make a better stroganoff from the thigh-thick interior filets that lie up under the ribs along the spine than you could buy in New York. Just as it would be difficult to describe the taste of beef to a person who had never tried it, so it is with hippo. The taste is mild, less than lamb and more than beef, slightly more marbled than usual venison. It tastes exactly like, well, hippo.

In Zambia, among the Chenyanja-speaking tribes, there was a typical example of the apparently meaningless taboos that often crop up in Africa. They had it firmly in mind that the eating of hippo flesh would cause boils and carbuncles. That I ate it regularly made no impression—it was just another case of *lo nsebenza ga lo Abelungu*, white man's business, the same weird reaction that a wild Bushman would show on seeing me speak through a single sideband radio to headquarters a hundred miles away. You would expect him to be agog with amazement; normally, he shows no reaction or surprise at all. You could flap your arms and fly like a bird and rouse little more interest. As far as the bush African is concerned, there's nothing a white can't do with his magic gadgets.

In East Africa, on the other hand, hippo is a delicacy among the blacks. In places like southern Sudan, they were hunted with harpoons by probing the river or lake bottoms until located, then stuck. In the ensuing festivities, a dead man or two was no rarity, which perhaps gave the meat the succulence of stolen grapes.

As hippo were not used by my safari staff, I normally tried to engineer that the hippo of the safari be taken before we tried for lion. Since lions are great scavengers, and a hippo after a day in the sun has little olifactory resemblance to Chanel No. 5, it usually did not take long for any resident pride to find the windfall and settle in for a protracted feed.

The trick was to get the bloody carcass out of the water, hopefully towing it with muscle power to some point where a Land Rover could be brought within rope length. Strong strips of hide are cut in an enlarging "whirlpool" design from the flank and back, knotted through flaps cut in the skin on the away-side of the carcass, and attached to the hunting car. A good dose of four-wheel drive will turn the carcass over toward you, gaining perhaps four feet, at which point the operation must be repeated until the hippo is in position to be staked down before first light, in the hope of catching a lion still feeding at dawn. It takes most of a day to make fifty yards in this manner, or with gangs of locals if a Land Rover cannot be brought in. All in all, there are more exciting things to do on safari than roll hippos around all day.

Like his prehistoric pal the rhino, the hippo is mostly a pain in the neck because you have to be so damned careful to avoid him. Despite his short-fuse temper, stunning power, and speed, he is very necessary to the balance of his range in Africa. But that doesn't mean you have to love him. I'll go along with Sir Samuel Baker, the Victorian explorer, who had enough brushes with hippos during his Nile expeditions to last a dozen lifetimes. "There is no animal," as Sir Samuel put it, "that I dislike more than the hippo."

199

6

Crocodile

"What's with the birdcage?" asked Paul Mason over his scrambled egg and impala liver breakfast. I glanced across the hard-packed earth of the safari camp to the slender figure of the young woman padding softly through the early light to the nearby lagoon.

"Fish trap, actually," I told him, ambushing a sausage from the platter Martin was passing. The woman disappeared into the bush, the cone-shaped cage of woven cane balanced lightly on her shaven head. "The women wade out into the lagoons along the river when they're low like this in the dry season and just slam the wide end of the trap into the bottom ahead of their feet. The bream and catfish are so thick when the water drops, they always get a few in the trap, then they just stick their hands through the open top and grab them."

Paul grunted, then spoke over his shoulder. "Martin! *Buisa maquanda futi!*" I was surprised that he even had the proper Q-click in the word for eggs. The old waiter, once the batman of a colonel of Kenya's crack regiment, the King's African Rifles, came to attention smartly, then trotted off to the kitchen for more scrambles. Mason grinned, proud of the Fanagalo he had picked up on his first two weeks of safari in the Luangwa. Even if it wasn't the formal language of the country, Chenyanja, the Tongue of the Lakes, Fanagalo did the same job for central and southern Africa as KiSwahili served on the east coast. And, a hell of a two weeks it had been. Still in his thirties Mason was fit and tough enough to hunt really hard, tracking twenty miles a day with nothing but an occasional breather, the kind of hunting that can produce the quality trophies he had taken. The third day out he'd busted a lunker lion from spitting distance with a better black mane than Victor Mature's and had built on that with a forty-eight-inch buffalo and a kudu that would necessitate an addition on his house if he planned to hang it on the wall. From the reports brought in by Silent, things looked pretty fair in the leopard department, too. The number three bait had been taken by a kitty that left a track like it was wearing snowshoes. Mason was

203

one of the really good ones, a humble man who never thumped his chest, a fine shot and a better companion, a genuine pleasure to bwana for.

"What say we just screw around with some *Zinyoni* today, then hit the leopard blind about four?" I asked. "There's any amount of francolin and guinea fowl over by the Chifungwe Plains, and we could shoot the water holes on the way down for ducks and geese. Always the chance of picking up a decent elephant spoor in that area, too."

"You just purchased yourself a boy," he answered. "But, how's about we pot another impala? This liver's out of this world."

"Sure," I told him, "you've got two left on your license and the camp is getting kind of low on meat. That kudu filet's about finished and . . ."

The scream was low at first, more a cry of surprise than alarm, then crescendoed into a piercing shriek of pure animal terror echoing hollowly through the *mukwa* hard- woods, up from the lagoon. Again it cut the cool morning air, even higher, a throbbing razor-edged wail that lifted my hackles and sent a shiver scampering up my spine like a small, furry animal. We both froze for an instant, Mason with a piece of toast halfway to his open mouth, his eyes wide in surprise. Reacting, I snatched the .375 H. & H. from where it leaned against the log rack on the low wall of the dining hut and loaded from the cartridge belt as I ran toward the lagoon. I heard Mason trip and curse behind me, then regain his feet and run, stuffing rounds into the magazine of his .404 Mauser action. My heart felt like a hot billiard ball in my throat as I bulled through the light bush along the 150 yards to the low banks of the lagoon, a reedy, dry-season lake that would join the Munyamadzi River 100 yards away at the first flooding rains. Bursting into the open, I could see a flurry of bloody foam fifty yards from shore, a slender, ebony arm flailing the surface at the end of a great, sleek form that cut the water with the ease of a cruiser. I raised the rifle. Should I shoot? What if I hit the woman? Like a mallet blow, I realized that even if I did hit her it would be a blessing, far better than being dragged inexorably, helplessly down by the huge crocodile. I lined up the sights and carefully squeezed off a 300-grain Silver-tip, which threw a column of water just over the top of the croc's head, then whined off to rattle through the trees at the far side of the lagoon. A second later Paul fired, the big .404 slug meeting empty water where the croc had been an instant before, the giant saurian submerging like a U-boat blowing positive. Slow ripples rolled across the calm surface, waving the dark, green reeds until they lapped the low banks. Once again, the lagoon was silent. We stood helplessly, shocked into muteness, thinking of the woman. We could almost feel the tent-peg teeth deep in her midriff, the rough scaliness of the croc's horny head under her hands as she used the last of her strength to try to break loose before her lungs could stand no more and she would breathe dark death.

"Jesus Christ," said Paul in a hoarse whisper. It didn't sound like a curse. Silent, my gunbearer, Martin, and Stomach, a skinner, came running up. A glance at the floating fish trap and at the woman's sandals on the bank told them what had happened. Wading to his knees, Silent retrieved the cane trap and placed the other effects inside. He started a slow trot that would carry him to the woman's village, a miserable huddle of mud and dung huts called Kangani. Slowly we turned back to camp, the shock of witnessing the most horrible death in Africa leaving us numb. I took the rifles and unloaded them, placing a cartridge bullet-first into the muzzle of each to prevent mud wasps from starting nests in the bores, a bit of Africana that has cost hunters their sight and even lives when they forgot it. Martin came over to us and spoke quietly in Fanagalo. "There is nothing for it, Bwana," he intoned with the exaggerated fatalism of the bush African. "It has always been so. Always has *Ngwenya* been waiting; always will he wait."

Ngwenya, the crocodile, has been waiting a very long time. For 170 million years he has been lurking, patient and powerful, in the warmer fresh and salt waters of this planet. Virtually unchanged from his earliest fossil remains, he demonstrates with deadly efficiency the value of simplicity in design. The crocodile is the master assassin, the African Ice Man, combining the ideal qualities of cunning with ruthlessness and cold voracity matched with a reptilian intelligence far greater than his small brain would indicate. He is little more than teeth, jaws, and stomach propelled by the most powerful tail in nature. He will eat anything he can catch and digest almost anything he can eat. Someday, if you spend enough time around the watery haunts of *Ngwenya*, that may include you or—Lord forbid—me.

In these days of moon landings and lasers, it can be difficult to fathom the fact that crocodiles are still a very substantial threat to human life in Africa. Most Americans, were you to conduct a poll, would probably offer some vague impression that crocodiles are teetering on the brink of extinction in Africa today, hardly any threat to man. I've got some big news. By the most conservative estimates of professional researchers, something approximating ten human beings are dragged off to a death horrible beyond description *each day* in modern Africa. The figure may even be considerably higher since successful croc attacks, unless witnessed, normally leave no trace whatever of the victim, who may have died by any of the methods Africa has developed to make evolution a working proposition. The facts boil down to this: *Crocodylus niloticus* is the one man-killer who, if he's big enough and you're available enough, will eat you every time he gets a chance.

I was taught in Sunday School, I dimly remember, that it's not nice to hate anything. Nonetheless, I do hate crocs, an opinion shared rather vocally by such ne'er-do-wells as Winston Churchill and Theodore Roosevelt. I do not believe in their being driven to extinction, heavens no, because we find to our infinite wonder that everything in nature has its place. On the other hand, I have not an ounce of regret at having been in on the killing of about a hundred of them, all legally shot, I might add, and not for their hides. I have often wondered what stand the ultrapreservationists would take if we were to stock a few hundred crocs in New York's Central Park, where their philosophizing might become more than the armchair variety next time they walked their poodles. I'm sure it would lower the crime rate, if nothing else.

As with snakes there has been a great deal of exaggeration as to the length crocodiles may attain and at the same time a lack of appreciation of the weights they may reach. Adventure books are full of vivid reports of twenty-five and even thirty footers, but few realize how truly immense even a twelve-footer is. The Luangwa Valley of Zambia probably has the largest population of crocodiles in Africa, perhaps the world. Never having been hunted for their hides in this area, they have flourished in untold thousands. In a normal afternoon of hunting along the banks of the Luangwa and Munyamadzi Rivers, it is not unusual to see hundreds sunning themselves on the sand bars and banks, their mouths agape in sleep, oxpeckers and tickbirds hopping around their jaws with impunity. Yet of all the thousands I have seen, I must conclude that a twelve-footer is big and one of thirteen feet edging up to huge. The biggest croc I have ever seen, besides the one who killed the woman in the lagoon, went about fifteen feet with three feet of tail missing, fairly common for some reason in very big crocs. That would make him roughly eighteen feet, which is one hell of a lot of crocodile. I've owned cars shorter than that! He crawled out to sun himself on a small island 150 yards from my camp one hot afternoon when I was between safari clients. I watched him for about a half-hour, out of film for my camera, of course, and God, but he was immense. He looked like a big, scaly subway car with teeth, that could have taken a buffalo and three wart hogs with one gulp. To tell you the honest truth, I came very close to killing him. Crocs that big are very often man-eaters, learning the habits of native women until they try a couple and find they're a lot easier to handle than trying to pull a rhino in by his nose. But, I didn't have a license and knew that the locals would turn me in for the reward offered for violators, so I reluctantly let him go. At least they can't take away your white hunter's ticket for what you're thinking. When the next clients arrived two days later, he was never to be seen.

One famous hunter, shooting years ago in Kenya's Lake Rudolph, which has some Godzilla-league crocs in it, swatted over one hundred, of which only three beat fifteen feet, and those only by a whisker. The largest crocodile "officially" recorded was killed by the Uganda Game Department in the Semliki River along the Congo border in 1953. It was only three inches short of twenty feet. I have seen a mounted croc in a museum that tapes sixteen feet, and he stands higher than my waist, so you can imagine how colossal that nineteen-footer was. When crocs get over twelve feet or so, they gain tremendously in weight for each inch they grow. You could practically shoplift an eight-footer, but you had best have three strong friends along if you want to even roll over a twelve-footer. I have never weighed a big croc, but I'll bet you a hangover that a fifteen-foot *Ngwenya* will outweigh a big buffalo, well over a ton. A croc this size will stand about four feet when walking and have a girth of about eight feet.

Crocodiles never stop growing their whole lives, so the age of an immense one must be very impressive. Consider that one Asian specimen, a salt-water crocodile, has been living in an American zoo for over thirty years and has grown only about four feet since his capture. Conceivably, a brute like the Semliki nineteen-footer may have seen two centuries turn over.

As much, if not more than, the lion, the history of African exploration is written around the crocodile. In fact, there is hardly an explorer or a missionary that doesn't mention a few squeaks with *Ngwenya, Mamba, Nkwena*, or whatever his local name may be, often with fatal results. By way of example, let's look at just one passage of the writings of Sir Samuel Baker on a military expedition in the great papyrus Sudd of southern Sudan:

"Among the accidents that occurred to my expedition, one man had his arm bitten off at the elbow, being seized while collecting aquatic vegetation from the bank. He was saved from utter loss by his comrades who held him while his arm was in the jaws of the crocodile. The man was brought to me in dreadful agony, and the stump was immediately amputated above the fracture. Another man was seized by the leg while assisting to push a vessel off a sand bank. He also was saved by a crowd of soldiers who were with him engaged in the same work; this man lost his leg. The captain of No. 10 tug was drowned [by a croc] in the dock vacated by the 108-ton steamer, which had been floated into the river by a small canal cut from the basin for that purpose. The channel was 30 yards in length and three feet deep. No person ever suspected that a crocodile would take possession of the dock, and it was considered the safest place for the troops to bathe. One evening the captain was absent and as it was known a short time previously that he had gone down to wash at the basin, he was searched for at the place. A pile of clothes and his red fez were upon the bank, but no person was visible. A number of men jumped into the water and felt the bottom in every portion of the dock, with the result that in a few minutes, his body was discovered; one leg was broken in several places, being severely mangled by the numerous teeth of the crocodile. There can be little doubt that the creature, having drowned its victim, had intended to return."

Several months later, sitting in the cool of the evening with Lady Baker and Commander Julian Baker, RN, Sir Samuel was accosted by one of his men, panicked almost into incoherency. To let Baker tell it:

"The man gasped out, 'Said, Said is gone! Taken away from my side by a crocodile, now, this minute!'

" 'Said! What Said?' I asked: 'There are many Saids!'

" 'Said of the No. 10 steamer, the man you liked, he is gone. We were wading together across the canal by the dock where Reis Mahomet was killed. The water is only waist deep, but a tremendous crocodile rushed like a steamer from the river, seized Said by the waist and disappeared. He's dragged into the river and I've run here to tell you the bad news.'

"We immediately hurried to the spot. The surface of the river was calm and unruffled in the stillness of a fine night. The canal was quiet and appeared as though it had never been disturbed. The man who had lost his companion sat down and sniffled aloud. Said, who was one of my best men, was indeed gone forever."

One can only hope that those of Baker's men working the No. 10 steamer got hazardous duty pay.

Arthur Neumann, the same chap who got the fifteen-minute battering from a bull elephant referred to earlier, was the horrified witness to a classic croc attack on New Year's Day, 1896, on a river near Lake Rudolph in modern Kenya:

"Late in the afternoon, I went down for another bathe, with Shebane (my servant) as usual carrying my chair, towels, etc., and did the same thing again. It is a large river and deep, with a smooth surface and rather sluggish current; its water dark-coloured and opaque, though hardly to be called muddy, deepens rapidly, so that a step or two in is sufficient at this point to bring it up to one's middle, while the bottom is black, slimy mud.

"Having bathed and dried myself, I was sitting on my chair, after putting on my clothes, by the water's edge, lacing up my boots. The sun was just about to set behind the high bank across the river, its level rays shining full upon us, rendering us conspicuous from the river while preventing our seeing in that direction. Shebane had just gone a little way off (perhaps a dozen yards) along the brink and taken off his clothes to wash himself, a thing I had never known him to do before when with me; but my attention being taken up with what I was doing, I took no notice of him. I was still looking down when I heard a cry of alarm, and, raising my head, got a glimpse of the most ghastly sight I have ever witnessed. There was the head of a huge crocodile out of the water, just swinging over towards the deep with my poor Swahili boy in its awful jaws, held across the middle of the body like a fish in the beak of a heron. He had ceased to cry out, and with one horrible wriggle, a swirl and a splash all disappeared. One could do nothing. It was over; Shebane was gone . . . A melancholy New Year's Day indeed!"

Because there are far more blacks than whites in the range of the Nile Crocodile, it follows that the preponderance of victims are black. Most are women, the traditional duty of that sex being to draw water from the river bank where they are most vulnerable. However, crocs are equally partial to white meat, as the grisly case of William K. Olson, a Cornell graduate and Peace Corps volunteer attests. Olson was recovered in large chunks from the stomach of a thirteen-foot one-inch croc who killed and ate him while he was swimming—despite warnings—in the Baro River near Gambella, Ethiopia, on April 13, 1966. The croc was shot the next day by a Colonel Dow, a safari client of my friend, Karl Luthy, a Swiss white hunter operating in Sidamo Province. I have seen the photos taken by Luthy of removing the body from the croc's stomach, and if you are interested to see what Olson looked like a,ter twenty hours in a croc's paunch, you may see one of them reproduced on page 200 of Alistair Graham's and Peter Beard's book, *Eyelids of Morning* (New York Graphic Society, 1973). I don't recommend it, however, unless you considered *The Exorcist* light comedy.

The inside of a croc's stomach is sort of an African junkyard. I have found everything from human jewelry to whole wart hogs to Fanta bottles and three-pound rocks inside them. One ten footer I shot in Ethiopia even had a four-foot brother tucked in his belly. According to a reliable writer-hunter, one east African man-eater contained the following horribilia: several long porcupine quills, eleven heavy brass arm rings, three wire armlets, an assortment of wire anklets, one necklace, fourteen human arm and leg bones, three human spinal columns, a length of fiber used for tying firewood, and eighteen stones. I wasn't there, but that sounds just a touch exaggerated if only for the simple amount of the inventory. Stones are commonly found in the stomach of crocs, but whether they are picked up accidentally when the croc lunges for a fish or whether they are meant as an aid to the digestive process like the grit in a bird's crop is unknown. Maybe they're used for ballast.

The collections of indigestible items found in the stomachs of crocodiles points out their fantastic digestive powers. I have found good-size antelope leg bones that were almost dissolved; they would have to be since they were far too large to be passed through the normal process. The arm bracelets are worn by African women very tightly on the bicep, and the only way for them to be found free would be for the arm to have been digested.

The Nile crocodile holds the unquestioned title as the most accomplished of Africa's man-eaters. Some individual crocs have been credited with hundreds of human victims and since the species is more or less limited to water, there is only one factor that makes this possible—the incredible sense of fatality that the African holds toward the crocodile.

There are innumerable cases of scores of women being taken by crocs at the *same spot* every few days as they draw water for their families. Crocs easily learn where to wait and, apparently, the fate of the last person who filled her jug from a particular place has no effect whatever on the next one who may have even been present when the last victim was taken. I have lived with Africans in the bush for many years, but I have found it impossible to understand their total indifference to horrible death. I have seen this phenomenon from Ethiopia to South Africa, so it is not a matter of one particular tribe but a continent-wide indifference that defies explanation. Ask a woman why she takes her water from the same place where her sister was killed the week before and she will just shrug. It's weird.

I was once crossing a river in Mozambique by cable pontoon, which is a raft drawn across the stream by cables operated by government personnel. One man jumped off near shore to unfoul a line and was immediately taken by a croc in a swirl of bloody water and never seen again. Yet when I returned the following day, the surviving raft operators were happily splashing and washing not twenty yards from where their fellow worker was killed!

Crocodiles are considered "saurians" by science (as in dinosaur) and are available in a wide variety of flavors. Among these are their cousins, the alligators, gavials, and caimans. With the exception of the African or Nile crocodile (the same animal, even though found nowhere near the Nile) and the salt-water crocodile of the warm Asian islands, most of the clan is relatively inoffensive. Of course, the American alligator has caused some deaths and injuries, including a fully documented fatal attack that took place in Sarasota, Florida, in August 1973. A sixteen-year-old girl was taken by an eleven-foot gator and, despite efforts of onlookers to prevent it, partially eaten. Between 1948 and 1971 there were an additional seven unprovoked attacks, which produced various injuries but no fatalities.

213

Although rare, there is an American crocodile reputedly as dangerous as the African breed.

The salt-water crocs of Asia are lumped under several types, including the marsh or mugger crocodile and estuarine types, all considered very dangerous. In fact, one of the greatest clashes between man and croc took place during World War II. At the time that Burma was being retaken by the Allies, about 1,000 Japanese infantrymen became caught between the open sea and the island of Ramree, deep in mangrove swamps crawling with crocs, expecting to be evacuated by ships that never arrived. Trying to retreat, they found themselves cut off by the British Royal Navy in such position that they could not regain the mainland. When night came, so did the crocodiles. Witnesses on the British ships have told of the horror of the mass attack on the men, of the terrible screaming that continued until dawn when only 20 men out of 1,000 were left alive. Certainly, some were killed by enemy fire and others by drowning, but all evidence points up that most were slaughtered by the big salt-water crocs.

Any animal as obviously dangerous as the crocodile is bound to have a thick layer of legend wrapped around its reputation. Of course, a lot of it is *marfi*, a polite term for droppings. Time and again tales are heard of people who have had an arm or leg removed, "snapped off in one bite," by crocs. Not so. One look at a croc's dentures point out that, because of their spacing and rounded design, they are intended for catching and holding rather than cutting. If you have ever tried to carve a London broil with a tent peg, you've got the idea. Anything a croc can get down his gullet at one try he will swallow whole, tilting his head back so the morsel falls to the back of his throat. Anything bigger, he must wait for decay to set in and soften the meat so that he can grip it and spin his body, ripping off a healthy chunk in the same way that a Frenchman tears off a piece of bread.

Another myth about the croc is his supposed ability to knock animals into his jaws by using his powerful tail, even from elevated river banks. No way. I have seen at least

twenty animals taken by crocs, both on banks and in the water. All were caught with pure speed and surprise. No animal of the size and bulk of a croc could possibly jump in such a way as to get his tail behind his meal and flip it toward him. Yet crocs have been reported as accomplishing this with animals on river banks six feet over them!

I had a good lesson in the speed a croc may generate late one afternoon when I was sitting in a leopard blind along the river. My client and I were watching a small troop of impala wander idly down a path to the water to drink, pausing thirty-one feet, by later measurement, from the river's edge. Instantly, a twelve-foot crocodile erupted from the water like a Polaris missile, crossing the ground to the nearest impala, a ewe, like a green blur. As she spun to escape, he was on her, grabbing her right rear haunch and effortlessly dragging her to the dark river. In less than a minute there wasn't even a ripple to mark where she had disappeared. Considering that the impala is one of the fastest of the African antelopes, the speed a croc can crank out over a short rush must be well over thirty-five miles per hour. I can tell you I didn't walk as close to the river after the demonstration.

The awesome power of big croc has been demonstrated on large game many times. In a Tanzanian (Tanganyikan) game park in the late 1950s, a party of tourists were photographing a black rhino cow as she drank at a water hole. She was fair sized for a female, probably shading 4,000 pounds. As she stuck her odd, prehensile nose into the scummy water, the water exploded and a big croc clamped down on her muzzle. There followed an amazing test of strength between the two armored monsters, the croc trying to pull the rhino into the water and the rhino trying to pull the croc out of it. After an hour of straining, with neither gaining more than a foot, the rhino was actually inched toward the water. Thirty minutes later, her head was held under and, after a final flurry, she rolled over, drowned. The croc was estimated as about fourteen feet by the ranger driving the tour car.

The crocodile is a cold-blooded creature in more ways than one. Like most nonmammals, his ability to hang onto the last shreds of life would make a vampire wild with envy. So tough is the croc that there is an old hide hunters' maxim quite as valid today as it ever was: A croc ain't dead until the hide's salted, and even then don't count on it! Besides the fact that really large crocs—twelve feet and over—are sneaky as revenuers, the felony is compounded by their anatomy offering only the smallest of targets for a fatal shot. I have heard other professionals claim that a lung-shot *Ngwenya* will leave the water before he drowns, although I have never witnessed this. But then, to be fair, I have never shot a croc in the lungs. For my money the only way to anchor a crocodile where he lies and thus prevent his certain escape to the river where he will be lost or eaten by his pals is to separate him from his brain. Smaller than your fist, it's located just behind the eyes, an angle that can almost never be made from dead on or astern without at least 30 degrees of elevation above the croc. The brain is encased in some very impressive bone (I once broke a steel spearhead in two trying to drive it through the skull) and just can't be reached from a flat angle. The only reliable position for the brain shot is from the side, where your target will be about two inches high by three inches wide. Joe Joubert, a fine professional hunter who had a camp near mine in Zambia, was once shot in the face by a ricocheting .22 bullet when an excited client bounced it off the skull of a big croc in an attempted *coup de grace*.

Just how much pummeling a crocodile can absorb came to my definite attention during a safari in Botswana's Okavango Swamps, which had been pretty well picked over by professional hide hunters years before. Yet, after the market shooting was stopped, the crocs had come back strongly, if warily. I spotted one of a dozen feet sunning himself half out of the water on the base of an old termite heap. He was a good 400 yards out, and open water prevented stalking any closer. But, the croc was a good one for

Okavango, and I knew my client to be an excellent shot with his "toy," a .257 Weatherby Magnum with a variable power telescopic sight, a flat-shooting iron too light for most game but perfect for a long shot like this.

We hunched along through the light *mswaki* scrub at the edge of a sand flat, the tsetse flies absolutely mobbing us. I have never seen them in greater numbers or more savage. Ignoring the saber-toothed mauling he was getting, my client rested the rifle across his hand on a broken wrist of branch, lined up with plenty of holdover, took his shooting breath, and sent one off Air Mail Special. I was amazed to see the little slug lash out and strike right on the money, a light mist of bone chips and brain matter erupting from the skull. Typical of a brain-shot croc, his prehistoric nervous system jammed in flank speed, his powerful tail whipping the water like a paddle wheeler gone aground.

As I watched through my binoculars, I could see the growing pink cloud in the water and the tail slowed to a stop. My gunbearers and skinners, who very wisely share a common sentiment of loathing anything to do with crocs, dead or alive, decided that they just weren't getting paid enough to help me drag that one back through open water. I stoked up the .470 with soft-points, removed my wallet, and, in the best Stewart Granger tradition, started wading. The water was only to my waist, and I wasn't nearly as worried about crocs as I was leery of the small herd of hippos who were eyeing me with some annoyance from seventy yards away. After a few minutes, however, the herd leader finally decided that I wasn't there to rape any of the ladies fair, and he ponderously ignored me. The big crocodile was lying mostly in the water, just his shattered head on the ant hill, so I was able to work him out into deeper water despite his bulk, which was largely negated by his buoyancy. With the end of his tail across my shoulder, I began to drag him back like a small ant with a dung beetle. I had made about forty yards when I noticed a tiny quiver through his body and began to reflect seriously on the prudence of my position. I didn't have much time to think about it because, with a tremendous wrench, he flattened me. The fist-sized crater in his head where his brains used to be had lulled me to the hasty conclusion that he was dead, a status he was clearly contesting.

I came up spitting muddy water, trying to get the double rifle free from where it was slung around my neck. He hit me again with his body, and I went back down, stumbling and thrashing to keep away from the jaws. I managed to break the rifle, pour the water out of the barrels and present the croc with 1,000 grains of high velocity tranquilizer right behind the smile. When the little pieces of the rest of his head stopped falling out of the sky, I grabbed him again and completed towing him back to shore. Polaroids appeared as if by witchcraft, and the client and I squatted down in the hero position and opened the jaws, the teeth gleaming like a nest of bloody *punji* sticks. Just as the camera clicked, there was a sound like an iron maiden being slammed, and people became very scarce. We jumped back as the croc began to thrash around, snapping his jaws and actually growling, a sound I have never heard one make before or since. My client belted him twice more with a .300 Magnum, his head looking like a jam jar somebody had stuck a grenade into. That calmed him down considerably. We finished the pictures and three of my men had to sit on the battered body to hold it down from nervous reaction as the belly skin was taken. Hunting back past the spot a few hours later, I was surprised to see the corpse surrounded by a ring of vultures, odd because normally they would have swarmed him and finished him up in short order. As we got closer, they flew off and I noticed something: a dead vulture was clamped tightly between the "dead" croc's jaws. That boy wasn't about to quit!

Paul Mason and I began to hunt the man-eater the same afternoon as the attack on the woman. I hadn't had much of a look at him beyond his obvious bulk, but that was so exceptional it would give him away if we ever saw him again. From the size of his head and the wake he was throwing, he had to be better than fifteen feet, and there just weren't many of that size anywhere. I decided to abandon the rule that the professional only shoots in case of a charge or imminent escape of dangerous game and split us into two groups on either side of the big lagoon, which was separated from the Munyamadzi by a sandy umbilical a hundred yards wide. We sat, rifles ready, through the long afternoon, watching the water until our temples throbbed for some sign of the huge croc, but not a ripple betrayed his presence. Crocodiles can hold their breath by only showing the tiniest tip of nostrils. As the last of the light disappeared, we pushed aching, cramped joints into action and returned to camp.

We ate early that night, not saying very much, and after a few belts of man's best friend went off to bed. It was still full dark when tea arrived and we shrugged off blankets in the chill morning air. Well before dawn, we were picking our way to the lagoon. Even in the growing half-light, I could see that we were too late. Across the sand spit lay a spoor like a half-track; a deep, wide belly mark flanked by huge tracks showed where the killer croc had crossed from the lagoon and entered the river. I said a bad word. We had a good chance of finding him in the limits of the lagoon, but now, in the expanse of river, where he could move at will, things looked much dimmer. Still, I thought, given enough time, hard work and a fifty-five-gallon drum of pure, Grade A, vitamin-enriched luck. . . .

Paul and I retraced our steps and wolfed down a fast breakfast of the remaining kudu steaks and plenty of sweet, black tea. Before heading for another long day on the river, I thought it best we check the "zero" of our rifles, having decided to switch from the heavier .375 and .404 to Paul's .25-06 Remington and my .275 Rigby Rimless, reasoning that any shot we might get would probably be a long one requiring the precision of the lighter rifles over the power of the heavier. My .275 didn't have the velocity of Paul's superhot Remington, but I had put so many rounds through it that holdover and windage were as indelibly ingrained in my subconscious as Raquel Welch's bustline. Satisfied that any misses could not be blamed on Messrs. Rigby or Remington, we headed back to the river.

In view of the fact that, considering the size of the area the croc could be in, our best approach would be a saturation campaign, I called all my staff together. There were twenty-six of them, a mixture of Sengas, Awizas, Baila, and even a couple of BaTonkas up from the Zambezi. There were cooks, waiters, skinners, trackers, gunbearers, water boys, laundry boys, *chimbuzi* boys, and firewood gatherers, all my bush family. Leaving only Martin to watch things around camp, I split them up into pairs with instructions to watch for the big croc at various vantage points on the river. If seen, one would stay while the other would come to fetch us. My strategy wasn't entirely hit or miss: it had been a cold night, and since crocodiles must regulate their body temperatures by alternate sunning and wetting, I was pretty sure that the man-eater would show somewhere within three miles in either direction of my camp. Therefore, I had somebody watching nearly every convenient sand bar.

The sun was an incandescent, white cueball on a blue felt sky when I saw the first smoke a half-mile downriver. Someone had seen the crocodile! I sent Silent to bring Paul, 300 yards upriver from me, and, when he arrived, breathless from running, we started off toward the tendril of smoke. On the way I met Chenjirani, partnered with Invisible, sent to fetch us if we did not notice the smoke. From a bend in the river, I climbed a small bluff and turned the binoculars on the shimmering water. Eight hundred yards away, the dark, water-wet form of a gigantic croc smothered the tip of a sand bar. It looked like we had him. I mentally marked a tree on the bank that was opposite the croc, deciding to use it as a firing point. I motioned to Paul that we should sweep in a large half-circle through the heavy brush so there would be no chance of the croc or his tickbird sentinals spotting us, and we came out at a point a few yards from the grass-skirted tree trunk.

It was a perfect stalk, the soft ground giving no warning that our tiptoe approach would set up vibrations that the animal could feel through the dense medium of water. The tree loomed nearer above the towering elephant grass until we were up to it. Ever so slowly, Mason moved up, slipping into firing position with the .25-06 clenched by the pistol grip ahead of him. We could see the edge of the upper part of the bar through the fringe of grass as I worked closer to Paul, ready for a backup shot if necessary. The croc should be only thirty yards away, sleeping in oblivion, a shot a blind man could make. I slid my hand forward to push the grass away from Paul's muzzle and we both popped up to find . . . *nothing. Nowhere. Empty.*

I was absolutely baffled. What in bloody hell could have spooked him? He must have just changed his mind about the sunbath during the ten minutes it had taken us to make the stalk. Or, maybe he had gotten to grow so big by realizing that to expose himself for any amount of time could mean the hot whiplash of a bullet. Whatever the reason, he simply was not there.

Two days later, our knees raw as minute steaks from crawling along the brushy banks looking for the croc, he still hadn't tipped his hand. I increasingly feared that, like many of his brethren who had achieved great age and size, he had figured out that safety lies in darkness.

"Paul," I said that night after dinner, pouring him something to dispel his mood, "we're gonna have to bait that croc to have any chance at him at all. I'm convinced he just isn't active during daylight or we would have seen him more than just once."

"Whatcha got in mind, Bwana?" he asked. "Want me to go fish trapping in the river?"

"Not 'til you pay your safari bill, I don't," I grinned back. "I think that big lizard has been hunted before. Shot at. Maybe he came all the way up from the Zambezi. After five months in this camp I've never seen him before or even cut tracks that big." I took a flaming splinter from the fire and lit the tip of a Rhodesian Matinee from the thirty-pack in my breast pocket. "Maybe he's not even in this section of river anymore, but I doubt that."

We ghosted the banks of the Munyamadzi the next morning until the sun was high in the cloudless, dry-season sky. September dust-devils swirled black grass ash thousands of feet up to rain back on us in a fine, greasy film until Silent joked that we were now dark enough that he might adopt us. Scores of crocs were basking on sand bars and small beaches, but nothing approaching the size of the man-eater. Then, as I swept the glasses across a stretch of calm water at the head of a pool, I caught two dark lumps that protruded oddly above the slick surface. As I stared, they disappeared without a ripple, as if they felt my stare. From the distance between the knobs, I knew they were the eyes of a monster crocodile, and I would take all bets that he was our boy. I crawled back from the bank and got Paul. We drove the hunting car quietly upriver a half-mile where a hippo herd lay in the tail of the current. Paul wedged himself into the sitting position and slammed a 400-grain .404 slug through the brain of a big, scarred bull, who collapsed without a twitch and disappeared into the black depths.

"How long, Silent?" I asked the spindle-shanked old gunbearer. He knelt down and felt the temperature of the water and glanced at the sun, calculating for a moment. A great poacher in his youth, Silent was never fifteen minutes off in predicting how long it would take a hippo's body to bloat and leave the bottom. Finally, he pointed to an empty piece of western sky where the sun would be when the hippo would rise to the surface. At five, we were back with the crew just in time to see the carcass balloon up and drift into a quiet eddy where we were able to rope it. After a long struggle we wrestled his tons into position where the Rover could winch him over in stages. When we were finished, he lay at the edge of a shallow bar beneath our ambush point, a low, riverine bluff thirty yards away and twenty feet high. Powerful ropes of his own hide held him to stakes driven deeply into the mud to prevent the crocs from pulling and tugging him into the current.

I showed Paul the big, wedge-shaped bites in the hide, tooth marks of crocs testing the degree of decomposition of the body. Usually, they would have to wait several days before the hide had rotted enough to be torn away, exposing the meat beneath, but this hippo would be table-ready. Already the skinners were busy struggling to slash away huge patches of the thick skin so the crocs could feed immediately. I suppose I should be able to tell you how crocodiles locate carrion, but I'm not really sure. I believe that they hunt living prey by both sight and sound of water disturbance, but I couldn't say how good their sense of smell is. Judging by the short time it takes a large number of crocs to find a decomposing carcass, though, they must have fairly decent noses, although whether they discern the odor from airborne scent or from tainted water evades me. Stomach brought over the corrugated ivory arcs of the fighting tusks and the smoother, amber rods of the interior teeth and presented them to Mason. Nearly dark, we drove back to camp and a couple of sun-downers followed by an excellent stroganoff of hippo filet. We were both dead to the world before ten o'clock.

"*Vuka*, Bwana, *tiye!*" I tried to drag myself back from deep sleep, the hissing glare of Martin's pressure lamp searing through my eyelids. I forced them open, taking the big tea mug and pouring the sweet, strong brew down in a few hot swallows. Martin laid out clean bush shorts and jacket for me, then refilled the mug.

"*Yini lo skati?*" I asked him, blearily squinting at my watch in the shadows.

"*Skati ka fo busuku*, Bwana," he answered. Jesus! Four A.M. I had better get moving if we were to be in position before first light. I shivered into the shorts and bush jacket and stepped into the sockless shoes, almost bumping into Mason on his way to the *chimbuzi*. He muttered something sleepily about idiots and disappeared into the toilet hut. I

227

had finished my third tea and, while he swilled some coffee, I checked the rifles, deciding to go back to the big guns. If we got a shot this morning, it would be barndoor stuff and the .375 and .404, with their express sights, would be better over the dimly lit short range with their express sights. If necessary, their big slugs would also penetrate water better.

Leaving the hunting car a full half-mile back on the track, I led the way toward the bluff in the velvety darkness, our bare legs and shoes soaked by the dew-wet grass before we had walked ten yards. A trio of waterbuck clattered off, caught in the slender beam of the electric torch, and an elephant could be heard ripping tender branches from a grove a hundred yards to our right. Somewhere in the night a hyena snickered and was taunted by the yapping of a black-backed jackal. Eyes sharp for the reflected sapphire of snakes' eyes, we sneaked closer until we were only fifty yards from the bluff. I kept the beam well covered even though I realized that the crocs on the carcass were deep in the hill's defilade and could not see it. After another twenty feet, I eased it off completely, slipping slowly forward in complete silence, the sugary river sand hissing beneath the soles of our shoes. Dully, from ahead, came the disgusting, watery sounds of crocs feeding on the hippo—the tearing rip of meat, the muffled clash of teeth, the hollow, retching, gagging sound of swallowing the big, bloody lumps of flesh. Ten feet from where I guessed the lip of the bluff was, Paul and I squatted and froze in the darkness awaiting enough light to slip up for a shot if the man-eater was there. If.

With maddening slowness, like a low fire heating the inside of a heavy steel barrel, the gun-metal sky began to blush. As we waited, cramped, listening to the crocs, the light swelled from mango to cherry to carmine tinged with thick veins of wavy gold and teal-wing blue. My outstretched hand began to take shape before my face. I nudged Paul to move with me to the edge of the overhang. The river was still black, but after a few seconds the darker blob of the hippo carcass loomed dimly, pale feathers of water visible as dozens of crocs swirled and fought over the meat. Behind a light screen of grass on the lip, I got Paul into a sitting position, his rifle eased up to his shoulder. Seconds oozed by like cold caramel as the dawn strengthened, the bulk of the hippo more discernible. I thanked our luck that we were on the west bank and would not be skylined by the growing light.

As I stared through the felt-gray shadows toward the water, smaller dark shapes began to take form and outline; then I saw one, partially behind the hippo, that was much larger then the others. I felt a thrill of triumph as I realized that our plan had worked. He was *there*, just thirty yards away, unaware that in a few seconds lightning was going to strike. A few more seconds and Paul could kill him. My stomach tightened as the giant length moved, then again. God, no! He was returning to the water with the dawn. The loglike outline moved again, two feet closer to deep water and safety, his head already in the river. Couldn't Paul see him? Didn't he understand that in a few seconds he'd be gone forever? Frustration coursed through me. I could not risk whispering. A tiny sound snicked through the half-blackness, and I realized it was the safety of the .404. Shoot, I willed him. Shoot now! He's still moving! He's going to . . . A yard of orange flame roared from Paul's muzzle, a brilliant stab of lightning that blinded me as the thunder-clap of the shot washed over my arms and face. I was deafened, great, bright spots exploding wherever I focused.

"I think I got him," Paul yelled over the ringing of my ears. Twice more, the big bore rifle fired as Mason opened up on the spot where the croc had been. Slowly, my vision began to clear with the growing dawn, the orange blossoms of light fading. I stared down at the dead hippo, my hope welling up as I saw the tremendous, dark shape beside it, half in the water. The great tail waved feebly as a shudder passed through the killer, then all was still. Paul knelt and put his last shot through the man-eater's skull. It was over.

Pounding each other's back in congratulations, we half-fell down the sandy bank and walked across the sand bar to the bodies, the odor of the dead hippo already sickly in our nostrils. Behind us came Silent and Stomach, their hands covering their open mouths in polite astonishment, muttering the usual, "Eeehhh, eeehhh," over and over. When two more men arrived, we were able to roll him onto dry land and examine him with mounting awe. Paul's first shot had been perfect, taking out the rear half of the brain as he faced away and below us. The rest hadn't mattered. One thing was for sure; he was the biggest croc I had ever seen up close, let alone killed. I put the tape on the two pegs we ran between snout and tail-tip, even though we couldn't get the tail all the way straightened out. The third unrolling of my six-foot measure totaled fifteen feet, two and one-half inches! We all guessed him at over a ton, perhaps quite a bit more. Crocs are very dense and heavy for their size.

After almost an hour had passed, the entire village of Kangani arrived to revile the dead reptile by spitting on him and kicking him in impotent frustration for the death of the woman. When Silent made two long incisions in the side and cut the stomach wall, we all gagged. From the slimy mass of hippo meat and crushed bones, slid the putrefacted arm of a woman, a copper bangle still tightly in place, gleaming dully from the croc's stomach acid.

Mason and I sat, smoking slowly in the warm sun, watching the men skin the man-eater and place what they could find of the woman in a plastic bag. Her head and one arm and shoulder were missing, as best I could tell. Somehow, the killing of the crocodile had felt anticlimactic, and I wondered if there wasn't something more to the episode than a woman being eaten and a croc being killed. No, I finally decided, it was exactly that simple. It had been going on for a million years and would continue as long as there were people, crocodiles, and water. But, at least, I thought on the walk back to camp, that's one *Ngwenya* who won't be waiting.

7

Rhino

It was a typical midwinter afternoon in late July, the sun warm and bright, yet the shadows oddly chilly in the dry Zambian air, when we broke for water and a cigarette under a *Brachystegia* tree near a vast ocean of tall, brown grass. We had been walking for two hours, hoping to cut the fresh spoor of a herd of evasive roan antelope I knew to be in the area. My clients, an American and his nineteen-year-old son, plunked down gratefully and the rest of my six trackers, skinners, and gunbearers hunkered, wrapping black shag tobacco in scraps of newspaper and smoking them with a smell like a hotel fire. Silent, laid up with a bad bout of malaria, was back in camp, and I was using a young Senga tribesman local to the area as a guide to the region, since we were many miles from my normal hunting grounds.

We all heard it at the same time, a strange sound like a distant locomotive chuff-chuffing, then another joined with it. I felt a shiver of apprehension as it dawned on me what the sound was: rhino, and coming this way fast. We got to our feet, straining to locate the noise exactly, the thudding of thick, short feet now audible with occasional squeals, muffled by the grass. Grabbing the rifles of the Americans, I handed them to my men and started them climbing with a boost up the tree. We had no rhino license, and I didn't want one of my buckos belting one of them in possible self-defense. I kept the .470 and got behind the wide trunk as my men dispersed similarly. Fifty yards away the grass waved wildly, stirring as the surface of the sea would just over the back of a couple of big sharks. As I watched from behind the tree, the grass exploded with a cow rhino, then a big bull, then yet another bull. The first bull had a nasty gore wound on his flank and the second began to overhaul him, slashing at his rump with his thick front horn. I held my breath as the cow thundered right by the tree, oblivious to our presence, followed by the males, snorting and foaming, to disappear into the bush thirty yards away. I mentally wiped my brow at our near involvement and was about to step back into the open when there was a particularly savage snort and a shout of fear from somebody in the direction the rhinos had passed. I immediately ran into the cover, the big rifle ready, hoping to hell I wouldn't have to use it.

As I got closer I could make out the form of a bull rhino dashing in figure eights around a buffalo thorn tree, in the very top of which was Charlie, the local guide. From twenty yards away, the rhino stopped and stared myopically at me, snuffling for my scent. Taking a chance before he took the initiative, I fired the first barrel between his front feet, stinging him with earth and pebbles from the slug. No good. He lowered his head and charged me with the speed of a polo pony. Close at hand was a climbable tree, so I took another chance and, holding carefully on the base of his second horn as he quartered toward me, I fired the second barrel. It caught the horn squarely and flattened the bull with the impact of the blow of 5,000 foot-pounds of bullet energy. In a few seconds he was back on his feet, wobbling around like a punch-drunk fighter until he finally took off straight through the bush and left for good.

When we got the party back together, I noticed that Charlie was not there, and we all went back to the tree where I had seen him roosting. When the rest of my men saw him, they collapsed with laughter, howling and rolling on the ground. In his haste to get away from the rhino, which had seen him and doubled back, he had chosen a very poor refuge. The buffalo thorn, or *Umphafa* as it's called locally, is a solid mass of the cruelest thorns imaginable. Charlie, in his haste, hadn't even noticed them on his way up; now it was a different story. Bleeding like a butchered hog, he couldn't figure out a way back down through the barbed branches. Perhaps the essence of humor is the unexpected, and despite the fact that poor Charlie was obviously in pain and punctured like a pincushion, his ridiculous expression of misery soon had all of us laughing until the tears flowed. Finally, one of the men tossed him a *panga*, and he was able to clear his return partially, although he needed a quart of Mercurochrome by the time he reached terra firma once more. I saw the rhino with the shattered

234

second horn a couple of times over the next few years, so he was no worse for wear from the incident.

Hunting in rhino country is rather like treading through an old minefield. If there is anything more innately stupid than a rhinoceros, then it has to be two of them. I cannot look at one without a wistful feeling for the days of yore, when he was a real game animal, a fair match for the flint-pointed javelins and arrows of our furry forbears. Today, he's like an arthritic, old soldier, a one-too-many-fight boxer who is losing his battle for survival. He's dimwitted right off the bottom of the scale, a nonachiever in the changing struggle for existence. As a legitimate member of the "Big Five," he is marginal in the face of modern firearms. His only qualification for inclusion in that heady quintet is the fact that he can and will kill you.

The rhino has a very simple philosophy: If anything gets in your way, knock it down and gore it. In the heavy covers of central Africa, where it is not only possible but common to inadvertently bumble into a rhino, the intent of the bumbler has little influence on the rhino's reaction. In fact, in the Luangwa Valley rhinos were by far the greatest threat as a species even when unwounded. They had been carefully protected for years in Northern Rhodesia and later Zambia until they had reached a local population density that made incautious poking around the boonies for other species very tricky fare. And, since hunters were limited to a total of five black rhino in a given country per year, the killing of one in self-defense became a nightmare of red tape and possible loss of one's professional ticket. Ken Woolfrey, a hunter with whom I made several safaris, *had* to bust one under similar circumstances as mine above, shooting it from a matter of feet to prevent its killing him or one of his clients, Bob and Bim Gill of Florida. Jesus, but what a hassle he went through with formal hearings and the whole schmear. He was finally exonerated, but only just. I have been in on the killing of two legal rhinos, and frankly, they are the only critters that really give me a sense of sadness to hunt. Except in a charge, they are relatively easy to flatten with a bullet of proper size, and with the passing of each one, I have a terrible, hollow feeling of having smashed a priceless artifact.

The rhino's biggest problem with staying on the program is his "horn." From most ancient times, this weird mass of fused or agglutinated hair (not horn at all) has been attributed with a variety of supernatural talents. In medieval times a cup made of the stuff was considered to be able to indicate the presence of poison by turning the liquid milky. This has been poo-pooed by most writers, but I believe that it may have a solid basis in fact. Being a loose, animal substance, it could well be that certain of the more primitive poisons would indeed affect the horn, showing a reaction that impervious glass or pewter would not. Today the horn, which is not even attached to the bone beneath it but rides in strong, fleshy sockets attached to the skin itself, is still considered a powerful aphrodisiac in much of the Far East. Powdered, it sells for astonishing prices in Oriental apothecaries. I've tried it myself, but found no reaction other than, shall we say, the normal under circumstances in which such a substance might be called upon. Both sexes of the rhino have horns, usually two per customer, the front commonly the longer although there are some individuals with equal-length horns or, rarely, the second one longer. The female horns tend to be longer although considerably thinner than those of the bulls. Particularly in east Africa, poaching over recent years has hit the rhino harder than any other species, with the possible exception of the elephant; yet the elephant has much greater populations than the rhino to start with.

The rhino, if we want to bite the bullet and face it, is an unsuccessful species in the face of modern encroachment by man. Even a hundred years ago, he was very common over nearly all of east and south Africa, but as soon as the blacks got guns, he was one of the first to start to wane. As a species, the animal will not become extinct because we have enough of them under management in game parks and reserves, yet the familiar sight of lone bulls and small family groups dotting the bushscape with archaic regularity is becoming a thing of the past.

When white men first came across African rhinos, they took the differences between individual animals to indicate that there were many species rather than just two. The more common is the "black" rhino, who is perhaps 1,000 pounds smaller than his cousin the "white" rhino, although infinitely more dangerous and aggressive. Of course, both "black" and "white" rhinos are the same color, the "white" coming from the Boer word for "wide" (*weit*), which referred to the different structure of the mouths of the two types. The black has a pointed, prehensile upper lip, which suits his needs as a browser, whereas the white has the flat muzzle of the grazer. Because of their relative docility and tractability, the white rhinos took the brunt of much of the early, indiscriminate shooting of the first explorers and their armed gangs. In fact, so severe was the shooting pressure that in the 1850s, the white or *Mahoho* rhinos was considered by William Cotton Oswell, one of the early hunters in central Africa, to be extinct. Happily, it was rediscovered at the end of the nineteenth century and now enjoys fair numbers in controlled habitats in parts of Rhodesia and South Africa.

The word "unpredictable" applies well to most of Africa's dangerous game, but the black rhino certainly demonstrates this trait to a greater degree than any other animal. It's likely that the problem lies in their very poor eyesight as much as with their rattle-brained IQs. I cannot recall a single instance of meeting a rhino that suspected my presence in which the animal did not advance, often in a series of half-circles, to test the wind with their excellent noses. The slightest sound, such as the click of a camera or rifle safety, will be heard and will precipitate a full charge. The rhino is gifted with astonishing speed and incredible grace for an animal that may weigh three tons, the second largest of the land animals. I have always enjoyed reading the fanciful renderings of people like Jean-Pierre Hallet in his *Congo Kitabu*, in which he smugly tells us how simple it is to sidestep a rhino's charge. It may make nice reading, but this is one boy who knows better! A full-charging rhino can stop in his own length and change direction faster than a mongoose. If you don't want to get hammered, you had better get up a tree, throw him a jacket or other piece of clothing to gore, or kill him. If you are armed, rhinos rarely follow through with a charge in the face of fire. A horn shot will turn most charges and a shot over the head or into the ground often will do the same.

Of course, it would be rididulous to presume that all advancing rhinos are actually warming up for a charge. The problem is that you just can't tell; probably the rhino doesn't know itself what it's going to do. If bluff tactics don't work, you'd better start measuring some handy trees.

The utter destructive power of a rhino's charge has been exhibited frequently in east Africa, where several railroad locomotives have been attacked and occasionally derailed! In most cases the rhino was killed—small compensation to the railway company. For the most part, the rhino is a tosser, lacking the freelance finesse of the elephant. I have the impression from experience that they tend to close their eyes a few feet from their target, although it may be that they are just squinting with concentration like a rifleman over his sights. At any rate, if one connects, you are probably not going to be very happy with the situation at all. Colonel Patterson, the great bwana who bungled his way to success with the coolie-eating lions of Tsavo, mentions a case that, if true (and I see no reason for him to fabricate here when having been fastidious with the veracity of his other tales), unquestionably accounted for the largest loss of human life by a rhinoceros at a single go. Twenty-one slaves were chained together by the neck on their way to the coast to be shipped. Passing through a thick stretch of bush, a rhino boiled out of some cover and spitted the middle man of the string, the impact of the charge breaking the necks of the remaining twenty men.

As might be expected, since the influx of sportsmen

into Africa, there have been plenty of people who had no better luck with rhinos than those slaves. A chap named Eastwood, who was associated with the Uganda Railways at the same time Patterson was, knocked over a rhino with a shot and made the old goof of thinking him dead. The rhino lurched to its feet and squashed the man, breaking several ribs and his right arm. When Eastwood got up again, the rhino shoved his horn through the man's thigh and tossed him a couple of stories straight up. When he came back down, the rhino stuck him a few times again and meandered off. Fortunately for Eastwood, some of his men saw the vultures gathering to finish up what the rhino had started and found him. As it was, he was damned lucky to lose no more than his arm, which had to be removed.

I doubt that any student of African hunting would contest that a man called J. A. Hunter, one of the finest professional safari operators and government hunters of East Africa, had more experience with rhinos, particularly the black rhino (*Diceros bicornis*) than anyone else. All in all, especially during the biologically tragic "Great Makueni Rhino Hunt," Hunter killed more than 1,000 personally, mostly on orders from the government. The Makueni Hunt was forced by the decision to open up large tracts of new land for resettlement of the Wakamba tribe in the Machakos District of Kenya about the middle of this century. Since the bush area was practically crawling with rhinos, many of whom had killed women gathering firewood, Hunter was ordered to clean them out so the bush could be cut. A basic reason for cutting the bush was to deprive tsetse flies of breeding grounds. More's the shame that after the rhino were slaughtered, the scheme never came to fruition, the great animals wasted.

Now nobody, not even a man like Hunter, goes off into very thick bush to kill 1,000 bull butterflies let alone rhinos without a consequent number of hairy encounters. Hunter himself was never caught, but some of his native hunters or scouts had some stories to tell their grandchildren. In one case, during a triple charge in very dense cover, Hunter had killed a bull and a cow when a third, another bull, whipped past him with one of his scouts hanging on the animal's horns for dear life. J. A. risked a shot and collapsed the bull, the young man's body shooting forward from the momentum. Convinced that he had killed both the scout and the rhino, Hunter was overjoyed to see the boy move. The bullet had missed him by fractions of an inch. When the rhino, surprising the scout, had lowered his head for the toss, the boy had desperately grabbed the front horn and held himself clear while the rhino bulled off with him clinging like a tickbird.

Many men, unable to avoid a charge, are caught between the legs by the horns or gored in the lower belly. Hunter records one native in Kenya who had been completely castrated by a rhino's toss and healed perfectly. I have heard of elephant carcasses being found with perforations that were almost certainly caused by rhino horns, and there's no question that an elephant will back off when confronted by old Dimwit.

Although various forms of rhinoceros existed in Europe and North America as contemporaries of the mammoth and cave bear, besides the two African species, there are now only three other Asian types. The Indian rhino, which, if you can believe reports, is even dumber than the African, is much more segmented in appearance than other rhinos. His skin is deeply creased into "compartments" and he has but a single horn. Considered very aggressive, he has developed a strange habit of biting his victims more than goring with the horn. The other members of the Oriental family are the Sumatran rhino, which has two horns, and the Javanese rhinos, which have only one. Both are just about finished as viable species, outside zoos.

The black rhino is constantly accompanied by several breeds of sentinel birds, both oxpeckers and tickbirds, as well as cattle egrets, which catch the insects stirred out of the grass by rhino and other large herbivores. I have read that tickbirds will nip meat out of the suppurating sores that rhino all have at their "armpits," where the thick skin rubs against itself. In examining these wounds, though, I have not seen any evidence that the birds do any more than eat the vermin from the deep, seamy folds of skin. Although rhinos are almost blind, the birds are very sharp-eyed and will alert a rhino instantly with their cries of alarm.

Black rhino have an interesting habit of scattering their droppings with their feet, scuffling up the bush quite a bit. I don't know the reason for their behavior but suspect it is some form of territory-marking device. During mating season bull rhinos can be tracked across open ground by following the snaky line left by their pizzles dragging in the dirt. It sounds somewhat uncomfortable to me but doesn't bother them in the least. Incidentally, a short, swordlike whip is made from this organ when dried and stretched. It's called a *sjambok*, and a blow from one can lay a man open like a straight razor.

Since rhinos are quite individual looking, one can often recognize the same one time and again. One such animal that I particularly remember was a big bull that lived alone near my camp on the Munyamadzi River, often wallowing and drinking within sight while we ate breakfast. Except for one burst of bad temper, in which he tried to eviscerate a Game Department vehicle, he was quite tame and was known locally as "Ralph" or "Lalph" by the Chenyanja-speaking tribesmen, who could not pronounce the letter r. One day, driving by, I pulled the Rover over in surprise. Ralph stood by the roadside looking like he'd been recycled. His front horn was ripped half off and hung over his nose like a nightcap, his flanks and legs tatters of flesh. Obviously, he was in horrible pain and dying. From his rear end hung a large piece of intestine, ripped free by a pack of hyenas. I would have given anything to have put him down, out of his misery, but the law strictly forbade dispatching any wounded animal found. It was inhumane, but would have given poachers an excuse to murder wholesale, then claim their prey was hurt and killed for humanitarian reasons. As it was, Ralph had to suffer another two hours until I could drive over and pick up a game guard who shot him. The Munyamadzi never seemed right without him. He had apparently tangled with another bull rhino, or for all I know, an elephant. Maybe he'd even fallen off one of the cliffs along the river. It was hard to tell. Weakened and sick, he hadn't been able to do much about the hyena pack that had chewed away most of his lower rear belly and equipment, then left him still alive. Africa has little compassion in such matters.

The white rhino is in a very odd ecological position these days. Although badly shot up because of its relative docility a century ago, there are some areas where the species is quite numerous, especially in South Africa. Despite the overall rarity of these beasts, some are cropped annually because of overpopulation, or exported. A friend of mine in Rhodesia recently obtained several from, I believe, the Natal Parks Department and they are doing very well on his ranch, where they once roamed naturally.

Today, one of the most deplorable mockeries of sport involves the white rhino and that fringe group of screwballs and chestbeaters that are sadly lumped in with sportsmen on the basis that they also use firearms. I'll tell you about it because it's true and it's only fair that I give you the bad with the good, even though it is the complete antithesis of sport hunting. If you have enough money, you can still shoot a white rhino today. I said shoot, not hunt. One will be driven into a large enclosure for you by official personnel. You may then walk up to the condemned beast and kill him, nice and neat, no walking, no risk. You can spend the air trip back home thinking up a nice, scary story of how you stopped his charge from mere inches when your white hunter lost his nerve and you had to save his life. The presence of a recently shot white rhino on anybody's wall is, to me, tantamount to mounting a red banner inscribed "FRAUD." Sure, there have been some honestly taken white rhinos, but I know of no place where they are available today on a real sporting basis.

There are only a few places left in Africa where one may hunt black rhino. No matter where you go, you had best be prepared to spend the equivalent of a down payment on a Spanish castle to hang Old Dimwit on your wall. In Kenya, for example, let's take a look at the costs involved, a major portion of which are ploughed back into wildlife management.

First off, you can't get a rhino license unless you have contracted a safari for a minimum of thirty-five days. At a bare minimum of $450 per day for a single client and one professional hunter, not counting about $2,000 in airfares to get there, your basic investment will be $15,750. Add to that your general license of about $250, then the rhino license itself of 2,500/- (shillings) at 14¢ and that's an additional $350. Then, when you do kill the rhino, it will cost you another $700 in Controlled Area Fees. Figure another $2,000 for shipping, taxidermy (don't bother if you live in the United States since rhino trophies may not be imported), and you have a rough cost, without airfare, mileage, booze, rental guns, ammo, tips, packing, dipping, and so forth, of a touch under $20,000. I wonder how much that is per pound? By the by, these are 1975 prices, and Africa has been marching right along with the rest of us in inflation, so I would honestly guess that the cost of a rhino would be, in current values, closer to $28,000 to $30,000.

Although man, more than any other factor, has been responsible for the downfall of the rhino, a large percentage of the dead were a result of the animal's simple inability to cope with natural conditions of existence. In time of drought, the elephant packs his trunk and heads off to greener pastures; failing that, he digs and tusks his way to water in dry riverbeds. Not the rhino. He stands around wondering what the hell's going on, then eventually falls over. Some enterprising chap whacks off his horns and retires for a six-month beer drink with the money he gets for it. He breeds slowly, and the very size of the critter precludes short generations. When you think about him, the wonder is that he's still around at all. And that's more than a shame. Thickets just don't have the same adventurous allure without the possibility of a snoozing rhino hammering down on you at any time. He ain't much, but I'll sure miss him. We've had some good times together.

8

snakes

October in south-central Africa is like a coy woman, a tease full of empty promise. From the first week the heat builds up like a kiln, the smooth daytime breeze of August and September a memory but for the dust-devils, those rude, insulting fingers that probe obscenely at the parched earth in whirling columns of airborne filth and ashes. As the spring days pass, even the scant shade offers little respite from the swelter of midday, which turns bush jackets alternately into muddy maps of moisture and stiff, crackling salt patches. It is very different from the winter, when the sun is warm and the shadows actually cold in the arid air. Now, the humidity grows slowly from the tie-dyed dawn, building like a filling bowl until your brain feels squeezed by the hot band of your skull.

No longer do the dozens of daily cuts and thorn scratches of bush living and hunting heal in the dry air under clean scabs, but even the smallest nick festers and turns septic as the newly active bacteria in the barber-towel air feed upon your wounds. Truly, October is a flirt. Great, sterile thunderheads build like puffy, lumpy fortresses on the horizon only to evaporate into wispy mares' tails, disappearing into the flat incandescence of colorless sky. At night, sudden gasps of hot wind howl through the hunting camps, whipping canvas and straining tent ropes, but the promised slash of rain never seems to come.

October is the month of madness. The water in the pans is down, foul with alkali and muddy with the stirrings of thousands of hooves. Elephant are evil tempered, tortured by flies and heat even under their armor of caked slime, and the mutual admiration societies of bull buffalo are not seen even at dusk or dawn. Lions seem to call more, often complaining in the heat of day. In the villages fights, murder, and suicide are far more common than at any other time of year, spearings and head cleavings practically nightly occurrences.

But, October is notable for more than heat rash and rasped tempers. You see, October is the first month of snakes.

One of the most common questions of people who have not been on safari is, "But, what about all the snakes?" *Well*, that depends. In most areas of reasonable elevation, snakes are not too much of a problem during the usual safari period of the May through September dry season. The reason is that it's just too cold for most species to be active. Snakes are, of course, cold-blooded and take their body temperatures from their surroundings. In many parts of Botswana and Rhodesia a bucket of water left out over night will freeze solid by morning, although daylight hours in winter are a delight of low humidity and warm sun. Because of this low moisture content of the air, the variations of temperatures between places very close to each other can be astounding, dry air not holding heat the way moist air does. A classic example was that difference between the *vlei* along the Mongu River in the Matetsi District of northwestern Rhodesia I hunted, and the hill on which headquarters was located, not 200 yards away and perhaps 250 feet higher. Returning from a day's hunting in the evening in an open Land Rover through this low spot was like being locked in a cryogenics chamber with a fan on you. By six o'clock the temperature was well below freezing, yet as you drove up the hill, it would magically warm to about 70 degrees Fahrenheit. As a consequence, one never saw a snake in the *vlei* during the dry season, but an eye had to be kept peeled around the headquarters building.

To tell you the truth, if anybody had any idea of how many dangerous snakes there really *are* in most parts of Africa, nobody would dream of going on safari, including Your Obedient Servant. If you want to look for them, though, they are certainly there. One man who did a lot of looking in an area just a few miles square in Tanzania actually caught over 3,000 green mambas in a matter of a few years. From October through May most of my safari range is literally crawling with snakes, and it is a happy chance that they are not so much in evidence during winter. There are enough "requiem" snakes to give a herpetologist the creepy-crawlies, including black and green mambas,

Boomslangs, regiments of adders and boxcar lots of cobras, not to mention a leg-long list of less poisonous types. To suggest that a visiting hunter doesn't take a risk of snakebite in the colder season would be irresponsible; yet to say that snakes are a full-blown menace blocking every path and festooned from every third branch would be an equal overstatement. Even though I have conducted many safaris where no snake was ever seen, one must also bear constantly in mind that just one bite from a black mamba or large cobra, let alone a small adder, can transform you into a neat, italicized statistic in one hell of a hurry. If you spend much time in Africa, sooner or later you will bump into dangerous snakes. Such confrontations are not much fun.

Peter Seymour-Smith, a pal of mine, has a very nice house, built from concrete reinforced with poachers' snares, on his Iwaba ranch in central Rhodesia. In the living room, behind the sofa at about neck level of a sitting person, there is a large gouge in the woodwork that looks like a point-blank shotgun blast. A closer look will confirm it to be just that. Peter was sitting in an armchair across the room when he noticed movement near his wife Jane's hair as they were having sun-downers one evening. A further glance showed it to be a dullish-colored snake lying along the top edge of the couch, a foot or so from Jane's neck. Used to the bush life, she did not ask questions when Peter told her to freeze as he edged across the room for his shotgun, propped in a corner. At his command, she hit the floor while he unstuffed the sofa, redecorated the wall, and killed the snake. Black mamba, about six feet long.

The following summer, in December, Peter was driving with Jane and the baby in an open, doorless Land Rover late one warm afternoon on an inspection tour of the cattle ranch. Watching some impala off in the bush at the roadside, he was surprised to hear his wife shout for him to stop the car quickly. He braked to a halt and was shocked nearly witless to see a huge black mamba rear up right along side the English-drive left fender with a hiss colder than Freon.

251

The snake struck immediately at Jane as she snatched the baby out of reach, the slender head somehow stopping a foot from her face. Peter grabbed her and the baby and bailed out the driver's side of the car as the big mamba kept striking the windshield and car body in a series of heavy jabs, flecking them with amber venom. When he was free of the car, Peter saw that by the weirdest quirk of luck, he had stopped the Rover with the tire over the snake's tail, pinning it to the ground and preventing it from reaching Jane or the child. Jane had seen the snake in the road when she shouted, but Peter hadn't since he was watching the impala. If he'd stopped a couple of inches either way, probably his wife and baby, if not himself, would be dead by now. He whistled up a Matabele herdsman, who killed the snake by spearing it. It was a bit over thirteen feet, packing enough poison to kill a football team.

That the black mamba is a fascinating snake in sort of a queasy way is obvious when you consider that he has probably been the subject of more legend than any other African snake. The very sight of a black mamba, *Dendroaspis polylepis*, is enough to send a shiver through anybody but a congenital idiot, and if you haven't seen one before, you'll still probably recognize the species at a glance. Mambas really *look* deadly, probably because of the sharp canthus, or angle, between the flat plane of the head and the cheek. Set into this head are a pair of glimmering black eyes that look into your soul like a fluoroscope. One of the most dangerous aspects of mambas, especially black ones who are not so prone to living in trees as are their green cousins, is their extreme aggression. If disturbed even at a distance while mating, or just sunning for that matter, they are inclined to attack, approaching with scary swiftness and rearing to a very impressive height. A high proportion of mamba bites are high on the body, often the face. Inside the black mouth (which is really the basis for the name "black" mamba), normally held agape, is as much lethalness as a hand grenade. Mambas swell their necks in threat display, although not as much as the cobras.

A further reason for the black mamba being one of the world's most dangerous snakes is that he is also one of the, if not *the*, fastest snake. I doubt that many people confronting mambas in the wild happen to have the inclination to check them with stopwatches, but estimates of their speed have been variously given as twenty miles per hour to "faster than a running horse." These are, in my opinion, vast exaggerations, although I also consider the "official" estimate of seven miles per hour a bit low. A black mamba in a hurry can probably crank out a good ten miles per hour over a short distance. Because of their rippling undulation, they seem to be going much faster than they actually are, and their terrifying ability to ghost in a flicker across the tops of chest-high grass stalks is practically supernatural. In any case experts agree they are at least twice as fast as any North American snake.

As mentioned, it is the dead-black lining of the mamba's mouth that gives this species its monicker, not the body coloration, which varies from a dull dun to a gun-metal gray. Newly hatched black mambas are very hard to distinguish from the Jameson's and green varieties, since they resemble their cousins in color until older. The black mamba's scales are lackluster, not as shiny as the cobra's, making him harder to see in cover.

Mamba poison, especially the volume that may be injected by a large individual, is fantastically toxic, and a solid bite, even with antivenin at hand, usually means a quick, singularly unpleasant death. Black mamba venom, which is twice as deadly as even the green mamba poison, paralyzes the breathing and, according to some herpetologists, affects the vagus nerve that controls heartbeat, letting the heart literally run wild. How quickly it can kill was elucidated a few years ago in Botswana.

In the Okavango Swamp of Ngamiland, quite near where I used to hunt, a white man was hunting crocodiles under permit at night, so the local story goes. (I personally suspect that since he was alone he was not actually hunting crocs although licensed to do so, because he would have had a gaffer and another assistant to help him recover the bodies. At any rate, he *was* in a small boat alone.) We'll never know how he bumped into the mamba that struck him—perhaps it had been hiding in his boat, maybe it had been swimming and the man disturbed it with a paddle. It may even have struck him from an overhanging tree. It's beside the point. His body was found in the boat next day, his antivenin kit open. He never had time to use it, presumably dying before he could administer the serum.

Well mixed through the African records are many reports of a single mamba killing several people. One such snake lived in the London Zoo in the 1950s, having been captured by the greatest of Africa's "Snake Men," C. J. P. Ionides, after killing seven people in a matter of months. Another black mamba, in Rhodesia, went deep-end and killed eleven people and several sheep, all the bitten expiring in less than half an hour. Dr. Phil Kahl, who recently returned from southwest Africa, told me of a game ranger bitten in 1977 who died in twenty minutes. The tendency of black mambas to get into the thatching of native huts in their hunt for vermin often leads to catastrophe. A man who worked for me in Zambia as a waiter told me that a black mamba had fallen from the roof of his brother's hut and killed him, his wife, and three children one night near Chipata, or as it was called at the time, Fort Jameson. There are so many cases of this happening that I have no reason not to believe him.

One of the major problems with black mambas is that they (as well as cobras and other species) are attracted by the mice and voles that so frequently take up residence around a safari camp. In 1969, when Peter Hankin gave up much of his hunting activities to maintain the base supply camp at Chitangulu on the Luangwa, the hub of outlying safari operations, he developed a positive plague of black mambas around the place. After he had killed a dozen or so within a two-week period, he ordered that every person working at or visiting the camp to carry two antivenin kits at all times, even while sleeping. Incredibly, nobody was bitten that season, although there were some close encounters. In the case of snakes, forewarned is forearmed.

One of the most terrifying encounters I have ever had with a dangerous snake took place on an early October morning in Zambia, on the Munyamadzi River. It had been very hot the previous night and I had slept under a mosquito net on a cot outside the hut with just a *kikoy* loincloth, lions or no lions. I awoke for the hundredth time at dawn, well basted in sweat, and padded bleary-eyed across the thirty yards to the *chimbuzi*, a wraparound, grass-walled latrine or "high-fall" on a bluff near the river bank. Still half-asleep, I started to enter and was chilled by a hiss like a ruptured air hose. Half across the open toilet seat, bolted to a cutoff fifty-five-gallon oil drum set into the top of the hole, reared an eight-foot black mamba. His head was as high as my throat, his tongue flickering from his partly open mouth. I clearly remember seeing a couple of strings of saliva stuck between his upper and lower jaws like thick spiderwebs. That I woke up in a hurry is a masterpiece of understatement. Without thinking, I threw the towel I had in my hand at his head and, not waiting to determine the results, bolted out of the latrine and across the space to my hut in a flesh-colored blurr like a Road Runner cartoon. Shaking the big buckshot loads out of the shotgun, I reloaded with birdshot and carefully, very carefully, approached the *chimbuzi* again. As I inched up, I peeked around the grass baffle. Nothing, no sign of the snake, which bothered me one hell of a lot more than being able to see it would have. The only thing worse than seeing a mamba at close quarters is *not* seeing a mamba at close quarters. After checking the grass walls carefully, I went outside and looked over the bare dirt. I couldn't even find a crawl track on the hard earth. Where in blazes had he gone? Aha! Obviously, he had gone down the open toilet and into the latrine hole, I reasoned. With the safety off, I edged back inside the roofless structure.

Sneaking up to the toilet seat, I pushed the muzzles of

the double-barreled shotgun up to the edge and levered them downward. There was no movement. In a flash I leaned over the seat and pulled off both barrels, one after the other, straight down the drop-hole. The secondary results were not unlike dynamiting a septic tank while sitting on it, and I certainly got a solid dose of the basic contents of the hole. After, as the British say, purging myself, I managed a cold shower from last night's water, shouting to my understandably confused staff (who might have been wondering what the bwana was doing blowing up the crapper) to keep an eye out for the snake until I was no longer *hors de combat* from my sneak raid on the can. Invisible brought over a flashlight and a couple of more shells for the gun, although if that mamba was in the hole, I strongly doubted that he would need any more persuasion. As Invisible held the torch, I held my nose and peered down into the black shambles of the shaft. Whatever else was in it, there was sure no mamba. Where he had gotten to in the less than a minute it took me to get the gun was beyond me, but I couldn't shake the idea that he might be in the walls or had even crossed over to my hut, where he could be hiding right now. Not about to spend the rest of the season wondering if there was a mamba under the bed, I took the only alternative. I got a live brand from the campfire and lit the *chimbuzi* after removing the toilet seat, a possession rarer than ambergris in the middle of the bush, and watched it burn merrily to the ground without a glimpse of the snake. Since my hut was the only other cover in sight, I had my men drag out the bed and metal footlockers with sticks along with the rest of my *katundu*, and fired the hut also. I felt a little stupid when it, too, had completely burned without flushing out the snake. It may have been somewhat extreme a gesture for a little peace of mind, but then, mambas really give me hives. Except there was one problem still remaining: Where was the flaming snake? The way my men were glancing at me sideways, I was starting to wonder if I'd been hallucinating.

Since I did not have a client at the time, the rest of the

day was spent building a new hut on the other side of the camp and digging another john. The following day, as I was eating lunch, one of the men came running over to say that there was a big mamba sunning near where the old latrine had been, on the edge of the bluff. I grabbed the scatter gun and killed him with one shot, his writhing carrying him over the edge and into the river. A few weeks later I was hunting across the river from the camp and suddenly realized where the snake had escaped to that day we met. Below the lip of the cliff were many deepish holes in the clay dug out by nesting colonies of carmine bee-eaters, one of Africa's most spectacularly beautiful birds, which breed there each year. Almost certainly, the snake had disappeared straight over the edge and into a hole while I ran for my gun. From our side of the river, the holes were invisible and because of the possibility of the undercut banks collapsing, nobody would have thought of walking out to the edge, over the croc-filled water, to investigate.

I was mightily relieved that the snake was finally dead. I have often wondered what might have happened had it been darker in the latrine or if I had sat down on him. I probably would have had hell's own time with the tourniquet!

With the exception of the black mamba, the mamba family is composed basically of tree dwellers: the eastern and western green mambas and Jameson's mamba. All have venom that can kill quite efficiently, although none has the size and potency of the black species. Since they live in trees, it follows that man's contact with the other mambas is considerably less and they are not nearly as aggressive.

Among the other potentially dangerous tree snakes of Africa are the Boomslang and the bird snake. Both are relatively inoffensive and have fangs in the rear of the mouth similar to the North American coral snake, limiting most bites to those handling the snakes. Boomslang venom is especially powerful and requires a special antivenin, although bites are so infrequent that the snake was not considered more than mildly venomous until a few years ago. There are two species of tree cobras, both happily somewhat rare. One is the gold's tree cobra, which looks much like a shiny version of a black mamba although it does not attain such length.

There is a charming selection of cobra forms all over Africa, many quite different in appearance but sharing the common ability to kill you quickly if you don't watch where you step or go reaching around dark holes in *kopjes* or ant heaps. The genus *Naja* has six members, including the Asian, or spectacled, cobra, five of which are Afros: yellow, forest, spitting, Egyptian, and a western cousin of the Asian cobra. This doesn't count the ringhals of Rhodesia and the Republic of South Africa, a highly specialized snake whom I have seen in action.

The ringhals cobra, *Hemachatus hemachatus*, is one of the two cobras uniquely evolved with the ability to "spit" or spray its venom with surprising accuracy over a distance of seven or eight feet through the use of a modified pair of front fangs. These short teeth have an orifice in the front of each that acts much as the nozzle of a child's water pistol. Powerful muscles around the venom sacs contract at will, providing the propelling force to project the venom through the hypodermic teeth, out the orifices in a spray toward the eyes. Contact with the eyes or broken skin can cause blindness in a few minutes and even death if untreated. It is my impression that the venom of ringhals (from an Afrikaan word that refers to the neck rings) is somewhat different from other cobra toxins in that it is very quickly absorbed through the conjunctiva, or white, of the eye. Although this snake is generally a pretty good shot, it aims for reflecting objects and may mistake a bright belt buckle or binocular lens for the eyes. The ringhals most likely uses this technique to blind and kill small animals out of reach, although it will bite like a proper son of a bitch if cornered, striking like the other cobras, chewing its venom deep into the wound as it holds on like a snapping turtle. There is another spitting cobra that, although common in much of Africa, is not well distributed in my areas of activity. This is the *Naja nigricollis*, which is generally (but not always, because of race variations) marked by a single, very broad black band under the hood. I have never run across one, but other hunters tell me he's not very pleasant.

In 1971, I was on a busman's holiday in the Ngamo-Sikumi Forest in west-central Rhodesia hunting sable antelope. This is quite thick grass and bush country, sometimes punctuated with *kopjes* of giant boulders many stories high, which are handy as lookout posts for spotting game movement. I was hunting with just a gunbearer and a tracker, on the spoor of what promised to be a very fine lone bull sable, when we came up to one of these *kopjes*. The tracker, a MaKalanga whose name I don't remember, scrambled ahead of me and was looking across a scrubby plain for the bull from atop a six-foot rock at the base of the pile. I was just behind him, about to join him with my binoculars when he gave a strangled shriek of pain and surprise and threw his hands over his face, his fingers digging at his eyes. Startled, I glanced around and saw just the last half of a heavily scaled snake disappear between two rocks in a jumble at about chest height, three-quarters in front of where the tracker was standing.

Chagga, the gunbearer, upon hearing me shout "*Nyoka*!" ("Snake!") grabbed the tracker's leg and pulled him off the rock. Despite the man's writhing and clutching at his eyes, Chagga pinned him down with a knee on his chest and pried his hands away. To my surprise, he then urinated in the man's eyes, yelling at me to grab his arms, holding the lids open with his fingers as best he could. When he ran dry, I dashed back for the water bag the tracker had been carrying and together we irrigated the horribly bloodshot eyes with the whole jaw-sack. After ten minutes, even though he was clearly in considerable pain, we were able to tie the man's shirt over his face and lead him the two miles back to the Land Rover, where I had two kits of polyvalent antivenin. I gave the MaKalanga the sensitivity test for horse serum, the basis of the antivenin, which can kill an allergic man quicker than the snake venom and, when there was no reaction, made a mixture of roughly five to one of sterile water and antivenin. Through the hypodermic syringe, I dripped this slowly into the eyes and after two hours, even though still horribly swollen and discolored, he had regained some sight and eventually recovered completely. Had the tracker been alone or had Chagga not applied such basic action, I doubt he would have ever seen again. He certainly caught a full dose. (Incidentally, I once told this story to a doctor client who told me that urine, as it issues from an undiseased bladder, is actually sterile! An interesting tidbit that might come in handy sometime.)

Just as is the case with the large, mammalian bad actors, so with the reptiles, there is vast disagreement as to which is Africa's most dangerous snake. Of course, "dangerous" is one of those slippery words open to wide interpretation. A man stuck in a telephone booth with an angry black mamba would be quite justified in voting for this species. On the other hand, it might also be said that the most dangerous snake is that which is most likely, on a statistical basis, to kill you. It would follow that this snake would also be the most likely to bite you because he's the most common of the deadly snakes. Following this logic, there is a clear, concise winner, albeit an unlikely one. He isn't featured in many pulp-fiction tales and most visitors to Africa have never heard of him, but he's practically everywhere. He's a heavy, well-marked, Argyle-patterned serpent that only reaches a couple of feet in length, yet attains considerable thickness and weight. He is the African puff adder, *Bitis arietans*, and he kills more people on that continent than any other snake. He has the very long fangs of the classic adder and packs enough venom to kill five men. Death by puff adder is typical of the agonizing and lingering horror caused by the hemotoxic venoms of the vipers.

The nocturnal habits of the puff adder are as much a cause of death as his powerful venom. Puff adders favor the smooth footpaths of the bushveldt, which stay warm with absorbed sun heat well after dark. Women and children are the largest group bitten; perhaps because of their weight they do not set up the warning vibrations to alert the snake, and so step upon it. This is also the problem with hunters stalking or tiptoeing quietly along the paths. Like the cobra the puff adder is a chewer, opening his mouth and extending his long fangs to literally stab the victim before he closes it to bite, driving a huge dose of venom deeply into the wound. So dreaded is the bite of a puff adder that many Africans have been known literally to die of shock and fear on receiving the strike.

Unfortunately, the puff adder is quite common and even on cold days will be found basking in the sun. I have seen many but take such care where I walk when hunting that I haven't had a close call with a live one. I say a "live" one because another professional once killed a big puff adder and, on the request of his client, took the head to dry as a curiosity. He propped the mouth open with a small stick and placed it on the roof of the hut we were sharing. I don't know if it blew off—I didn't know it was there in the first place—but I stepped on it with bare feet and a fang lightly punctured my right great toe. Although it scared the screaming bejeesus out of me, there was no venom injected. (Injection of venom is largely voluntary on the snake's part.) Call it sufficient to say that the other gentleman and I discussed the matter at some length.

Though the bite of a puff adder results in hemorrhage of the mucous membranes and death in about twenty-four hours, often sooner in untreated cases, even with prompt antivenin application gangrene and wide tissue destruction may result with the ultimate consequence of "sloughing" the flesh of a foot or hand. This you can do nicely without, take my word for it. As I wear only bush shorts and sockless Clark's desert boots, I spend a great deal of time watching the ground, yet, except for aggressive species such as black mambas near camp, I don't believe in killing snakes. Certainly, the deaths of the few a hunter might shoot would make no difference locally, and they do play their part in the overall scheme of things.

A discussion of the large constrictor snakes such as the python could fill most of another book this size. Like so much to do with snakes, there has been no dearth of misinformation and hairy tales generated by travelers as well as misinformed "experts." African pythons do reach very large size—up to the thirty-two feet mentioned by the very reliable and experienced Bernhard Grzimek for the rock python, although the biggest I have seen was about eighteen feet.

It would seem that not all tales of man-eating snakes are necessarily so much fiction; a few cases appear to be genuine, especially in the situation when the victim has been a woman or child. As Grzimek so accurately points out in *Among the Animals of Africa*, giant snakes do not kill by "crushing their prey to a pulp" as much fiction tells us, but by asphyxia, the prevention of chest expansion so critical to the breathing function. Also, no constrictor snake coils about its prey without first obtaining a solid grip with its jaws, which are studded with six layers of back-slanted teeth as effective as barbed wire or fish hooks. Therefore, if there exists any potential danger with the python, it's that of a very nasty bite and possible later infection. That even a huge snake would attack a grown man unprovoked for the purpose of eating him is so remote as to rank with death by meteorite. It's possible and it has happened, but I wouldn't lose much sleep over the matter on your next safari.

Underrated Killers

The most disconcerting thing about living and hunting in remote African regions is the mathematical fact that you have to make so many right decisions to stay healthy, whereas it requires just one thin slice of bad luck or simple indiscretion to get yourself crippled or dead. In the long run the odds have an annoying way of winning out, not an especially comforting consideration to wake up to each morning, and a hunter, the longer he hunts, has more and more unfortunate friends each year to reinforce the validity of the hypothesis.

Odds are tricky, shifty little rascals. If you are going to make a living cropping elephants or hunting lions, it's understandable to expect that one day you may run into that particular lion or elephant who is the personal representative of Kismet. Okay, that's reasonable. But, somehow it just doesn't seem fair to be so careful around the obvious dangers and then have Fate pull a switchblade one fine morning when you find yourself trapped between a Land Rover body and the slashing hooves of a screaming, biting, kicking, lousy zebra who was supposed to be dead and wasn't, as a pal of mine found out a couple of years ago to the tune of six months on his back. Or, have a wrist-thick sliver of steel-hard, dried *mopane* wood somehow flip up under your car and impossibly come right through the metal floor like a lance, as it did through another friend's leg. Or have a cocoon half-blind you when putting on spare glasses without checking them, driving spiky filaments deep into your pupil, as happened to Peter Hankin in 1969. Or be bitten by the fatal tsetse, the fate of Johnny Blacklaws. I, too, have learned the price of vigilance—more than 300 stitches, one cut femoral artery, and three severed tendons repaired with silver wire. All stupid, all useless. But I never got severely caught by a "dangerous" animal, which means any animal. They're all dangerous if they get a chance and you're just as dead from a bushbuck horn as an elephant's tusk.

The only thing more abundant in Africa than life is death. It takes a thousand forms, each of infinite variety as opposite as the slashing lunge of a crocodile or the lingering tragedy of the bilharzia snail fluke. It walks, crawls, creeps, flies, swims, and runs in untold disguises, but in no shape is it so brazen, so completely polished, so jaw-snappingly efficient and universally loathed as in the Cape hunting dog or wild dog, *Lycaon pictus*. Even the great cats are but casually respected by their prey, who merely keep a distance just past the danger point. Only the presence of the wild dog in thick bush country creates the mindless horror of death unique among predators.

It was tea time at Khwaai Lodge, at the edge of the great Okavango Swamp. My wife and I were relaxing under the tremendous *Ngamo* fig tree, on the stone terrace that had been built around the base. As we chatted with Lassie Allen, who with her husband, Jan, ran the lodge at the time, we watched the constant stream of sable, impala, wildebeest, baboons, wart hogs, and other animals filing down to drink at the artificial pan we had created by sinking a bore hole and hooking up a pump which provided the only water for some miles at the height of the dry season. Over the months it had come to support a sizable population of assorted critters, most of whom were quite used to the lodge and reasonably tame.

As we sat there in the cool of the late afternoon, a sudden shiver seemed to run through the herds, a signal we could not detect. Then, in an instant, every one of the several hundred antelopes swung about to face the thick bush bordering the *vlei* some 300 yards away. I grabbed my binoculars in curiosity and turned them on the area. From the distant shadows movement flagged, and a small herd of impala burst out onto the plain, racing and jumping in soaring bounds straight at us. Forty yards behind them a dozen wild dogs, big-eared and brindled, streamed in their dust, eating up the distance with inexorable certainty. We stared, open mouthed, as the moving tableau grew closer and one of the impala ewes with a half-grown calf at foot was wedged away from the rest of the herd, eight of the wild dogs swerving after her as four others continued straight for us, singling out a yearling for the touch of death. Fifty yards from the terrace, one of the lead dogs closed on the calf, snapped for a hind leg and dissolved into a boil of dust as it pulled the little fellow down. Realizing the inevitable end of her calf, the mother stopped short, another dog whipping past her in a twisting turn. In a split second the others were on her, her stomach and intestines spilling out, ripped into red flags and partially eaten even before she fell over, swarmed by the powerful, rending jaws. Within heartbeats, she was literally torn completely apart, legs, body, and head, some of the wild dogs dashing in different directions with scarlet chunks of her still-twitching flesh staining the grass. I tore my gaze away to the other four, pursuing the young ram, who sailed right past the edge of the verandah, smack at Jan Allen who was reading in a hammock along the sunny side of the building. To our astonishment, the desperate impala leaped straight over the hammock, startling the half-dozing Jan half to death. As it hammered off behind the lodge, the wild dogs also cleared the side of the building and braked to a screeching halt practically at Jan's feet. He fetched them one hell of a shout, and they withdrew a few yards, making squeaking sounds. We were completely stunned, a hundred yards from the nearest rifle. Jan shouted again, clapped his hands, and took a step forward, to our unspeakable relief, while they turned and trotted past the porch and back out onto the *vlei*, which was as empty as a desert but for a lingering haze of hoof dust and the other dogs.

"Get your bloody camera, man," shouted Jan, gesturing to my forgotten Pentax on a nearby chair. Not knowing what he had in mind, I cocked it and without thinking followed him off the terrace. To my growing panic, he was striding big as life straight for the still-feeding pack! As we got closer and closer, I began to wonder if old Jan had been into the aftershave lotion because he started making a *wooo-wooo* sound like a faraway train, softly under his breath. I should, in retrospect, have realized that he knew what he was doing, since he had been chief game warden of one of Kenya's largest national parks before coming to Botswana. However, the idea of walking unarmed on purpose into a pack of feeding wild dogs (a 35mm. single-lens reflex camera being, in my humble opinion, a bit light for dangerous game) was not and is still not my concept of the apogee of applied prudence. But, what the hell. I couldn't exactly turn tail in front of the memsahib, and so started *woooing* myself.

To my considerable interest, we were not eaten on the spot, although we approached to within about fifteen feet of the pack, which was somewhat involved tugging and chewing sundry tatters of the late lady impala's anatomy, the calf being long gone. It was one hell of an odd feeling standing there, not overly helped by a close-up demonstration of those terrible jaws at work. After five minutes among the wild dogs, during which they polished up the remains and drifted away, after giving us the once-over balanced on their hind legs, I snapped off a whole roll of film of the killers. They had treated us with more curiosity than either fright or aggression, not especially unlike the reception one would expect in a bad but cheap restaurant. I later gave the roll of film to a "friend" to have it processed and, since I never saw it again, presume the pictures were pretty exceptional. I assure you I never went to the trouble to obtain others like them, although Jan said he had pulled that stunt several times before.

The presence or pursuit of wild dogs can produce extraordinary behavior in some animals, completely eliminating their fear of man. There are many confirmed cases of animals hunted by wild dogs approaching a man to within inches, obviously using him as a bodyguard. After quite a few years in wild dog country, I finally saw a case of this in Zambia when a semitame, old wildebeest bull named Charlie actually walked into my safari camp at Nyampala, chased by a pack of wild dogs. I shouldn't say I witnessed the event, but my nonhunting camp staff told me about it in great wonderment when I returned home from the field that day. Old Charlie had walked right up to the kitchen within a few feet of the cook and a waiter, who came outside and saw the wild dogs. They drove them off with clods of earth and Charlie hung around all afternoon until nearly dark, then went back to the bush.

I have seen wild dogs kill a variety of prey on perhaps six or seven occasions and their bewildering efficiency never fails to gag you. Whereas they will tear a smaller animal like a young impala completely apart in seconds, the slaughter of something the size of a zebra is an even more chilling spectacle. A large part of the basic wild dog technique, unlike that of the cats, who have claws to hang on, is to pull alongside the luckless animal and with a razor snap of their jaws bite through the flank or the thin skin near the genitals, exposing the internal organs, which fall or are pulled out and eaten. Obviously, nothing tends to travel very far after a dose of this treatment. In the process of one kill I saw, that of a zebra stallion, the lead dog grabbed it by the nose or lip while the others disemboweled it, not a cowardly act as zebras have tremendous fighting fangs.

Depending upon whom you listen to, or what terrain they are hunting, the estimate of percentage of successful hunts by wild dogs varies from about 50 percent to a reported 25 of 28 tries in Ngorongoro Crater in Kenya. Except for the case at Khwaai, where man interfered, I've never seen an unsuccessful wild dog hunt.

It's quite likely that animals caught by wild dogs and dragged down are in a state of terror-induced anesthetization as they have never, in my observation, shown indications of pain, although they are literally being eaten alive for the first minute or longer of their ordeal, living slabs of meat ripped out of the backsides and bellies wolfed before their glazing eyes. Death is normally mercifully quick, but there have been many accounts of animals living as long as fifteen minutes, later displaying the unquestionable symptoms of agony as the shock wore off. This sort of performance doesn't do a hell of a lot for the sensitivities of the Disney crowd.

I was surprised by the comments and photographs of Hugo and Jane van Lawick-Goodall, who have done extensive research on the wild dog in East Africa, showing that in their open, clear plains country, prey animals do not flee at the first sign of wild dogs, but treat the intruders much like lions. This is not the case in my experience in the thick *miombo* and woodlands of central Africa. Possibly because visibility is so much lower here, a mere whiff of wild dog is tantamount to a bomb warning. It may be that they can not keep a watchful eye on the wild dogs as they can on the plains. And, after all, an animal would have to run over the horizon to get out of sight with the type of visibility in Serengeti or Ngorongoro.

I find it interesting that any visitor who has seen African wild dogs kill is invariably affronted, revolted by them basically because of their extreme, somehow detached skill and the heart-wrenching violence of their methodology. Of course, this is just another example of humans labeling animals with supposed virtues or faults we value or despise in ourselves. On this reasoning lions are "noble," elephants "wise." Koala bears and bushbabies are "cuddly." Wild dogs are "evil." Well, so it goes.

In actuality, wild dogs have an extraordinarily complex and formal social structure, rich in elaborate behavior mechanisms and abstract ceremony. They are unquestionably very intelligent and much of their ritual has to do with submission and dominance of individuals arrived at by nonviolent means. They are one of the only wild mammal predators that will permit young pups to feed on a kill before adults do. Yet, for all their brightness, unless they have been shot at or molested, they display almost no distrust of man, which has led to the out-of-hand slaughter of untold thousands of them at the judgment of rifle-wielding idiots who believe they are saving other soft-eyed creatures from horrible death and thereby, through some hazy logic, assisting the balance of nature.

It is very good news for man that there has never been a confirmed case of man-eating among wild dogs. This strikes me as singularly strange because their diet includes any meat they can catch, even adult lions according to reliable sources in various parts of Africa. This being the case, what is it about man that incurs this gastronomic snub? It just might be that one of the oldest theories of the success of man, who has no natural physical weapons, is true: he simply smells too bad to eat to a sensitive creature like a wild dog. We're ripe enough from any animal's viewpoint, but you can bet that the early prototypes of our model were surely no bunch of lilacs! There have been a lot of reports of people supposedly treed by packs of wild dogs, but the fact remains that nobody has ever reliably been reported as eaten. I suspect the mere presence of the dogs was interpreted as an attack rather than their usual curiosity, and you may be assured that the story lost nothing in the retelling.

The wild dog, because man in his infinite wisdom has declared him unworthy of life, is much reduced in numbers all over Africa. Over the last ten years, however, a few people have seen the light, and protection has been provided in many countries. That's good news. For my money, he's one of the great reminders of the facts of life in Africa: life feeds on death in the exact ratio that death feeds on life. One *is* the other and it is only one's viewpoint that varies.

The sound of Africa is not the thundering rumble of a distant lion, nor is it the hollow trumpet of a bull elephant. If Africa has a voice, it is the hyena. Deep in the blackness of night it gropes through the bush in rising and falling echoes that come from nowhere, yet everywhere, insane choruses of whoops, chortles, chuckles, giggles, shrieks, and howls that have a way of reaching out into the guts of a man as he sits by a lonely, dying fire and of raising the hackles of ancient, long-forgotten apprehension. From the first, faraway *wooooo-uppp* of the pack gathering to the sniggering chitter of the kill, the hyena is telling you something you don't want to be reminded of: *you're just meat after all and your day will come*.

It may be the reluctance of man to admit to his protein mortality that has led him to his low opinion of the hyena. We call the animal a cowardly, sneaking, stinking, stupid scavenger. He is none of these except, possibly, a better sneak than we are. It's not news any more that the spotted hyena is a predator of great efficiency, hunting with deadly dedication animals much bigger and stronger than himself. Certainly he'll take the wobbly newborn and the broken-down sick and old. It's easier fare. But he will also execute the strong and able with better technique than the big cats, who have a very low attack-kill ratio. As for being a scavenger, many lions live off the hyena's leavings and if the latter's taste for less than fresh meat is a character defect, remember the "high" Scottish grouse or woodcock, hung by the neck until the body rots free before cooking. Maybe you never thought of a pork chop as the flesh of a long-dead pig or two fried eggs as the unborn embryos of chickens. Tuna is nothing but dead fish, but humans don't think in terms of a dead fish salad sandwich. It would appear that scavenging is a relative trait.

If you consider the hyena cowardly or stupid, you have never seen him systematically brave the arched swords of the sable antelope with the discipline and elan of a squad of crack Green Berets. I know he doesn't stink; I've sniffed him. He smells rather like a recently washed dog although he is more closely related to the cats than the canines, despite appearances. The hyena is one of the world's most accomplished food processors. His jaws and teeth are as powerful as a steel scrap shredder, his bite worse than a tiger's. He looks neither strong nor quick with his shifty, shuffling, cringing gait, an impression formed by his massive upper chest and head and his sloping, seemingly half-crippled rear. Yet, he can manage a confirmed forty miles per hour flat out or twenty-five while carrying a forty-pound young antelope clear of the ground in his jaws. I know it's true because I've been passed by hyenas at night in a Land Rover.

Fisi, as he is reviled in KiSwahili in East Africa, or *Pirri* in Botswana, or *mPisi* in the Sindebele Zulu dialect of Rhodesia, can and will eat any bloody thing, dead, alive, or inanimate that might produce nourishment. The strange, white dung of the spotted hyena illustrates that he regularly crushes and eats the heaviest bones. He will also mangle binoculars into trash for their leather and glue coverings, taking a camera along for dessert. If you leave them out, he'll gobble a rifle sling or even your shoes for the leather. He'll actually chew iron spearheads from which the blood has not been cleaned until they look like bad *objets d'art*. I had a fine Randall-made knife that I used for skinning trophies, which had a leather handle. Of course, blood scent was well impregnated into the handle. One night it disappeared and was later found a few hundred yards away by one of my men, the handle completely eaten away by a hyena. In Botswana a fresh elephant tusk of some eighty pounds was taken one night from my camp. Debalo and I followed the drag track more than a mile, where we found the tooth in a thicket, most of the thinner base ivory crushed away and eaten. (This hyena damage didn't exactly thrill my client, but a taxidermist was able to repair the injury to the ivory perfectly.)

I rather doubt that, after considering the hard facts of history, anybody would question that more human flesh has gone down hyenas' throats than down those of any other animal. It is still the comforting custom of some tribes to drag out the old and weak to be taken, dead or alive, by prowling hyenas. Even the shallowly buried dead rarely enjoy their privacy; hyenas are very good diggers. Paleontologists tell us that this is why very ancient human remains are so rare. Hyenas crushed up and scattered the relatively light bones of our dim ancestors too frequently and badly for them to survive as fossils. The voice of the hyena has always been the reminder of finality to the Africans, and at one time to the Europeans as well. In Pleistocene Europe the cave hyena undoubtedly did as efficient a job of human disposal for Neanderthals and Cro-Magnons as he does for Africans today. Maybe that accounts for the strange feeling

I get of "somebody standing on my grave" whenever I hear old *mPisi* tune up.

It has been suggested by several experienced writers that, in some areas, the hyena is a greater man-eater than the lion and the leopard put together. It may be true. Certainly, there is no lack of reliable reports of man-eating, as many as four or five deaths per month at one time in Nyasaland, now called Malawi, on Lake Tanganyika. The spotted hyena, *Crocuta crocuta*, is the invariable culprit. There is a striped hyena ranging through parts of Kenya and Ethiopia and on through Asia, although he is not nearly so dangerous as the spotted variety.

The biggest problem with sharing the bush with hyenas is less that of being completely eaten than being partially eaten. It's not all that rare to run across Africans with cheeks, noses, or even whole faces missing, wounds so horrible Homer wouldn't have included them in the *Iliad*. Most tell you that the cause was lion; it's not usually so. The risk a heavy native drinker takes in Africa is not his liver; rather, it's having a hyena dine off his profile as he lies unconscious by a dying fire, stoned motherless on beer. *Mpisi* hangs around a camp or village, listening to his stomach rumble, smelling all the lovely odor of food, skins, and blood. Eventually, he can't resist and sneaks up on a sleeping person. In one ferocious snap that shears bone and meat like a butcher's cleaver, he removes somebody's face. Or worse. Some, not so lucky, are gelded.

Hyenas, especially in areas where antelopes, zebra, and other prey have been eliminated, can live in symbiosis with man. Of course, this tends to reduce their fear of man and can lead to very dangerous conditions. Hyenas may greatly increase in numbers under plague circumstances and, when the sickness finally abates, be forced to turn to eating live people. An artificial example of this occurred near Nairobi after World War I, where huge packs of hyenas were living nicely on the scraps from a slaughterhouse that discarded the heads and bones of slaughtered cattle. When the war was over, the troops left and the slaughtering stopped. The hyenas, desperate for food, swarmed the place, eating everything that wasn't red-hot or nailed down, including clothes, stained cooking pots, brooms, and finally several women working in the mealie patches.

The social order and adaptability of the spotted hyena have been explored quite a bit recently, especially in a fascinating book by Hugo and Jane van Lawick-Goodall, *Innocent Killers* (New York: Houghton Mifflin, 1970). It especially points out that in many parts of their range, hyenas operate almost entirely as predators and not scavengers. This was also confirmed by the South African authority, F. C. Eloff, who reported that of 1,052 hyenas watched while feeding, 82 percent were eating only animals they had killed themselves. Yet hyena behavior seems to vary considerably from place to place, pack to pack, which may explain why man-eating may be highly developed in some parts of Africa and not in others. It still remains, though, that a hyena used to eating bodies would probably not show much reticence about taking a live person if he had the opportunity.

I found out how quickly these very intelligent animals learn at a water hole near Khwaai Lodge in Botswana when I ran it for a while between safaris. Around dusk, I would often drive a few miles, taking one or two of my men, to treat myself to a half-hour's sand grouse shooting. There was an open field upwind of the water hole where the sand grouse came to drink at last light, and, still riding the wind like feathered blobs of ectoplasm against the darkening sky, they offered some of the most challenging pass shooting I have ever experienced. Inevitably, a bird or two would drop into cover and be lost to my men. Hyenas, coming in to drink, would pick up the scent of the birds and clean them up. After the third time I shot there, they had made the clear association between the sound of the shotgun and easy food. After I had a half-dozen "sandies" down, I was surprised to see four big hyenas galumphing across the field and even more so when they sat down with perfect nonchalance forty yards away watching me expectantly. Sure enough, the next bird I killed, two of them raced for it, far beating my human retriever. Being armed, I wasn't worried that they would give us any trouble and so kept experimenting to see just how bold they would become. Incredibly, they would charge in and grab a bird as close as five yards, and that was after only three "lessons." It's no wonder they pull off peoples' faces from time to time. At least one thing's for sure: a pet hyena would make one hell of a bird dog!

Because, in older times, so many men ended up inside of hyenas, man shares a closer mystic relationship with them than with any other animal, particularly in the realms of black magic and witchcraft. Hyenas are traditionally, in many tribal cultures, the lovers of witches who are said to ride on their familiars' backs on nocturnal journeys. The lion and the leopard are also quite mixed up in this macabre portfolio of spookies, but I think the legends of the hyenas are the most fascinating. In some places in Tanzania wild hyenas are not considered to exist, all of the local *Fisi* or *Lipwereri* being thought of as special, extra-big were hyenas, belonging to the local witches, mostly female, who rent them out for revenge murders. Witching and warlocking must be a very popular profession since there are a hell of a lot of hyenas around this location. The proposition doesn't sound too convincing to an outsider, but then consider that good old George Rushby shot several hyena that had beads knotted into their fur as well as strange, symmetrical scars cut into them, marking ownership. One, if you are ready for this, was wearing a pair of khaki shorts! I wonder if they were Sanforized.

Weird? Sure. Impossible? I don't think so. Too much of this sort of thing has been reported by people who know what they're talking about. I doubt that we'll ever know the truth of the matter, but as the hyena is such a bright animal, there's no reason why "witches" could not tame them as has been done in many wild animal shows and zoos. Even if a witch was to catch several young hyenas and tie beads in their fur or cut designs into their hides and then release them, the discovery of these marks in later life would add a

pile of credence to the witch's claims to have hyena "familiars." That a witch could train a hyena to kill on command is no less possible than our own training of German shepherds or Dobermans to do the same thing.

In a few regions witches are thought to be able to turn themselves into hyenas and back again—shades of Transylvania. The writer Peter Matthiessen, in *The Tree Where Man Was Born* (New York: E. P. Dutton, 1972) tells his favorite tale of lycanthropy in which white hunter Bror von Blixen was asked to kill a marauding hyena, which the tribesmen were afraid to tackle because of retribution from the witch. Finally convincing a gunbearer to come along, he wounded the creature by moonlight and it crawled off into some bush. Following the blood spoor, the men flushed it out and von Blixen's second shot killed it. When they got up to the carcass, there was no sign of a hyena. There lay, instead, a dead African with two bullet holes. It's not an unfamiliar theme in our own culture, which you might know if you watch as much late-night television as do I.

Of course, all this magic business is just so much bull dust. Isn't it? We civilized people know that such goings on are ridiculous gibber, don't we? Sure we do: we don't trust anything but our good, reliable horoscope.

One of the odder but most understandable legends about the hyena is that he, she, or it is hermaphroditic, having the sex organs and many of the secondary sex characteristics of both genders. The fact is that both the male and female hyena have organs extraordinarily similar in appearance, if such matters interest you. They are not, however, interchangeable, much to the relief, I'm sure, of the hyenas themselves.

I don't know another hunter who doesn't—even if quietly—share my affection for the spotted hyena. The wild savagery of the animal's song is to me the symphony of the beauty, the horror, and the reality of life and death in the long grass, finally and at last, the truth. But, sometimes I think perhaps I've sneaked into the concert hall without buying a ticket. You see, I've decided to be cremated.

* * *

The vast percentage of shooting done on a modern safari is centered about the antelopes, which vary in size from ten pounds to the ponderous eland, which may top a ton. For the most part these animals are no more dangerous than white-tailed deer, unprovoked attacks of any consequence almost unheard-of. Yet, when they are wounded, there's not a one that can't put you away if you get cute with them. They all have horns and know how to use them.

My vote for the noblest, fiercest, most handsome, horned game on the African continent goes to the sable antelope. The first time you see one, you won't have to ask your hunter what it is. Although for many years the British favored the name Harrisbuck, in honor of the man who discovered the species, the term "sable," descriptive of the glossy, anthracite black of the mature bulls' hides, has gained in popularity until these days it's the only one used. Sable have an air about them, almost a chip-on-the-shoulder attitude. With big, lone bulls it's practically an aura. They are large animals, a bull tipping in at somewhere around the quarter-ton mark, 500 pounds of iron, rippling muscle from their deep, thick chests to trim, wasp-waisted hindquarters. The eight-ball black of their upper bodies ends abruptly with a switch to creamy bellies, the borderline of the two colors swinging up in the middle of the animals like an inverted bow.

Both sexes of sable have thick, bristling manes and facial patterns of chalky white probably better described as war paint than clowns' markings. Both cows and bulls sport horns and are not shy in their use, although the females' weapons are generally shorter and less massive than those of the bulls. The horns of the adult male sable are considered by a wide proportion of well-traveled sportsmen to be the *pièce de résistance* of African antelope trophies. And with good reason, too. Unlike the long spiraling corkscrews of the greater kudu, his most popular rival of the "glamor" game, sable horns show at first glance that they were not constructed for decoration. Close to the skull the horns are tightly knurled, these corrugations running like the carved grip of a giant sword to within a foot and a half of the heavy, rapier-sharp points. This last section of horn is nice and smooth to permit easy penetration into meat when the sable is goring. Sables' horns are as functional as Samurai blades, making most other species of antelope seem as if they're wearing a pair of butter knives in comparison.

The sable, joined by the oryx tribe and the little bush-bucks, are the most aggressive of the antelopes. Try getting clever with a wounded one and you just might wish you'd stuck to duplicate bridge. A lone sable bull won't back down from a lion; in fact I've seen small herds of sable chase lions from a water hole, so you will appreciate that they don't hold too high an opinion of man, either. Perhaps that's their great attraction, besides their wonderful looks—their raw machismo. They could care less.

One of the most attractive features of Khwaai Lodge was the rustic bar just off the patio under the Ngamo Fig Tree, the rear wall of which backed up to the swimming pool enclosure. It was an area fenced with very strong wire and bound with grass, surrounding the pool apron. So the tourists wouldn't have to share the facilities with buffalo or hippo, a baffle door provided entrance, an arrangement set up like the *burladero*, or slab of fencing, painted with a bulls-eye that the matador can duck behind when inspecting a fresh toro. To an animal's eye the fence would appear solid, humans just walking around the baffle into the pool area.

One evening about ten o'clock I was sitting with guests at the bar, tossing a few. Hyenas were carrying on outside like a floor show from hell. I had heard a lion grunt earlier, quite close, but since he had not called again, I figured he was stalking a kill, one of the many impala around the lodge. Five minutes later the pool enclosure began to sound like a hi-fi replay of the Barnum and Bailey train-wreck, wood crashing and splintering, lions snarling and roaring, and another heavy animal furiously grunting. Hooves rang against the flagstone accompanied by loud snorts, a stran-

287

gled sound, and a heavy splash. I grabbed the .470 from behind the bar and stuffed in a pair of 500-grain soft-points, snatching at the flashlight. Safety off, I sneaked around the building and edged my head into the entrance past the baffle, swinging the light in a short arc. Two very bright green eyes reflected in the beam about fifteen feet away. There was a snort and a further rattle of hooves, so I ducked back out of the way behind the baffle. With a soggy *crunch*! 500 pounds of sable bull hit the barrier where I had been, his long horns sinking through the fencing and sliding by my midriff. With incredible strength he ripped back his head, tearing free the heavy staples that held the wire to the posts like buttons popping from a fat man's vest. Trailing thirty feet of fencing from his horns, he trotted, muttering, out of the enclosure and into the night.

When I was sure he was gone, I went into the pool area and picked out the corpse of a large lioness on the pool bottom in the beam of the light, her diffusing blood turning the water a rosy pink. Another blood trail ran across the stone apron and over the fence at the far side of the enclosure.

I called several of the lodge employees to lend a hand, and we fished out the dead lioness, a heavy, mature animal. A four-inch section of sable horn protruded from the top of her head like a small antenna. The sable's riposte had caught her charging, and the point had penetrated from below the jaw up through the bottom of the skull, through the brain and out the top of the head. The horn had broken off when the bull tossed the 325 pound cat into the pool. There was no question that she had died instantly.

Two days later the hyena- and vulture-tattered scraps of a male lion were discovered two miles away. After the garbagemen had finished with him, it was not possible to say definitely that it had been sable wounds that killed him, but it's almost beyond question that his was the blood trail leading over the fence. Except for a series of claw marks on one shoulder, the sable was doing admirably the last time I saw him, although his humor had not much improved.

Frederick C. Selous, the great naturalist and sports-man-explorer who wandered thousands of miles through central African sable range in the last century, was a great admirer of the animal. Traveling along the Umniati River in the 1880s, a lovely stream I have also hunted in central Rhodesia, Selous' Boer companion fired from his wagon and wounded a fine male sable his men wanted for meat. At the shot Selous' pack of experienced lion dogs took out after the hard-hit bull, who made for a depression near the river bank. By the time the men could run the 200 yards to finish off the sable, he had killed four of the ten powerful dogs stone dead, wounded four more seriously (one of which soon died), and torn open the throat of Selous' favorite bitch. Nine out of ten lion dogs dead or disabled within seconds gives some idea of the sable's ferocious swordsman-ship, even when badly wounded. Selous also records, about this same time, the death of a Zulu warrior from the village of Churchin who had wounded a cow sable with his *asseg-ais*—short throwing or stabbing spears. The cow killed him with one sweep of horn, placing his kidney neatly *en brochette*.

Sable are among the more difficult, pound for pound, of the African antelopes to kill, sharing the trait of the buffalo if merely wounded by the first shot. Their systems produce large amounts of adrenalin, which goes a long way toward immunizing the animal from further bullet shock effect. Sometimes they will almost shrug off wounds that would floor a bull elephant.

To demonstrate the principle, let me call again upon the late Mr. Selous. He and his native helpers were elephant hunting when they spotted a grand sable bull. Although reticent to fire because of fear of disturbing the jumbos they were following, Selous decided that the superb length of horn was worth the price of a shot. Taking the most accurate of his two elephant guns, he had his men lie down while he stalked the bull to 120 yards, when the sable sensed or saw the man and turned to stare at the bush behind which Selous was hiding. Realizing he could get no closer,

Selous rose slowly to his knees and fired the huge 4-gauge at the center of the chest. The sable staggered to his knees at the strike of the four-ounce ball but rebounded instantly and galloped full speed for a hundred yards, where he fell. Selous' bearers speared the bull to death. Selous was pleased with the shot:

> "Considering my weapon, a smooth-bore elephant gun, carrying a four-ounce round bullet, backed by *fifteen drams* of coarse powder . . . the ball, after entering the chest rather low, and passing through the whole length of the body . . . made its exit by the left thigh, grazing the heart on its passage."

If the ability to travel a hundred yards after having had a .93-caliber ball driven completely through the body lengthwise isn't a fair demonstration of resistance to bullet energy, I'm sure I don't know what is!

Although sable are exceptionally well armed and active when wounded, they are not the only antelopes that bear great care in following up. The roan antelope is also very determined, as may be waterbuck, oryx, and even wildebeest, not to mention the zebra, which is a holy terror with a kick like a pile driver and a bite like a hyena. But, when it comes to pure heart and determination, the bushbucks take the prize in the lightweight division.

Bushbucks are widely distributed throughout the heavier cover of most of Africa and are not herd animals, usually living in pairs. They range in size from the will-o'-the-wisp, 300-pound bongo of Chad, the Central African Republic, and the rain forest of Kenya to the smaller, striped and spot-marked harnessed and Chobe races, typical of the many moderate-sized members of the clan. There are more than forty species of bushbuck, and they are the smallest of the spiral-horned antelopes, which include eland, sitatunga, nyala, and the greater and lesser kudus. They range between seventy-five to eighty pounds and as much as one hundred pounds more than that, exotic-looking beauties that flit through the dense bush in shadow-mottled camouflage. A wounded bushbuck, despite his unimpressive size, can be hell on hooves to a following hunter or poacher. When I was in Zambia in the 1960s, there was a case of a native who had caught a bushbuck in a snare. As he approached it to finish it with his tomahawk, it lunged at him, breaking the worn snare and goring him in the stomach. The man died in about an hour, from all signs of internal hemorrhaging.

On another occasion a client hunting in the Luangwa Valley had wounded a fine male bushbuck, which disappeared like a flash into heavy bush. Before I could stop him, a new tracker I had hired took off after him, trying to impress me with his keenness, armed with his throwing spear. After quite a bit of shouting, we found him treed, the little bushbuck pacing below as determinedly as any lion, the tracker's spear stuck in the ground where he had missed his throw. He looked like a wrestler treed by a Chihuahua and took such a ribbing from the rest of the men that he drifted away that night and went back to his village. The bushbuck, incidentally, spun around as soon as he saw us and started a charge, which I was obliged to stop at somewhat sticky range.

That dangerous animals are unpredictable is axiomatic. With roundhouse logic, it may follow, therefore, that the most unpredictable creature capable of sending you West is the most deadly. Humor me with the further conclusion that something that doesn't itself know which way it's going to jump can hardly be anticipated and therefore defended against. If you are interested in one man's opinion—guess who's—the most potentially dangerous item in Africa is a nervous client, anxious to make good, tiptoeing along behind somebody else with a cocked, unsafetied rifle in his sweaty mitts while semisuppressed fear plays a banjo solo on his intestines. As the blind hog stumbles over the occasional acorn, so have I developed the

Professional Hunter's Survival Axiom, also modestly known in very limited circles as Capstick's Law, which says, "*Never, but absolutely never, permit a person with a cocked rifle behind you.*"

Sorry, nothing personal. I know you've been hunting all your life and know how to handle guns safely. So did the man who almost shot me.

It was an ordinary day during which we were hunting out of Mwangwalala Camp on the Luangwa, easing slowly through the bush in hope of cutting some fresh buffalo spoor. The client was a very likeable older American, a good shot with slathers of experience on North American game. He was following behind me with his rifle sling-slung over his shoulder, a potent .375 H & H Magnum borrowed for heavier game from another professional in camp. We had been out for three weeks, and I knew that he was extremely cautious in the way he handled firearms, so I didn't think about it when I spotted a very fine, record-book-class waterbuck a hundred yards ahead. I sneaked ahead to find a shooting rest along a big tree and motioned him forward to get into position. I was kneeling as he edged in behind and to my right, and the world exploded in a smashing, white-hot, deafening flash.

I lay on the ground, numbed, sure I was dead, my head ringing like Judgment Day. Gradually, over the sound I heard voices and tried to open my eyes. So far, so good. Being dead wasn't as bad as I had figured. Cautiously, I began to explore for bullet holes on the presumption I had not been struck by lightning. Except for a burning sensation growing on my neck, I was forced to the conclusion that either this wasn't The Day, or my Sunday School teacher had been overpessimistic about where I would end up. Stupefied, I managed to wobble to my feet and saw the client, face white as a newly plucked chicken, staring at me open mouthed. The rifle lay on the ground, a wisp of cordite smoke still sneering from the muzzle.

It took a while to put it all together. Somehow, the man's rifle had gone off as he scrunched into position alongside me. The big 270-grain soft-point (soft-point!!) had bored and tugged neatly through both rolls of the collar of my bush jacket two inches up from the juncture of the right side of my neck and my shoulder, creased my neck—raising a welt like a *sjambok* stroke—and went on to blow a slab from the side of the tree the size of a beer tray. The bush jacket and a good bit of my neck and hair were scorched with powder burns, but I was so delighted that I could feel it hurt that I practically collapsed with relief.

In fairness, I don't know who was the most frightened, the client, me, or my men. I really began to worry about the American having a heart attack, he was so pale and shaken, gasping like a stranded carp. Fortunately, no one has written a description of what I looked like. After a while the shock began to wear off us all, although the realization of the fact that the slug had whipped right across my jugular, a skin thickness away, was still pretty spooky. When the client and I were both coherent—I was too frightened to be angry—I asked him just what had happened, and he said he just couldn't figure it out since his hand had not been near the trigger but just on the safety catch. I took the rifle and unloaded it for an examination. Cocking it on the empty chamber, I put on the safety catch and then slipped it off. An ominous *click*! sounded as the firing pin fell on the dead chamber. Jeesus! Imagine a rifle that would fire when the safety was released without touching the trigger!

Thinking it was something he didn't know, I brought it up to the white hunter who had loaned the gun and listened as he had the unbelievable gall to tell me that he was aware of the problem but had forgotten to mention it to the client. Forgotten? Perhaps it was the aftermath of the tension of the incident or simple frustration with his murderous stupidity that had almost got me sweet, young body wrapped in a blanket with a large hole in its neck, but I lost my temper, threw the rifle in the river and had to be pulled off him. It might be said we were never the best of buddies after that. Of course, you might know that although I had never seen the client with his rifle pointed carelessly, it would be the microsecond it was lined up with my neck that he awkwardly settled down for a shot and it chose to go off. Maybe the Chinese are right: machinery does have spirits.

Whose fault was it? All of ours. Mine for breaking my own rule and being in front of somebody with a loaded rifle, safety catch or no, the client's for having the muzzle in my direction, and the lender's for permitting the man to use a rifle he knew to be dangerously defective. After all, once somebody gets shot, whose fault it was takes on very little value to the shootee.

Many clients take personal exception to the seeming overcaution of professional hunters when it comes to firearms and their handling. Most of the pros I know choose a big tree or other landmark several hundred yards outside camp, where they stop the hunting car and all guns are unloaded and not reloaded until an equal distance from home. It sounds childish, I know, but I had three accidental discharges in camp by clients before I made it a rule early in my career. One man, excited over having killed a lion under hairy circumstances, was certain he had unloaded and to prove it, leveled his rifle before I could stop him and shot one hell of a hole in my water storage tank. It scared and embarrassed him so he didn't hunt the next day. After that, he became a fanatic about gun safety. Also remember that if your hunter prefers to have a gunbearer carry your rifle uncocked and with an empty chamber, go along with him. All he is trying to do is lighten up on the odds that the long grass doesn't grow over his grave—or yours—any sooner than it has to. He's seen too many close ones, unintentional little goofs by well-meaning and genuinely careful people, amateur and professional, to take the slightest chance.

Throughout this book, we've discussed a lot of the stranger things that seem to happen in the *bundu* world of central Africa as well as some of the not-so-obvious relationships between man and animal. It's not my aim ever to embarrass any clients by betraying my professional responsibility to their privacy, but through the dark veil of anonymity of person and place, this book would not be complete without mentioning one of the strangest evenings of my life, perhaps best called the "Tale of the Man-eating Lady."

It was a two-man professional safari of twenty-one days, the law not permitting a single white hunter to bwana for more than two shooting clients. The guests were European, a husband and wife and the husband's brother, who was my charge, while the second professional, let's call him George, was guiding the couple. We were quite a long way out, hunting elephant from a small fly camp, and had been getting along famously over the first few days. The sun had dropped like a hot rock and, after dinner and a few dollops to keep off the dew, George and I had said good night and bedded down in the small tent we shared a hundred yards from the larger clients' tents.

We were just about asleep a half-hour later when cries of "Petair! George! Come queekly!" shot us bolt upright and snatching for rifles, flashlights, and snakebite kits. We threw on bush shorts and dashed barefoot for the tents, horrified at what we might find. As we pulled up puffing, the husband hunched out of the tent, his arms streaming blood, and stood alongside the brother, who was sucking a nasty looking laceration on his hand. George and I stared at each other in complete confusion, then at the tent as the husband switched to English. "Een there! Een there!" he shouted. I took the light, George covering me with a rifle as I threw back the flap, expecting at least a wholesale lot of lions to come boiling out into my lap. I looked around. Except for the diminutive wife, the tent was empty! She was in a nightgown, half-smiling at me. I walked over for a look under the bed and to ask her what in the world was going on, when she lunged at me, grabbed at my hand, and, growling like a honey badger, tried to bite me!

I shouted for George to get the hell in there as I struggled with her, trying to keep her jaws away with all my strength as she snapped, snarled, and bit like a certifiable banana, slippery as an eel and twice as fast. It was like one of those heavy-dessert nightmares in which you have a huge snake by the throat that keeps slipping away. The power of the small woman was terrifying despite the fact that I outweighed her by ninety pounds and was a good foot taller. George ducked in and gaped in amazement until I finally got him to get with it and grab an arm. Together, we struggled to pin her to the bed where she ultimately lay, hardly gasping. She closed her eyes and suddenly stopped trying to pull her wrists free, relaxing like a wet sock. Feeling a bit stupid, we released her, thinking she had come to her senses. She lay for a few seconds watching us through half-closed eyes as we tried to reason with her, then in a lightning lunge wrapped her arms around George's leg and sank her teeth into his bare calf. He gave a most unprofessional bellow of pain and we peeled her off, George wilting the canvas with a spontaneous offering of very colorful Rhodesian idiom suited to the occasion. Switching from George, she then concentrated on gnawing off my thumb, an activity at which she was not entirely without skill. I yowled and shook loose, wrenching her wrists behind her until George worked up the nerve to dodge past her kicking feet, grab them, and lever her back onto the bed.

She stayed relatively quiet for several minutes although we knew better than to release our grip. After a long pause, having garnered her power, she slowly concentrated her supernatural strength on her right arm, which I was holding down. To my disbelief, she raised me right off the bed, forced my hands away, and tried to bite me again. To tell the truth, we were not a little frightened for her or us. She was clearly completely out of her skull, although it didn't seem at all like a fit wherein I imagined she would foam at the mouth or do something else picturesque. Her actions seemed too deliberate, with too much strategy to be entirely wild, yet what cculd account for her unbelievable strength? I'd heard of women rolling cars off their trapped children single-handed under duress, but what could have caused this?

Bit by bit her attacks grew less frequent, and she

slipped away for a few moments of sleep although she would still try to bite us any time she had an opening. Eventually, after three hours, she fell deeply asleep and showed no more signs of violence. We watched her for another hour and then suggested the brother and husband play bachelor in the second tent while George and I split the watch the rest of the night.

The next morning the lady was up and dressed by dawn, as rested and vital as if she'd had a full night's sleep. She seemed puzzled when she found me outside the tent and the husband in with his brother, both of them looking like sheiks in Mercurochrome wrappings, yet she apparently remembered nothing of the night before. I left it up to the family to explain, but what in the world they might have told her I couldn't imagine. The incident was seemingly ignored, if not forgotten. The best guess George and I could make was that it had been some kind of wild reaction to a combination of antibiotic, antimalarial prophylaxis and whiskey she had mixed that night after dinner. Whatever, it sure did a lot to shore up my flagging belief in possession by demons.

Maybe George summed it up best later, inspecting the wound on his leg. "Well," he mused laconically, "that's bloody Africa for you. Everything bites."